Leadership - New Insights

Edited by Mário Franco

Published in London, United Kingdom

IntechOpen

Supporting open minds since 2005

Leadership - New Insights
http://dx.doi.org/10.5772/intechopen.95224
Edited by Mário Franco

Contributors
Joseph Crawford, Lindall Elaine Adams, Ibrahim Al Zaabi, Marion Williams, Mohd Faridh Hafez Mhd Omar, Neil E. Grunberg, Erin S. Barry, Maureen Metcalf, Michael Morrow-Fox, Iffah Budiningsih, Tjiptogoro Dinarjo Soehari, Elif Bilginoğlu, Ahmad Rafiki, Miftahuddin, Atika Rizki, Anurag Mishra, Holger Pfaff, Natalia Zhuravleva, Milos Poliak, Tessie H.H. Herbst

First published in London, United Kingdom, 2022 by IntechOpen
IntechOpen is the global imprint of INTECHOPEN LIMITED, registered in England and Wales, registration number: 11086078, 5 Princes Gate Court, London, SW7 2QJ, United Kingdom
Printed in Croatia

British Library Cataloguing-in-Publication Data
A catalogue record for this book is available from the British Library

Additional hard and PDF copies can be obtained from orders@intechopen.com

Leadership - New Insights
Edited by Mário Franco
p. cm.
Print ISBN 978-1-83969-926-9
Online ISBN 978-1-83969-927-6
eBook (PDF) ISBN 978-1-83969-928-3

For EU product safety concerns:
IN TECH d.o.o., Prolaz Marije Krucifikse Kozulić 3, 51000 Rijeka, Croatia, info@intechopen.com or visit our website at intechopen.com.

Meet the editor

Mário Franco is an Associate Professor of Entrepreneurship and SME Administration at the Department of Management and Economics, Beira Interior University, Portugal. He received his Ph.D. in Management from Beira Interior University in 2002. In 1997, he was a doctoral candidate and participated in the European Doctoral Programme in Entrepreneurship and Small Business Management in Spain and Sweden. He is the director of the 2nd Cycle (Master) of Management. His research focuses on strategic alliances, business networks, innovation, and business creation. He is a member of a research unit at the Center for Advanced Studies in Management and Economics of the University of Beira Interior (CEFAGE-UBI) and is currently involved in several research projects on SMEs. He has authored several articles published in journals such as Long Range Planning, R&D Management, International Entrepreneurship and Management Journal, and Management Decision, and some books and book chapters published by international publishers.

Contents

Preface

Organizations are part of increasingly volatile societies marked by rapid digital and technological transformations. The technological life cycle tends to be shorter now than it has been in the past and this is impacting organizational performance. In the face of this rapid evolution, the obsolescence of business technology is a short-term reality if organizations are not in tune with reality.

In this context, leadership is viewed as an important issue because the continuity of organizations and their success depends on their leaders and the behaviours they demonstrate. How a leader behaves or how they access and "use" the various leadership styles can impact all stakeholders. Leadership responsibility can enable organizations to achieve a successful future. Thus, leadership plays an important role in how workers interpret and carry out their activities. Leadership and its influence on organizations are key concepts in how organizations/companies work and how they are insighted. Leadership is a process that influences the behaviour of leaders to perform proposed tasks and achieve defined objectives.

In this sense, understanding leadership is extremely important for an organization as well as the environment around it, since organizations are inserted in a social, economic, and environmental context where actions have effects and impacts. In addition, leadership should align with the goals and objectives of organizations to facilitate the achievement of those same goals and objectives. The leadership style that a leader presents can have a considerable impact on organizations because the market in which they are located is volatile and there are too many factors that condition their survival. Leadership, when linked with the organization's strategy, can influence the organization's entire process, as it establishes a path towards better involvement and performance of the parties involved.

However, leadership has become a complex, difficult, and multi-faceted issue for organizations because it entails challenges and issues, for example, determining what is the best type of leader. Therefore, research in the area of leadership has been obscured rather than discussed. Despite the significant body of literature on the subject, leadership remains quite misunderstood in the organizational world.

Leadership has given rise to several studies and involves a wide spectrum of relevant frameworks to explain the components of leaders' behaviour; however, there is still a vast field for research in search of more conceptual transparency, intrinsic characteristics, and the impact it has on everything that surrounds it. Therefore, the importance of leadership has been widely recognized in the literature, evidenced by the notable increase in relevant publications in the past few years. As such, this book is devoted to the study of different perspectives, contexts, and new insights into leadership.

The book includes four sections and eleven chapters.

Chapter 1, "A Contemporary Approach to Learning Transfer from the Perspective of Constructivist Theory: Marathon Running as a Leadership Development Strategy for Millennial Leaders" by Elif Bilginoğlu, presents a literature review of the research on marathon running as a leadership development strategy, especially for millennial leaders with a postmodern worldview who are searching for authentic and innovative solutions and who support divergent thinking.

Chapter 2, "Turning Bad Leaders into Good Leaders: Diminishing the Theory X Style" by Lindall Elaine Adams, Marion Williams, and Ibrahim Al Zaabi, explores e-micromanagement as a Theory X style of leadership and identifies indicators such as lack of trust and high staff turnover as the primary reasons why leaders fail to "lead" the "ship."

Chapter 3, "Humane Leadership in Islamic Approaches" by Mohd Faridh Hafez Mhd Omar presents some approaches to human leadership in an innovative context, i.e., Islamic. This leadership style has an important role in the organizations' performance and is essential for their growth and success.

Chapter 4, "Strengthening Innovative Leadership in the Turbulent Environment" by Iffah Budiningsih and Tjiptogoro Dinarjo Soehari, discusses a content analysis of several leadership types helpful for anticipating turbulent environmental changes, including leadership in the turbulent era, innovative leadership, leadership with high integrity, and leadership with high emotional intelligence (EQ).

Chapter 5, "Optimizing Innovative Leadership and Followership" by Neil E. Grunberg, Erin S. Barry, Michael Morrow-Fox, and Maureen Metcalf, proposes an innovative framework that combines several approaches to help leaders increase self-understanding and optimize the performance of organizations. The proposed framework focuses on Leader Type, Developmental Perspective, Resilience, Situational Analysis, and Leadership Behaviors and Mindsets.

Chapter 6, "Spirituality Leadership Applications in Small and Medium Enterprises (SMEs)" by Ahmad Rafiki, Miftahuddin, and Atika Rizki, explores a new leadership style in small and medium-sized enterprises. This sector plays a central role in several countries since they are extremely important in job creation, which contributes to regions' well-being and development.

Chapter 7, "Defining Post-Pandemic Work and Organizations: The Need for Team Belongingness and Trust" by Joseph Crawford, shows how the COVID-19 pandemic has brought forth substantial unrest in the ways in which people work and organize. Thus, this chapter provides a position for the future state of work and organizing, drawing on the belongingness hypothesis, to characterize a revised method of human connection that acknowledges unique differences in online connections.

Chapter 8, "Do Organizations Need Emotionally Intelligent Leadership at the Workplace?" by Anurag Mishra, presents an empirical study, the findings of which help in understanding individual and collective behavior and its effect on the quality of work. The results suggest that a transformational style of leadership should be encouraged in an organization.

Chapter 9, "Leading in Times of Disruption: Reimagining Leadership and Repositioning Leaders" by Tessie H.H. Herbst, explores how leaders and leadership paradigms have been disrupted and why the old model of fear and control does not work.

Chapter 10, "The Social Infrastructure of Organizational Resilience, Agency Capacity and Resilience Spirals: Starting Points for Resilient Leadership" by Holger Pfaff analyzes the social preconditions and dynamics of organizational resilience and the role of leadership in managing these conditions and dynamics. The chapter emphasizes the importance of leadership in building and maintaining the social infrastructure of resilience and in managing resilience spirals.

Finally, Chapter 11, "Green Transformational Leadership and Green Growth" by Natalia Aleksandrovna Zhuravleva and Milos Poliak, presents an empirical study to substantiate a scientific hypothesis of the impact of transformational leadership on green growth. The findings suggest that transformational leadership incorporating intersectorality is becoming a new type of management activity that ensures the growth of long-term profitability from green investments.

Mário Franco
University of Beira Interior,
CEFAGE-UBI Research Center,
Covilhã, Portugal

Section 1

Leadership Guided by Theoretical Perspectives

Chapter 1

A Contemporary Approach to Learning Transfer from the Perspective of Constructivist Theory: Marathon Running as a Leadership Development Strategy for Millennial Leaders

Elif Bilginoğlu

Abstract

This paper includes a literature review of the research on marathon running as a leadership development strategy especially for the millennial leaders while they have a postmodern worldview, searching authentic and innovative solutions and supporting divergent thinking. Furthermore, it points out the importance of learning transfer from the perspective of constructivist theory. In this respect, first, constructivist learning theory and learning transfer are explained. In the next two sections, leadership development for the millennial generation and how marathon running is handled as a leadership development strategy in the literature are determined. At the end of the paper, practical implications for leaders and organizations are suggested.

Keywords: Leadership development, marathon running, constructivist theory, millennial leaders, learning transfer

1. Introduction

The Millennial generation (born 1982–2003), whose dominating presence will make its behaviors the major motif of corporate life in the next decade, are quickly taking on leadership roles [1, 2]. The research indicates that this generation of emergent leaders lack managerial experience, thus their leadership skills are not fully developed. This means that Millennials are being promoted into managerial roles before they are ready and there is a need for ongoing mentorship and coaching to deepen their leadership skills [3–5].

Learning and development opportunities are one of the top things Millennials are looking for in an organization. They want to work for an organization that offers enough development opportunities that will allow them to grow and improve their skills [6, 7]. Besides, they do not see development and training programs offered to them as a sign of weakness, but rather a path to greatness, so to offer them leadership development training will not only make them better managers but will also excite them [4]. However while this generation has different preferences from prior generations; in terms of how they prefer to learn and how they view the programs they are offered, the organizations who would like to retain millennial talent cater to their unique needs rather than forcing them to fit into pre-existing patterns and practices. Millennials have been taught a postmodern worldview, which makes them have very different ideas about leadership and may lead to some disruption to traditional leadership. They also have different expectations of leadership development programs. Thus, the organizations should create innovative approaches to effective leadership development and offer adequate leadership development for these leaders. This will help their transition into leadership roles so that they are better positioned for success and they will provide long-term value to their organization [8–15].

While leadership learning and development initiatives are increasingly becoming complex in nature, organizations are using innovative and unusual approaches [16]. Innovative leadership development programs are effective, efficient, and establish true leaders because they focus on the stepwise completion of objective assignments that align with business strategy [17]. The present study aims to confirm that leadership development is a continuous process that can take place anywhere [18] and constitutes an answer to the call of Hamilton and Bean [19] who suggest further systematic study of leadership development that will lead to a better understanding of how to create shared meaning in context. Thus it suggests to move away from traditional leadership development courses and develops the core learning experiences from a diverse domain namely marathon running. Leadership and marathon running together provide a knowledge base that integrates understandings from diverse domains with closely linked field experiences to bridge theory and practice. As several authors have established that marathon running and leadership development share experiential commons (e.g. [20–34]), this paper introduces marathon running as an opportunity for human resources executives to facilitate leadership development for the millennial leaders and builds a theoretical foundation for academic studies.

This chapter consists of two main headings. In "Theoretical Background" section, first, the relevant literature on constructivist learning theory, learning transfer and learning transfer from the perspective of constructivist theory are explained. Then leadership development for the millennial generation and how marathon running is handled as a leadership development strategy in the literature are determined. The "Conclusion" section summarizes the results of the investigation and the results of different studies that support the present investigation's results. At the end of the paper, practical implications for leaders and organizations are suggested.

2. Theoretical background

2.1 Constructivist learning theory

The contemporary movements in the philosophy of science converge on the idea that knowledge must not be considered an objective representation of an external observer-independent environment ([35], p. 135). Constructivism is a philosophical view on how people come to understand or know ([36], p. 31). Constructivism generally casts learners in an active role. Instead of just listening, reading and working through routine exercises, they discuss, debate, hypothesize, investigate and take viewpoints ([37], p. 7). In this way, they are encouraged to constantly assess how the activity is helping them gain understanding. In ideally becoming "expert learners" by questioning themselves and their strategies, they obtain ever-broadening tools to keep learning [38].

Currently, many organizations are replacing the traditional classroom-teaching style of training with the constructivist problem-based learning style in professional training. Professional trainers prefer the problem-based learning system, because it facilitates learner autonomy and easier curriculum negotiation. Furthermore, when it is combined with small group work, it includes communication and collaborative skills that are missing in traditional professional education [39].

2.2 Learning transfer

Learning is a process of acquiring ideas, applying these ideas, embodying the ideas, reflecting on our experiences, and refining ourselves and our practice (Yeomans as cited in [40], p. 10). A central and enduring goal of training is to provide learning experiences that are useful beyond the specific conditions of initial learning ([41], p. 431). Transfer of learning refers to the use of past learning when learning something new and the application of that learning to both similar and new situations ([42], p. xiii). In the organizational training and development programs, learning transfer occurs when the learned behavior is generalized to the job context and maintained over a period of time on the job ([43], p. 63). As Fogarty et al. [44] claim, real transfer happens when people carry over something they learned in one context to a significantly different context.

While transfer of learning is the very foundation of learning, thinking, and problem solving ([42], p. xiii) and while transfer is theoretically indistinguishable from learning ([45], p. 109), there is no more important topic in the whole psychology of learning than transfer of learning ([46], p. 2).

2.3 Learning transfer from the perspective of constructivist theory

Transfer of learning enables the application of knowledge learned in one setting or for one purpose to another setting and/or purpose ([47], p. 235). According to constructivist learning theory, the learner is extremely open to new knowledge and reconstructs the information he/she acquired in his/her mind by comparing with the old information and thus begins to understand the world around him/her better ([48], p. 44). Several authors consider learning transfer from a constructivist perspective, where it is highly dependent on how a learner is able to personally integrate and apply lessons learned ([49], p. 86). Thus, it can be asserted that the aim of research on learning transfer is identical to the aim of constructivist approaches that deal with the problem of flexible applicability of knowledge ([50], p. 316). The principles of constructivist theory are also important in the context of adult approaches to learning and have important implications for learning transfer ([51], p. 9).

Although an important characteristic of learning transfer is that it does not necessarily require content overlap between the different domains [52], when the knowledge transfer in human intelligence is examined, it can be found that the individuals do not rely on low-level relatedness to transfer knowledge across domains. They are able to make analogy across different domains by resolving the high level structural similarities even when the learning domains are seemingly irrelevant. Understanding of these structural similarities helps to abstract away the details specific to the domains, and build a mapping between the abstractions. The mapping builds on the high level structural relatedness of the two domains, instead of their low level literal similarities ([53], p. 513).

2.4 Leadership development for millennial leaders

Millennial professionals are one of the most discussed and researched subjects of recent times ([54], p. 148). While they represent the majority of the workforce and about half of the manager population, they are the leaders of today [55]. Research reveals that these generation of leaders will need to be equipped to take leadership positions in organizations sooner than any other generation in history [56] thus training them for leadership is a business necessity now [57].

Leadership was always regarded as a challenge [58]. While the workplace has changed tremendously over the years, the need to develop strong, capable leaders to succeed in this fast-paced organizational environment has remained the same ([59], p. 10). Leadership learning and development is the critical priority in many of today's large, global organizations. As the degree to which an organization's leaders are effective critically affects all aspects of the business, today a more strategic and integrated approach which broadens the traditional view of leadership development and training is an absolute must ([60], p. 4; [61, 62]).

Leadership development is a highly personal learning experience that can provide new and relevant insights into one's strengths as a leader as well as the key areas to work on for further development [63]. As previous research on generational cohorts suggests that managerial practices, human resource management practices, and development strategies should be generation-appropriate [64–66], the human resources executives should architect millennial specific development avenues that accelerate professional growth and streamline success [67].

As millennials are aces at discovering information and they do not value a piece of information for its own sake, rather for its relevance to their lives [68], they are characterized as active learners, sharing the active learning style [69–71]. Research reveals that millennial leaders want experiences, not training. Rather than traditional classroom lectures, they prefer to take action and practice in the context of their real work. They find the traditional leadership development strategies too slow and believe that there is a need to redesign the leadership strategies [72]. Maybe this is because that the Millennials never accept how things were done before and always seek a new way of doing things. Innovation is one of their most attractive stereotypes [73]. The research also revealed that they believe that their organization's leadership development programs were aligned with its business needs. They stated that "poor content, insufficient thinking and expertise from outside sources, and a failure to make a compelling return-on-investment case" were the biggest barriers to training program effectiveness [13]. These findings reveal that the organizations require innovative solutions to create leadership development programs that the employees want and need. Focusing on what participants want is very important to designing any type of learning environment, so researchers and human resource executives need to design contemporary learning methods for the new generation leaders. Traditional leadership development programs generally offer classroom-based instruction pertaining to the theories, attributes, and behaviors of leaders ([74], p. 69). However millennials quickly tire of such training methods, especially if they do not see clear connections between the content and their day-to-day responsibilities. The classroom oriented training is now seen as obsolete, while the modern view is that the new design of training should be personalized, learner-directed, collaborative, interdisciplinary, offering strong connections to business and setting the stage for lifelong learning. Millennials are a cohort that constantly seeks inspiration and want to have fun [75, 76]. Besides, many of them are driven by competition. Thus the idea of incorporating game elements into training may keep them motivated and engaged in their continuous development. The organizations should consider offering this generation of leaders more diverse and engaging programs which will lead to an evolution in the leadership training and development approaches over time. These programs will not only make them better leaders, but will also excite them [4, 11]. These findings are consistent with the findings of the research which revealed that leadership development should not be simply an exercise in information download but the facilitation of a more self-directed learning process [63] and these programs need an update to reflect today's working world [77]. Research also revealed that 80 percent of business leaders believe that greater innovation was needed in learning techniques used in leadership development programs [13]. While today's world of the millennial leaders calls for a renewed focus on what constitutes genuine leadership development programs aiming to develop leaders ready to get ahead of tomorrow's challenges, it is time to challenge the status quo and push the leadership development efforts to the next level [78]. It is a fact that a leadership development program is only as good as its practical applications [79] and effective leaders learn from significant life experiences, such as inspirational experiences. The strategy of reflection used by leaders in significant life experiences can be utilized as an effective learning tool in leadership development [80].

The organizations should respond to these issues with the enhancement of existing leadership development programs that aim to develop this new generation of leaders. In light of the above discussion and following the notion of thinking about new and creative methods to reach the hearts and minds of the millennial leaders, the present study proposes a novel approach to alleviate the problem of the traditional classroom leadership development programs. More specifically, it aims to integrate the leadership and the learning research and make a contemporary approach to learning transfer from the perspective of constructivist theory in articulating the variety of leadership behaviors desired and clarifying the way learning by an inspirational experience such as marathon running influence those behaviors.

2.5 Marathon running as a leadership development strategy

A marathon is not just a 26.2 mile endurance race to run. In fact the marathon journey is a lot longer than that and it involves a lot more than just running [81].

Leadership is in many ways like marathon running. Numerous characteristics are adequate for both. From boardrooms to meetings, successful leaders often have many marathons against them when it comes to running, literally. Running a marathon which is seen as one of the greatest feats of human endurance [82] and the ultimate human challenge ([83], p. 348), requires continuous learning as does leadership [84]. As leadership development is a process that occurs in contexts, which are value-laden environments ([19, 85], p. 344; [86]), determinants of marathon running success may apply to leaders and offer them parameters of a life-long training regimen for success in this challenging profession of leading. Thus marathon running may constitute 26.2 miles of leadership lessons.

The most fundamental ideal required to understand learning transfer is that two tasks may differ yet share some common components, which provide the basis for intertask transfer ([87], pp. 15–16). Based on this claim, the present study offers a comprehensive list of leadership lessons one can learn by training for and completing a marathon, as well as commentary on the reasons of learning and living those lessons are a requirement for anyone who wants to be a leader.

A marathon is not just running 26.2 miles on race day. It is about putting in roughly 600 miles over a four to six month training period leading up to race day [33]. Crossing the finish line of a marathon is a great feeling. But for many, the journey of getting to the start line is more important than crossing the finish line.

If a runner has decided to take up running or signed up for a marathon, he/she has completed the first step to becoming a marathon runner. A runner should not shy away from taking that first step because he/she is afraid he/she will not be able to achieve his/her goal exactly how he/she pictures it. The first step to goal setting is to have absolute belief and faith in the process [88, 89]. A runner, who gets to the start line, will get to the finish line. While we all are capable of more than we think we are, although to take the first step is also the hardest one for the leaders, a leader should not wait for the moment when everything is in perfect alignment. Once a start is made, the following steps will be slightly easier, and there begins the journey towards achieving the goal. The leader shall align with his/her leadership goal and reach forward by placing one foot in front of the other. Before he/she knows it, he/she will gain momentum and move to the next phase called "second wind". Thus, a leader should focus a lot on getting the projects to the start line. With the support of his/her team, he/she will get it to the finish line [81, 90–92].

Running a marathon is a major commitment. It requires long periods of meticulous planning and a strict physiological and mental training regime [93]. This means several months of arduous, painstaking preparation which includes a careful diet and a regimented program of progressively longer runs [82, 94]. This is a must for the runners so that they know where they are going and that they are focused on establishing and reaching their goal. Aside from focus, it is also important for runners to have a race-day strategy which is based on training data such as total mileage, average pace and races completed during the training period. A solid strategy, careful planning, a strong focus and the ability to stay on the course are keys to success not only in running but also in leadership [95]. Goals do not only maintain motivation and desire to meet targets, but they also give the individual something tangible to aspire for and create a blueprint to stay focused and disciplined [32, 96]. Leadership involves skills, competencies and strategies that focus on collective action to achieve common goals [97, 98]. To achieve these goals, leaders should make plans so that they do not go in numerous directions, trying to figure out what to do next [34, 99]. The leaders focus their own attention because attention is the basis of the most essential of leadership skills - emotional, organizational, and strategic intelligence [100]. They also focus on ensuring the sustainable productivity of the ones in their organizations [101, 102]. By being able to remain focused at work and by careful planning, the leader gets connected to his/her sense of purpose and values.

To rise to the challenge of the marathon and complete the 26.2 mile can require speed and endurance, but most of all; it requires a huge expenditure of effort and determination [25, 95, 103]. Leadership is not different. Research shows that self-determination is essential to effective leadership based on the frequency with which attributes of self-determination are identified as elements of effective leadership [98, 104]. Leaders should have abundant passion and high intentionality. For leaders it takes steadfastness to stay determined in the face of challenges and successes ([105, 106], p. 235; [107]).

Experienced runners advise the beginners to expect the unexpected and to be prepared for it when it comes to running a marathon. Most unexpected things that happen during a marathon are like; breaking a shoelace, a heart rate monitor that will not stay on, messing up the GPS watch, chafing, wearing too little or too many clothes, cold symptoms or heat exhaustion, potty problems, blisters and black toenails, getting tripped by another runner or getting to a water station only to find out that they are out of liquid. When the unexpected occurs during a race, the runner should try not to get too upset and keep running [32, 108–110]. It is also possible that the worst happens on marathon day and the runner has to pull out, or gets injured. In such a case, he/she should try to think positively and focus on what he/she has achieved and not on what he/she has not. Top performers look at these things as learning experiences and let it be a motivation to get themselves in shape for the next opportunity. This is the time to start questioning "If I were going to do it again, what would I learn from that? What would I do differently?" and look for areas of improvement. That fires the brain towards a newer goal rather than away from it [111]. This happens also in leadership. Even the most experienced and skillful leaders have been confounded and frustrated by the inconsistent outcomes of careful planning [112]. Leaders need to keep an open mind and adjust their plan if necessary. It is the key to react to external changes, such as competition, customer feedback and new technologies [34]. A leader should also acknowledge that there will be setbacks. It is important to keep in mind that there are lessons learned from each failure [20, 113].

Although running is considered as an individual sport [114, 115] and not a team sport, no one gets to the finish line without support. Even though the runners compete individually, they often train with a training partner or in a team environment and often in opposition to their partner or teammates [116, 117]. By drawing inspiration and energy from each other, they push each other in order to achieve greater levels of performance. Furthermore, the training regimen of a runner includes gym trainers, masseurs to keep supple, pilates instructors, nutritionists, coaches and podiatrists. On the day of the marathon, there is a large psychological and small drafting advantage to running in a group, so it is better to stay with other runners [113, 118]. Besides, the committed individuals from fellow runners to friends, volunteers and spectators cheering on the marathon runner, lift the runner's spirits and her/his chances of success by their engagement. It would have been much harder to cross the finish line without all this support [26]. Leadership is also not a solo mission; it is a team sport. Leading an organization is so complex and multi-faceted that it is dangerously misguided to believe that one person has all the superhuman qualities that some may often claim they possess. The essence of leadership is accomplishing worthy goals through the combined effort of others [24, 119–121]. Without a diverse team and broad support, the victories can be somewhat hollow [21, 122].

A key requirement for optimal marathon performance is optimal pacing. A runner needs to become a master at pacing himself/herself in order to maximize his/her potential on the marathon day [118, 123]. To avoid getting burned out he/she should not go too fast on running or should not push himself/herself too fast in the beginning or for too long [24]. Pace also matters for long-term performance in an organization. A leader should recognize that everyone in the organization is not working at exactly the same speed and while achieving results he/she should vary the pace. In order not to use his/her own individual work pace as the standard which may usually lead to unrealistic expectations and frustrated co-workers, he/she should sometimes pause the action and create some space in the intervals between major events. In this way, energy may be conserved across the organization to lead high levels of performance for the long haul [124–126].

Marathon runners are not born. They are made. They train to become marathon runners. When a runner starts training for a marathon, unless he/she regularly runs that kind of distance (26.2 miles), he/she starts off being unable to run it. As capabilities build over time; the body transforms slowly to handle more running at faster speeds. That is the way of becoming a better runner [113, 127–129]. What makes runners and leaders is their willingness to learn and push themselves. Leadership also takes practice. The effective leaders grow in their roles. Through continuous learning and practicing, they enhance their strength, stamina and effectiveness as a leader. As they practice and develop their leadership endurance, they can run a bit longer than their last time [22, 28, 34, 84, 130].

Running a marathon requires a set of principles regarding physiology, psychology, nutrition and training [131, 132]. Like marathon runners, leaders require a set of principles that guide their actions and activities. This set of principles can be referred to as leadership ethics [84]. As ethics is the heart of leadership ([133, 134], p. 14), leading without ethics is no leadership at all [135].

Many spectators will see runners hunched over throughout the marathon, but even more so near the end. The reason is the increase in the amount of lactate in their muscles, which results in cramps. Lactate builds up when a runner burns glucose at a faster rate than he takes in oxygen, for instance, during the final sprint. Towards the end of a marathon is also when the effects of tissue damage on the muscles and joints really start to be felt, too. Unfortunately this damage is unavoidable. Resilient runners can cope with adversity and complete the marathon because they have the psychological ability to cope with both physical and mental fatigue. As the mind has great influence over the body, if the mind does not give up, the body will follow no matter how tired. Once the runner hits her/his stride, those thoughts will go away and he/she will experience a "runner's high" ([21, 136, 137], p. 23; [138, 139]). Like marathon running, leadership will also empty one's tank. At some point, the leaders' natural energy which keeps them running, influencing, stable and encouraged diminishes. As a result they need to make a lot of effort with all their resources and they burn out. In order to be able to respond to challenges and finally not burn out, a leader should keep in mind that they have unused reserves and push themselves, often one mile at a time. Otherwise, they will not realize or experience the depths of those reserves [28, 33, 140, 141].

A marathon is a massive physical challenge for the body. Recovery and self-renewal are absolutely essential and as important as activity [20, 142, 143]. Thus, following the marathon training cycle, a runner needs to spend a fair amount of time not running and instead resting, recovering and recuperating, both mentally and physically. Furthermore he/she should prevent injury and maintain hard-earned fitness by slowly and gradually building back up. Muscles need time off to heal and strengthen themselves. More rest and recovery is better than less, and a recurring theme is to listen to the body and back off until it says it is ready to go. This is the time to celebrate the past success and plan for future ones. Although similarly, leaders cannot attempt to be active all the time, recovery and renewal are often ignored in business. The research shows that working long hours on a continuous basis reduces overall effectiveness [144–146]. As the leaders cannot deal effectively with challenges and cannot manage stressful situations without a baseline level of emotional well-being, they need to give themselves time to relax and recharge [130, 141, 147, 148].

The glory of the most recent run remains with the runner only for a short time. Then comes the time to do it once again. The finish line of a marathon is the start of a new one. After the recovery is over, it is time to start the next season or cycle to set new goals and build on the strengths and weaknesses of past training. As goals are made to be achieved, either for a runner or a leader, it is suggested to decide on a greater and longer term goal. For a marathon runner, this may be to run another marathon or do one in a new and exciting location. For the leader, this may be a new project or a greater organizational success. New goals are set and the cycle of "challenge and accomplish" is repeated [149].

This review reveals that there is no one trait that will guarantee the runner a marathon success, but several rules of thumb that come together to give him/her the best chance. Likewise, many studies were conducted in the area of leadership trait theories to discover a list of physical and psychological traits or qualities that account for leadership effectiveness. However, none of them has come up with a universal list of traits that all successful leaders possess, or traits that will guarantee leadership success. Although there is no list of traits that guarantees leadership success, traits that are related to leadership success have been identified ([150, 151], p. 16; [152, 153]).

3. Conclusion

This research deals with the leadership development concept from the perspective of constructivist theory from a viewpoint of learning transfer and reveals that the participants of a marathon which is regarded as one of the greatest feats of human endurance [82] and the ultimate human challenge ([83], p. 348) can develop their leadership skills which can directly be applied to today's organizations.

Marathon running has become a popular sport globally in recent years. This can be partially reflected by the rapid growing number of marathon participants all over the world [154]. Although marathon running is one of the most demanding sports in the world, highly successful people enjoy this sport. While they have character traits such as focus and persistence, they can achieve success both in a marathon and in the business world [155]. Several studies revealed that a character trait of the millennial generation is also a desire to succeed [156, 157] and being a runner is part of their identity [158]. Thus, it is no wonder that they have been dubbed "the running generation" [159].

Sport, as a sphere of human life which is dominated by the continuous competition, naturally creates and shapes leaders [160]. Business leaders are keen to understand the athletes' passion for excellence and translate this formula for success into the corporate world [121]. While leadership is a lifelong marathon that one must endeavor to run with distinction so that he/she may get his/her due reward [161], the leaders know that they have a long distance to run and it is not speed but other traits like stamina and endurance that will carry them through [113].

In today's rapid-paced organizations, dynamic leaders are needed more than ever. The qualities that one has to replicate to thrive as a leader and to run a marathon are the same and marathon running has a structure similar to today's business environment with its compelling and dynamic conditions. Today the companies are looking for ways to offer their millennial leaders enough opportunities to develop and grow in ways that fit their preferences and styles. This study provides guidance on how marathons constitute more experiential while less didactic and thus unique learning environments for the millennial leaders to develop new perceptions of what they are trying to accomplish, what are the obstacles that stand in their way, and what they can do to overcome them and thus observe the challenges they will face. Today organizations seek to extend training beyond the basics. The present study wants to encourage them to break the traditional mold in their leadership development processes to open up to new and innovative ideas on these programs by the development of a methodology of marathon running to be translated into a mindset that will improve leadership performance.

Today leaders have to go through various learning processes which have both cognitive and behavioral complexity [162]. Previous research has emphasized the value of leadership development, offered insights on leadership preparation and revealed that leadership encompasses a learned set of knowledge, skills and attitudes [163, 164]. Leadership training and development programs which include a process of learning for problem solving, decision making and strategy formulation, have become a popular technique [165, 166]. As Covey [167] claims: "No person can persuade another to change. Each of us guards a gate that can only be opened from the inside." To ensure a positive learning transfer, a leadership development program must create the appropriate learning environment by providing learning experiences that are applied beyond the specific conditions of initial learning and make learners learn by observation, interpretation, analysis and questioning.

Running a marathon helps to build the mental skills and attitude necessary for traversing the challenges of the business. It does not only have profound benefits for mental health [168] but it also helps the individuals to develop mental toughness [169] which is a skill that the magnitude of the success of a leader depends on [170]. Furthermore, it offers a dynamic, experiential course for leadership development and opportunities to develop one's personal leadership style to inspire his/her team, motivate the staff and transform the organization. As learning environments with strong applicability to future experiences have greater potential for a more positive transfer of learning ([171], p. 230) marathons have a positive effect on the leadership skills of the participants and contributes to leadership development. Runners also claim that marathons provide vivid leadership development lessons [23, 33]. The findings of the present study suggest the Millennial professionals, the next generation of leaders who were raised by the concept of "team dynamics" and "everyone's a winner" in the school classroom [172], to take on new athletic challenges and run a marathon in order to make it a part of their leadership development. Although running a marathon is not on everyone's bucket list, it is a fact that the ones in leadership roles are (metaphorically) training for marathons every day they turn up for work.

The present paper presents a contemporary approach to leadership development and suggests the organizations to design leadership programs that will benefit from the learning transfer that identifies the common factors between marathon running and leadership. Marathon running may be a brilliant idea for the leaders to undertake leadership exercises in order to stretch their leadership skills. When coupled with training classes for developing leadership competencies and specific development goals, such an assignment may constitute a wonderful platform for leadership development and a rich growth opportunity that yields many benefits to the leader as a learner. Although scholars claim that it is difficult to predict whether transfer of learning will be positive or negative in particular cases because of incomplete knowledge of what was learned originally and how the transfer task is represented ([173], p. 4), the findings of the present study support the idea that the implementing of descriptive processes of marathon running programs in leadership development programs possesses relevance to leadership development issues with elements of valuable context. The results of this study, therefore, may help break new ground in comparing the effectiveness of traditional approach versus constructivist approach in leadership development programs.

The particular frame presented in the present study supports the experiences of several others (e.g. [20–34]) that marathon running and leadership development share experiential commons. Regarding the findings of the present study, it is suggested to the human resource executives who will decide to organize such leadership development programs, to choose running programs which have levels of difficulty that suits the participants' athletic levels and to encourage the individuals to participate these programs, even a marathon. As training for a marathon, takes planning, discipline and serious preparation, the challenge will be incredible and deliver several lessons for a leader. The leadership development programs which will combine traditional corporate classroom lessons with marathon training sessions will make the corporate leaders develop their leadership skills with their constructivist sessions. This approach also helps to eliminate the transferability issues that are typically present in leadership development programs in the corporate world and in academic settings.

There has been a considerable increase in the number of participants running marathons over the past several years [174]. Many leaders believe that a motivation to keep running is that it leads to business success by reducing stress, creating a balance in their lives and fostering a mental toughness that can bring rewards in the boardroom [175]. They are also running marathons because they are very success-oriented people and the marathons make them experience an even greater sense of achievement [176]. Previous research revealed that there is a positive relationship between leader fitness and firm value [177] and participation in sport influences leadership skills, style and career development and constitutes a powerful motivator for executives [178]. Previous research also revealed that despite the negative stigma associated with burnout resulting from marathon training, 85.7 percent of marathon runners believe that training did not negatively impact their ability to do their job. As the dedication and commitment involved in training can actually equip participants with a whole range of transferable skills that they can apply in the workplace, it can have a positive impact on overall career success. This makes marathon runners possibly even better employees [93]. These findings are consistent with the findings of the present study which reveal that marathon runners become better leaders. Despite the pain of it, running a marathon and testing the limits of the body and mind helps the leaders build the mental skills and attitude necessary for beating leadership challenges.

Written in 1908, the Olympic Creed states "The most important thing in the Olympic Games is not to win but to take part, just as the most important thing in life is not the triumph but the struggle. The essential thing is not to have conquered but to have fought well." [179]. True leaders understand that leadership development is a journey that never ends. And they keep in mind that success is not about finishing on top or making the most money. They are in a learning journey of constant growth, evolving and developing creative thinking capabilities and competencies. As the one who runs a marathon, runs against the distance, not against the other runners, it is more important for the leaders to learn from the journey and reach their potential [33, 180–182].

4. Practical implications

Previous research suggests that leader development programmes should be realistic and challenging while providing an opportunity for growth in knowledge and skills through self-reflections and external assessments [104, 183]. Leadership development programmes which are poorly matched to participants' expectations can be harmful and create negative experiences ([184], p. 435). The researchers should suggest a new paradigm of leadership that will operate for the new generation leaders of the 21st century, not the old paradigm of leadership that has dominated the literature for years. Taken together, the findings of this study have significant implications for the understanding of how marathon running promotes leadership development.

5. Limitations and further research

Regarding the findings of the present study, the corporate marathon running programs are expected to demonstrate the ability to produce beneficial outcomes in critical areas of leadership development. However, some scholars and human resources executives may question whether these programs truly benefit leaders and their respective organizations. While the findings of the present study may speak favorably for these programs, how these changes are affected by differing cultures and organizations remains unclear. The future research should focus on the lack of clarity around these variables as well as the effectiveness of certain facilitation practices in achieving desired leadership development objectives for the organizations.

As the primary purpose of the present study is to offer new insights into leadership development of millennial leaders, the researcher hopes that the findings could help the design of these programs to become more effective in leaders of the new generation leaders.

Author details

Elif Bilginoğlu
Independent Researcher, Turkey

*Address all correspondence to: elifb@ada.net.tr

References

[1] White, S.K. (2016, September 06). 5 tips to better understand millennial managers. Retrieved at https://www.cio.com/article/3116157/leadership-management/5-tips-to-better-understand-millennial-managers.html

[2] Winograd, M., Hais, M. (2014). *How Millennials Could Upend Wall Street and Corporate America.* Washington, DC: Governance Studies at Brookings.

[3] Deloitte (2016). The 2016 Deloitte millennial survey: Winning over the next generation of leaders Retrieved at https://www2.deloitte.com/content/dam/Deloitte/global/Documents/About-Deloitte/gx-millenial-survey-2016-exec-summary.pdf

[4] O'Donnell, J.T. (2016, April 27). 4 mistakes to expect from millennial managers. Retrieved at https://www.inc.com/jt-odonnell/why-you-can-expect-these-4-mistakes-from-millennial-managers.html

[5] Workplace Trends (2015, November 10). *The Multi-Generational Leadership Study.* Retrieved at https://workplacetrends.com/the-multi-generational-leadership-study/

[6] Bentley University (2014, November 11) Millennials at Work. Retrieved at https://www.bentley.edu/newsroom/latest-headlines/mind-of-millennial

[7] Deloitte (2018). 2018 Deloitte millennial survey: Millennials disappointed in business, unprepared for Industry 4.0. Retrieved at https://www2.deloitte.com/content/dam/Deloitte/global/Documents/About-Deloitte/gx-2018-millennial-survey-report.pdf

[8] BestWork, Inc. (2018, June 04). Millennials in the Workplace: The Importance of Developing Millennial Leaders. Retrieved at https://bestworkinc.com/millennials-workplace-developing-millennial-leaders/

[9] Brennan, M. (2018, April 04). Millennials, Boomers & The Leadership Gap. Retrieved at https://www.hrtechnologist.com/articles/leadership-succession/millennials-boomers-amp-the-leadership-gap/

[10] Brousell, L. (2015, August 04). How millennials challenge traditional leadership. Retrieved at https://www.cio.com/article/2956600/leadership-management/how-millennials-challenge-traditional-leadership.html

[11] DeRosa, D. (2018, July 17). 5 Ways to start training millennials for leadership roles. Retrieved at https://www.onpointconsultingllc.com/blog/5-ways-to-start-training-millennials-for-leadership-roles

[12] Fries, K. (2018, January 18). 7 ways millennials are changing traditional leadership. Retrieved at https://www.forbes.com/sites/kimberlyfries/2018/01/18/7-ways-millennials-are-changing-traditional-leadership/#14fa97557dae

[13] Harvard Business Publishing Corporate Learning (2018). *State of Leadership Development: Meeting the Transformation Imperative.* USA: Harvard Business School Publishing.

[14] Hopkins, J. (2017, July 08). Millennial managers: A guide For successful management. Retrieved at https://www.forbes.com/sites/jamiehopkins/2017/07/08/millennials-managers-a-guide-for-successful-management/#9c9e6c72ac30

[15] Moore, K. (2014, August 14). Authenticity: The Way to the Millennial's Heart. Retrieved at https://www.forbes.com/sites/karlmoore/2014/08/14/authenticity-the-way-to-the-millennials-heart/#3432e2574531

[16] Edwards, G., Elliott, C., Iszatt-White, M., Schedlitzki, D. (2015). Using creative techniques in leadership learning and development: An introduction, Advances in Developing Human Resources, 17(3), 279-288. doi: 10.1177/1523422315586616

[17] Hummel, B. (2016, October 08). Innovative approaches to leadership development. Retrieved at https://www.linkedin.com/pulse/innovative-approaches-leadership-development-brad-hummel

[18] Fulmer, R. M. (1997). The evolving paradigm of leadership development. Organizational Dynamics, *25*(4), 59-72. doi: 10.1016/S0090-2616(97)90037-1

[19] Hamilton, F., Bean, C.J. (2005). The importance of context, beliefs and values in leadership development, Business Ethics: A European Review, *14*(4), 336-347. doi: 10.1111/j.1467-8608.2005.00415.x

[20] Byrne, B. (2017, October 05). Six leadership lessons I learned from running a marathon. Retrieved at http://www.imi.ie/six-leadership-lessons-learned-running-marathon

[21] Dixit, R.K. (2016, January 24). Leadership lessons from running a marathon. Retrieved at https://www.linkedin.com/pulse/leadership-lessons-from-running-marathon-ravi-kant-dixit

[22] Edwards, C. (2016, February 08). Why leadership is like running a marathon. Retrieved at http://www.croftandcompany.com/why-leadership-is-like-running-a-marathon/

[23] Gergen, C. (2013, December 12). Leadership lessons from the marathon trail. Retrieved at https://www.ccl.org/articles/leading-effectively-articles/leadership-lessons-from-the-marathon-trail/

[24] Lalonde, J. (2017, October 18). Leadership lessons from running a half marathon at 3AM, Retrieved at https://www.jmlalonde.com/leadership-lessons-running-half-marathon-3am/

[25] Mahoney, R. (2016, November 07). Leadership and running a half marathon lessons applied as a pacer. Retrieved at https://www.linkedin.com/pulse/leadership-running-half-marathon-lessons-applied-ron

[26] Moyo, D. (2015, April 18). What leaders can learn from a long run. Retrieved at https://blogs.wsj.com/atwork/2015/04/18/running-a-marathon-and-leadership/

[27] Skinner, S. (2015). Leadership is like running. Retrieved at http://www.halogen.org.au/content/leadership-is-like-running/gjzqnw

[28] Suderman, J. (2016, January 28). Half-marathon leadership lessons: Perseverance & push. Retrieved at http://jeffsuderman.com/half-marathon-leadership-lessons-perseverance-push

[29] Tredgold, G. (2013). *Leadership: It's a Marathon Not a Sprint - Everything You Need to Know about Sustainable Achievements.* UK: Panoma Press.

[30] Tripathi, R. (2017, November 24). Leadership lessons from a marathon: Musings from my long-distance runs. Retrieved at https://www.digitalistmag.com/future-of-work/2017/11/24/leadership-lessons-from-marathon-05525557

[31] Waldschmidt, D. (2012, November 02). 5 leadership lessons I learned while running a marathon, Retrieved at https://www.businessinsider.com.au/5-leadership-lessons-i-learned-dan-waldschmidt-2012-11

[32] Wallor, E. (2010, September 07). Leadership and the marathon runner: 7 words to lead by. Retrieved at https://

artpetty.com/2010/09/07/leadership-and-the-marathon-runner-7-words-to-lead-by/

[33] Walsh, G. (2018, May 20). Leadership is a marathon. Retrieved at https://www.geraldwalsh.com/blog/leadership-is-a-marathon/

[34] Yudelman, E. (2017). Six important lessons I learned about running that apply to leadership. Retrieved at https://centricconsulting.com/blog/six-important-lessons-about-running-and-leadership_boston/

[35] von Glasersfeld, E. (1989). Cognition, construction of knowledge, and teaching, Synthese, *80*(1), 121-140. doi: 10.1007/BF00869951

[36] Savery, J.R., Duffy, T.M. (1995). Problem based learning: An instructional model and its constructivist framework, Educational Technology, *35*, 31-38.

[37] Perkins, D. (1999). The many faces of constructivism, Educational Leadership, *57*(3), 6-11.

[38] Saini, R. (2015). Constructivism in Education, DAV Academic Review, *1*(1), 97-105

[39] Bines, H. (1992). Issues in Course Design. In H. Bines & D. Watson (Eds.) *Developing Professional Education* (pp. 11-56). Oxford: SRHE and Open University Press.

[40] McCord, S.L. (2016). *Innovation and Leadership Development for the Millennial Generation.* Southern Illinois University Carbondale Honors Theses. Paper 415.

[41] Lobato, J. (2006). Alternative Perspectives on the Transfer of Learning: History, Issues, and Challenges for Future Research, The Journal of the Learning Sciences, *15*(4), 431-449. doi: 10.1207/s15327809jls1504_1

[42] Haskell, R.E. (2001). *Transfer of Learning: Cognition, Instruction and Reasoning.* San Diego: Academic Press).

[43] Baldwin, T.T., Ford, J. K. (1988). Transfer of training: A review and directions for future research, Personnel Psychology, *41*(1), 63-105. doi: 10.1111/j.1744-6570.1988.tb00632.x

[44] Fogarty, R., Perkins, D., Barrell, J. (1992). *The Mindful School: How to Teach for Transfer. Highett*. Australia: Hawker Brownlow Education.

[45] Kimball, D.R., Holyoak, K.J. (2000). Transfer and expertise. In E. Tulving & F.I M. Craik (Eds.). *The Oxford Handbook of Memory* (pp. 109-122). London: Oxford University Press.

[46] Leberman, S., McDonald, L., Doyle, S. (2006). *The Transfer of Learning: Participants' Perspectives of Adult Education and Training.* Hampshire, England: Gower Publishing Limited.

[47] Gagne, E. D., Yekovich, C. W., Yekovich, F. R. (1993). *The Cognitive Psychology of School Learning.* New York, HarperCollins College

[48] Karadağ, E., Korkmaz, T. (2007). Yapılandırmacı öğrenmeye genel bakış. In E. Karadağ & T. Korkmaz (Eds.). *Kuramdan Uygulamaya Yapılandırmacı Öğrenme Yaklaşımı - 1-5. Sınıf Etkinlik Örnekleriyle* (pp. 38-58) Ankara: Kök Yayıncılık.

[49] Sibthorp, J., Paisley, K., Furman, N., Gookin, J. (2009). Long-term Impacts Attributed to Participation in Wilderness Education: Preliminary findings from NOLS. In *Ninth Biennial Research Symposium* (Vol. 115, pp. 86-103). NewYork: Coalition for Education in the Outdoors.

[50] Prenzel, M., Mandl, H. (1991). Transfer of learning from a

constructivist perspective. In T. M. Duffy, J. Lowyck, D.H. Jonassen & T.M. Welsh (Eds.) *Designing Environments for* Constructive Learning (pp. 315-329). Berlin: Springer Verlag.

[51] Kirwan, C. (2009). *Improving Learning Transfer: A Guide to Getting More Out of What You Put Into Your Training.* England: Gower Publishing.

[52] Moreno, O., Shapira, B., Rokach, L., Shani, G. (2012). TALMUD – Transfer Learning for Multiple Domains, Proceedings of the 21st ACM International Conference on Information and Knowledge Management - CIKM '12. doi: 10.1145/2396761.2396817

[53] Wang, H., Yang, Q. (2011). Transfer learning by structural analogy, *Proceedings of the Twenty-Fifth AAAI Conference on Artificial Intelligence,* 513-518.

[54] Srivastava, M., Banerjee, P. (2016). Understanding gen y: The motivations, values and beliefs, Journal of Management Research, *16*(3), 148-164.

[55] Skidmore, K. (2017, December 14). How to develop leaders in 2018: 5 top trends in leadership development. Retrieved at https://www.flashpointleadership.com/blog/how-to-develop-leaders-in-2018-5-top-trends-in-leadership-development

[56] Morin, A. (2016, July 27). Want to train millennials to lead? 6 things you should know about the millennial mindset. Retrieve at https://www.forbes.com/sites/amymorin/2016/07/27/want-to-train-millennials-to-lead-6-things-you-should-know-about-the-millennial-mindset/#425059ff4782

[57] Buckley, J. (2013). Leadership Training for Millennials Done Right. Retrieved at http://www.jaredbuckley.com/steps-train-millennials-for-leadership/

[58] Kouzes, J.M., Posner, B.Z. (2007). *The Leadership Challenge.* San Francisco, CA: Jossey-Bass.

[59] Ketter, P. (2013). The seven decades of leadership development. Retrieved at https://www.td.org/magazines/td-magazine/the-seven-decades-of-leadership-development

[60] Heffner, S., Kennedy, S., Brand, J., Walsh, P. (2011). Develop your leaders, transform your organizations, Retrieved at https://www.harvardbusiness.org/sites/default/files/16843_CL_Whitepaper_Transform_Organization_0.pdf

[61] Loew, L. (2013). Learning and development: A key component of an integrated talent management framework. Retrieved at https://trainingmag.com/learning-and-development-key-component-integrated-talent-management-framework/

[62] Society for Human Resource Management (2017). Leadership development. Retrieved at https://www.shrm.org/hr-today/trends-and-forecasting/special-reports-and-expert-views/Documents/17-0396%20Research%20Overview%20Leadership%20Development%20FNL.pdf

[63] Telfer, G. (2014, March). Facilitating leadership development (Through experiential learning). Retrieved at https://www.leadershipthroughexp.com/article.php?id=17

[64] Kupperschmidt, B. R. (2000). Multigeneration employees: Strategies for effective management, The Health Care Manager, *19*, 65-76.

[65] Marston, C. (2010, August 27). Employee training and development across the generations. Retrieved at https://trainingindustry.com/articles/

strategy-alignment-and-planning/employee-training-and-development-across-the-generations/

[66] Lancaster, L.C., Stillman, D. (2002). *When Generations Collide: Who They Are. Why They Clash. How to Solve the Generational Puzzle at Work.* NewYork: Harper Business.

[67] BasuMallick, C. (2018, August 14). 4 Essentials of a Millennial-First Leadership Plan. Retrieved at https://www.hrtechnologist.com/articles/leadership-succession/4-essentials-of-a-millennialfirst-leadership-plan/

[68] Laskaris, J. (2016, March). How to engage millennials: 5 important moves. Retrieved at https://www.efrontlearning.com/blog/2016/03/5-strategies-to-engage-the-millennials.html

[69] Jain, A. (2016). Don't teach me, let me learn! Millennial learning, Indore Management Journal, *8*(1), 60-67.

[70] Roehl, A., Reddy, S.L., Shannon, G.J. (2013). The flipped classroom: An opportunity to engage millennial students through active learning strategies, *Journal of Family & Consumer Sciences, (105)*2, 44-49.

[71] Toohey, S.L., Wray, A., Wiechmann, W., Lin, M., Boysen-Osborn, M. (2016). Ten tips for engaging the millennial learner and moving an emergency medicine residency curriculum into the 21st century, Western Journal of Emergency Medicine: Integrating Emergency Care with Population Health, *17*(3), 337-343.

[72] Happ, A. (2017, June 30). Developing millennial leaders. Retrieved at https://trainingindustry.com/articles/leadership/developing-millennial-leaders/

[73] Altman, I. (2017, March 18). 3 surprising keys millennial leaders need for success. Retrieved at https://www.forbes.com/sites/ianaltman/2017/03/18/3-surprising-keys-millennial-leaders-need-for-success/#3d6ad7497902

[74] Grimard, C.M., Pellerin, S. (2018). Developing leadership through leadership experiences: An action learning approach, Developments in Business Simulation and Experiential Learning, *45*, 69-77.

[75] Long, J. (2017, July 10). 10 Millennial Leadership Qualities That Contribute to a Positive Office Culture. Retrieved at https://www.entrepreneur.com/article/296851

[76] Nair, P. (2011, July 29). The classroom is obsolete: It's time for something new. Retrieved at https://www.edweek.org/ew/articles/2011/07/29/37nair.h30.html

[77] Waters, S. (2017, July 24). It's time to update leadership development. Retrieved at https://www.shrm.org/hr-today/news/hr-magazine/0817/pages/its-time-to-update-leadership-development.aspx

[78] Skidmore, K. (2018, December 11). Design leadership programs that succeed in 2019: 5 top trends in leadership development. Retrieved at https://www.flashpointleadership.com/blog/leadership-program-design-2019-top-trends-in-leadership-development

[79] Donnelly, T. (2010, July 26). How to create a leadership development program. Retrieved at https://www.inc.com/guides/2010/07/how-to-create-a-leadership-development-program.html

[80] Meers, R. P. (2009). *How Effective Leaders Learn from Life: A Grounded Theory Study of the Impact of Significant Life Experiences Upon Leadership Development.* ETD collection for University of Nebraska - Lincoln. AAI3386556.

[81] Scully, J. (2016, March 03). Ten things every first-time marathon runner needs to know. Retrieved at https://www.theguardian.com/lifeandstyle/the-running-blog/2016/mar/03/ten-things-every-first-time-marathon-runner-needs-to-know

[82] Barford, V., Kelly, J. (2012, March 21). Could you run a marathon without training? Retrieved at https://www.bbc.com/news/magazine-17456672

[83] van Dijk, H., van Megen, R. (2017). *The Secret of Running: Maximum Performance Gains through Effective Power Metering and Training Analysis.* UK: Meyer & Meyer Sport.

[84] Auxier, B. (2014, May 13). Leadership is like running a marathon, Retrieved at https://billauxier.com/leadership-is-like-running-a-marathon/

[85] Gibson, K. (2016, October 05). Context In Leadership Training: Without Context, Leadership Training Will Fail. Retrieved at https://elearningindustry.com/context-in-leadership-training

[86] Klimoski, R. (2013). Commentary: When it comes to leadership, context matters. In M. G. Rumsey (Ed.), Oxford library of psychology. The Oxford handbook of leadership (p. 267-287). Oxford University Press.

[87] Gick, M.L., Holyoak, K.J. (1987). The cognitive basis of knowledge transfer. In S.M. Cormier & J.D. Hagman (Eds.) *Transfer of Learning: Contemporary Research and Applications* (pp. 9-46). San Diego, California: Academic Press.

[88] Foster, B. (2013, July 05). 10 steps to successful goal setting. Retrieved at https://www.huffingtonpost.com/bradley-foster/how-to-set-goals_b_3226083.html

[89] Galloway, J. (2017). 10 steps to start running. Retrieved at https://www.active.com/running/articles/10-steps-to-start-running

[90] Elizaga, K. (2013). *Find Your Sweet Spot: A Guide to Personal and Professional Excellence.* Guilford, Connecticut: skirt!

[91] Patel, N.V. (2015, November 02). What causes 'Second Wind' in runners? Retrieved at https://www.inverse.com/article/7687-what-causes-second-wind-in-runners

[92] Usher, I., Anderson, V. (2014). *7 Simple Steps to Goal Achieving Success - Including 100 Tips to Help You Achieve Your Goals and Live the Life You've Always Imagined.* USA: Wider Vision Publishing.

[93] Larkin, N. (2016, April 22). Why running a marathon is good for your career, Retrieved at https://www.cv-library.co.uk/career-advice/work-life/running-marathon-good-career/

[94] Noakes, T.D. (2001). *Lore of Running.* Champaign, IL: Human Kinetics

[95] Mills, S. (2014, April 15). 10 ways running can make you a better leader. Retrieved at https://www.business2community.com/leadership/10-ways-running-can-make-better-leader-0848340

[96] Velde, T. (2014, March 15). The 3 Ds of marathon success: Discipline. Dedication. Determination. Retrieved at http://archive.boston.com/sports/marathon/blog/2014/03/the_3-ds_of_marathon_success_d.html

[97] De Lacerta, T.C. (2015). Understanding leadership effectiveness in organizational settings: An integrative approach. Universidade de Lisboa, Unpublished Doctoral Dissertation.

[98] Johnson, J.R. (1999). Leadership and self-determination, Focus on Autism and Other Developmental Disabilities, *14*(1), 4-16.

[99] Tredgold, G. (2018, January 28). Three reasons why good leaders spend time planning. Retrieved at https://www.inc.com/gordon-tredgold/three-reasons-why-good-leader-spend-time-planning.html

[100] Goleman, D. (2013). The focused leader. Retrieved at https://hbr.org/2013/12/the-focused-leader

[101] Neubert, M.J., Dyck, B. (2021). Organizational Behavior: For a Better Tomorrow. Hoboken, NJ: John Wiley & Sons, Inc.

[102] Paul, M., Stroh, D.P. (2018). Managing your time as a leader. Retrieved at https://thesystemsthinker.com/managing-your-time-as-a-leader/

[103] Nerurkar, R. (2012). *Marathon Running: From Beginner to Elite.* London: Bloomsbury Publishing.

[104] Solansky, S.T. (2015). Self-determination and leader development, Management Learning, 46(5), 618-635.

[105] Bachus, T. (2013, April 12). What it takes to be a determined leader. Retrieved at http://training.hr.ufl.edu/resources/Leadership Toolkit/transcripts/WhatItTakestoBea DeterminedLeader.pdf

[106] Dallas, J.R. (2019). We Need to Have a Word: Words of Wisdom, Courage and Patience for Work, Home and Everywhere. Illinois: Hillview Digital.

[107] Li, J, Zhang, J., Yang, Z (2017). Associations between a Leader's Work Passion and an Employee's Work Passion: A Moderated Mediation Model, Frontiers in Psychology, 8, 1447.

[108] Connelly, R. (2011, January 28). Five of the most disgusting marathon pictures ever, Retrieved at https://www.houstonpress.com/news/hisd-board-turns-down-partnership-proposal-11081667

[109] Gruber, K. (2017, March 28). Marathon training week 18: Expect the unexpected. Retrieved at https://www.thepittsburghmarathon.com/Blog-Item-Marathon-Training-Week-18-Expect-the-Unexpected

[110] Middlebrook, H. (2018, March 14). Weird, gross and unexpected things that happen when you run. Retrieved at https://edition.cnn.com/2016/12/13/health/weird-and-unexpected-side-effects-of-running/index.html

[111] Barton, A. (2015, April 16). How to run a marathon in your mind: 12 tips for winning the mental fight. Retrieved at https://www.theguardian.com/lifeandstyle/the-running-blog/2015/apr/16/how-to-run-a-marathon-12-tips-mental-fight

[112] Dym, B., Hutson, H. (2005). *Leadership in Nonprofit Organizations: Lessons From the Third Sector.* Oaks, California: Sage Publications.

[113] Nair, D. (2015, January 30). 8 leadership lesssons from marathon runners. Retrieved at https://www.rediff.com/getahead/report/career-8-leadership-lessons-from-marathon-runners/20150130.htm

[114] Frank, A.M. (2003). *Sports and Education: A Reference Handbook.* Santa Barbara, California: ABC-CLIO.

[115] Karageorghis, C.I. (2017). *Applying Music in Exercise and Sport.* London, UK: Human Kinetics.

[116] Evans, M. B., Eys, M. A., Bruner, M. W. (2012). Seeing the "we" in "me" sports: The need to consider individual

sport team environments. Canadian Psychology / Psychologie canadienne, *53*(4), 301-308. doi: 10.1037/a0030202

[117] Widmeyer, W. N., Williams, J. (1991). Predicting cohesion in a coacting sport. Small Group Research, *22*, 548 –570. doi:10.1177/ 1046496 491224007

[118] Pfitzinger, P. (2009, October 14). Marathon pace perfect. Retrieved at https://www.runnersworld.com/advanced/a20783113/marathon-pace-perfect/

[119] Crawford, V. (2016, September 09). 5 ways running can make you a better leader, Retrieved at https://www.forbes.com/sites/worldeconomicforum/2016/09/09/5-ways-running-can-make-you-a-better-leader/#31c47cc5685a

[120] Dotsenko, S. (2016, June 11). How running a maraton made me a better entrepreneur, Retrieved at https://www.fastcompany.com/3065164/how-running-a-marathon-made-me-a-better-entrepreneur

[121] Fenning, R. (2012, August 08). The lure of Lycra: Is leadership a team sport? Retrieved at https://www.forbes.com/sites/richardfenning/2012/08/08/the-lure-of-lycra-is-leadership-a-team-sport/#4010db172c2d

[122] Maxwell, J.C. (2010). *The Complete 101 Collection: What Every Leader Needs to Know*. Nashville: Thomas Nelson.

[123] Gaudette, J. (2012, October 18). Learn to pace like a pro. Retrieved at https://www.runnersworld.com/advanced/a20847773/learn-to-pace-like-a-pro/

[124] Canaday, S. (2014, July 05). Pace and productivity: When faster and more isn't always better. Retrieved at https://www.huffingtonpost.com/sara-canaday/pace-productivity-when-fa_b_5274293.html

[125] Eyring, A. (2017). *Pacing for Growth: Why Intelligent Restraint Drives Long-term Success*. Oakland, CA: Berrett Koehler.

[126] Quandt, S. (2006). *Sudden Impact on the Job: Top Business Leaders Reveal the Secrets to Fast Success*. San Francisco, CA: Jossey-Bass.

[127] Beverly, J. (2017). *Run Strong, Stay Hungry: 9 Keys to Staying in the Race*. Boulder, CO: VeloPress.

[128] Falchuk, B. (2017, September 20). 3 lessons marathon training taught me about success - and what you can learn, too. Retrieved at https://www.inc.com/bryan-falchuk/3-lessons-marathon-training-taught-me-about-succes.html

[129] Fitzgerald, J. (2012). The principle of progression: How to consistently get faster. Retrieved at https://strengthrunning.com/2012/02/the-principle-of-progression-how-to-consistently-get-faster/

[130] Simanoff, D. (2018, October 08). 10 things leaders can learn from runners. Retrieved at https://www.businessadministrationinformation.com/leadership/10-things-leaders-can-learn-from-runners

[131] Watson, R., Wykes, D. (2017, March 01). Principles of the marathon. Retrieved at http://impactmagazine.ca/fitness/training-plans/principles-of-the-marathon/

[132] Zinner, C., Sperlich, B. (2016). *Marathon Running: Physiology, Psychology, Nutrition and Training Aspects*. Switzerland: Springer.

[133] Ciulla, J.B. (2014). *Ethics, the Heart of Leadership*. Santa Barbara, California: ABC-CLIO.

[134] Odom, L. (2010). *Leadership Ethics: Is Doing the Right Thing Enough?* USA: Xlibris Corporation.

[135] Sanchez, B.K. (2016). Leading without ethics is no leadership at all, GPSolo, *33*(5), 34-37.

[136] Betancourt, S. (2017, April 17). How running a marathon puts your body through hell. Retrieved at https://gizmodo.com/running-a-marathon-puts-your-body-through-hell-1794380470

[137] Lilliefors, J. (1978). *The Running Mind.* Mountain View, CA: World Publications.

[138] Lobby, M. (2009, September 24). Mind over matter. No, really, it works! Retrieved at https://www.runnersworld.com/advanced/a20825087/mind-over-matter-0/

[139] Paul, S. (2015, October 06). Understanding why you hit "The Wall" - Training your body to work more efficiently will help you out on race day. Retrieved at https://www.runnersworld.com/training/a20854502/understanding-why-you-hit-the-wall/

[140] Hotchkiss, J. (2015, February 23). Leading with margin & Why you should do it. Retrieved at https://www.gentlemansgazette.com/leading-with-margin/

[141] Kassel, P. (2017, February 27). Are you leading on an empty emotional fuel tank? Retrieved at http://www.phillipkassel.com/?p=515

[142] Canadian Running (2016, October 25). Post-marathon recovery: How to recharge following a marathon. Retrieved at https://runningmagazine.ca/explains/post-marathon-recovery/

[143] Therrien, A. (2018). Is marathon running bad for you? Retrieved at https://www.bbc.com/news/health-43211447

[144] Carmichael, S.G. (2015, August 19). The research is clear: Long hours backfire for people and for companies. Retrieved at https://hbr.org/2015/08/the-research-is-clear-long-hours-backfire-for-people-and-for-companies

[145] Chan, J. (2017, January 30). 3 scientifically backed reasons why working less leads to more productivity. Retrieved at https://www.huffingtonpost.com/jonathan-chan/3-scientifically-backed-r_b_14509568.html

[146] Williams, I. (2018, February 15). An updated formula for marathon-running success. Retrieved at https://www.theguardian.com/lifeandstyle/the-running-blog/2018/feb/15/an-updated-formula-for-marathon-running-success

[147] Lennick, D., Kiel, F. (2005). *Moral Intelligence: Enhancing Business Performance and Leadership Success.* New Jersey: Pearson Education, Inc.

[148] Masood, S. (2018, May 30). A career is a marathon, not a sprint. Retrieved at https://leaderonomics.com/personal/a-career-is-a-marathon-not-a-sprint

[149] Crook, C.L. (2015, August 24). #10 The finish line is the start of a new race - Ten things I learned training for a marathon, Retrieved at http://www.techleadershipacademy.com/10-the-finish-line-is-the-start-of-a-new-race/

[150] Kirkpatrick, S.A., Locke, E.A. (1991). Leadership: do traits matter?, Academy of Management Executive, 5(2), 48-60.

[151] Lussier, R.N., Achua, C.F. (2010). *Leadership Theory, Application, & Skill Development 4e.* Mason, OH: South-Western Cengage Learning.

[152] Patel, D. (2017, March 22). 11 Powerful Traits of Successful Leaders. Retrieved at https://www.forbes.com/

sites/deeppatel/2017/03/22/11-powerful-traits-of-successful-leaders/?sh=35df8656469f

[153] Worthey, C. (2016). Optimism and Positive about People: Key Traits to Hospital Leadership Success? Benedictine University, Unpublished Doctoral Dissertation.

[154] Sin, E.L.L., Chow, C., Cheung, R.T.H. (2015). Relationship between personal psychological capitals, stress level, and performance in marathon runners, Hong Kong Physiotherapy Journal, *33*, 67-72. doi: 10.1016/j.hkpj.2015.03.002

[155] Harpham, B. (2016). The 9 career hacks of successful marathon runners. Retrieved at https://www.lifehack.org/315847/the-9-career-hacks-successful-marathon-runners

[156] Curtin, M. (2016, April 27). Why millennials should stop trying to be successful... Immediately. Retrieved at https://www.inc.com/melanie-curtin/why-millennials-feel-more-pressure-to-succeed-than-any-other-generation.html

[157] Rainer, T.S., Rainer, J.W. (2011). *The Millennials: Connecting to America's Largest Generation. Nashville.* Tennessee: B & H Publishing Group.

[158] Plunkett, M. (2016, March 15). Millennials have embraced running as a lifestyle. Now race organizers must adapt. Retrieved at https://www.washingtonpost.com/lifestyle/wellness/millennials-have-fully-embraced-running-as-a-lifestyle-now-the-industry-must-adapt/2016/03/14/0b40eefa-e55d-11e5-b0fd-073d5930a7b7_story.html?noredirect=on&utm_term=.1c64b7dce026

[159] Lane, K. (2016, March 17). Millennials: the running generation. Retrieved at https://nationalpost.com/health/millennials-the-running-generation

[160] Gulak-Lipka, P. (2016). The role of trust for leadership in team sports, *Journal of Corporate Responsibility and Leadership, 3*(3), 39-54. doi: 10.12775/JCRL.2016.015

[161] Seleme, C. (2017, August 25). Leadership is not a quick 100m race, it is a lifelong marathon. Retrieved at https://www.news24.com/MyNews24/leadership-is-not-a-quick-100m-race-it-is-a-lifelong-marathon-20170825

[162] Karaevli, A., Hall, D.T.T. (2006). How career variety promotes the adaptability of managers: A theoretical model, Journal of Vocational Behavior, *69*, 359-373. doi: 10.1016/j.jvb.2006.05.009

[163] Barnett, B.G., Caffarella, R.S., Daresh, J.D., King, R.A., Nicholson, T.H., Whitaker, K.S. (1992). A new slant on leadership preparation, Educational Leadership, *49*(5), 72-75.

[164] Phillips, J., Phillips, P., Ray, R. (2012). *Measuring Leadership Development: Quantify Your Program's Impact and ROI on Organizational Performance*. New York: McGraw Hill.

[165] Kolb, A., Kolb, D. (2009). Experiential learning theory: a dynamic, holistic approach to management learning, education and development. In S. J. Armstrong & C. V. Fukami (Eds.) *The SAGE handbook of management learning, education and development* (pp. 42-68). London: SAGE Publications Ltd doi: 10.4135/9780857021038.n3

[166] Wagner, R.J., Campbell, J. (1994) Outdoor-based experiential training: Improving transfer of training using virtual reality, Journal of Management Development, *13*(7), 4-11, doi: 10.1108/02621719410063350.

[167] Covey, S.R. (2015). *The 7 Habits of Highly Effective People: Powerful Lessons in Personal Change*. USA: Franklin Covey Co.

[168] Martynoga, B. (2018, June 21). What does running do to your brain? Retrieved at https://www.theguardian.com/lifeandstyle/the-running-blog/2018/jun/21/what-does-running-do-to-your-brain

[169] Ross, J. (2018, August 01). 4 expert-backed ways to build mental toughness. Retrieved at https://www.runnersworld.com/runners-stories/a20783068/four-ways-to-build-mental-toughness/

[170] Mariama-Arthur, K. (2016, January 25). Why every leader needs mental toughness. Retrieved at https://www.entrepreneur.com/article/250989

[171] Gass, M. (1999). Transfer of learning in adventure programming. In J.C. Miles & S. Priest (Eds). *Adventure Programming* (pp. 227-234). State College, PA: Venture Publishing.

[172] Jones, D. (2017). Millennial managers: 7 skills for the next generation of leaders. Retrieved at https://business.udemy.com/blog/millennial-managers-skills-leaders/

[173] Cormier, S.M., Hagman, J.D. (1987). Introduction. In S. M. Cormier & J.D. Hagman (Eds.) Transfer of Learning: Contemporary Research and Applications (pp. 1-8). San Diego, California: Academic Press.

[174] Hamstra-Wright, K. L., Coumbe-Lilley, J. E., Kim, H., McFarland, J. A., Bliven, K. C. H. (2013). The influence of training and mental skills preparation on injury incidence and performance in marathon runners. Journal of Strength and Conditioning Research, *27*(10), 2828-2835. doi: 10.1519/JSC.0b013e31828a4733

[175] Hoak, A. (2007, October 04). Executive endurance. Retrieved at https://www.marketwatch.com/story/executives-mix-business-and-pleasure-on-the-marathon-course

[176] Sicking, D. (2012). *Professor Bosses total verrückte Karrieretipps.* Deutschland: Monsenstein und Vannerdat Verlag.

[177] Limbach, P., Sonnenburg, F. (2014). CEO Fitness and Firm Value, SSRN Electronic Journal, doi: 10.2139/ssrn.2489967

[178] Ey (2015). Where will you find your next leader? Retrieved at https://www.ey.com/Publication/vwLUAssets/EY-where-will-you-find-your-next-leader/%24FILE/where-will-you-find-your-next-leader-report-from-EY-and-espnw.pdf

[179] Toohey, K., Veal, A.J. (2007). *The Olympic Games: A Social Science Perspective.* UK: CABI International.

[180] Eikenberry, K. (2013, September 09). Leadership is a marathon, not a sprint. Retrieved at https://blog.kevineikenberry.com/leadership-supervisory-skills/leadership-is-a-marathon-not-a-sprint/

[181] Fein, P. (2017, February 01). Finding wisdom throughout the leadership learning journey. Retrieved at https://www.td.org/insights/finding-wisdom-throughout-the-leadership-learning-journey

[182] White, B.J. (2006). *The Nature of Leadership: Reptiles, Mammals, and the Challenge of Becoming a Great Leader.* USA: AMACOM.

[183] Dragoni, L., Tesluk, P.E., Russell, J.E.A., Oh, I.S. (2009). Understanding managerial development: Integrating developmental assignments, learning orientation, and access to developmental opportunities in

predicting managerial competencies, Academy of Management Journal, 52(4), 731-743.

[184] Kjellström, S., Stålne, K., Törnblom, O. (2020). Six ways of understanding leadership development: An exploration of increasing complexity, Leadership, 16(4), 434-460.

Chapter 2

Turning Bad Leaders into Good Leaders: Diminishing the Theory X Style

Lindall Elaine Adams, Marion Williams and Ibrahim Al Zaabi

Abstract

While not everyone is born with the talent to lead, many businesses have been plagued by accidental leaders. Such leaders have no prior experience managing others. A bad leader can do more harm than good to a company. They are frequently the cause why employees decide to leave a company. Controlling and manipulative leaders have a negative influence on employee morale and have the potential to damage the organization's corporate culture. Furthermore, employees do not depart because they are unsatisfied with their jobs. They leave the company because they are unhappy with their leaders. This chapter explores micromanagement as a Theory X style and identifies indicators such as lack of trust and high-staff turnover as the primary reasons why leaders fail to "lead" the "ship." The chapter concludes that effective leadership necessitates leadership skills and training.

Keywords: Theory X, micromanagement, trust, staff turnover, disease

1. Introduction

This chapter begins with a quotation from President Theodore Roosevelt: "*The best executive is one who has sense enough to pick good people to do what he wants done, and self-restraint enough to keep from meddling with them while they do it*" [1].

Humans are born with an innate need to follow leaders. The earliest leaders are documented in historical and religious artifacts, from ancient civilization to modern-day leaders [2]. The ability to lead groups of people has been a highly valuable and highly sought-after skill from early times.

Good leadership forms an essential part of managing employees and directing the organizations' objectives, directing individual and group goals, guiding employees effectively, and increasing employee productivity [3]. Effective leadership as noted by [4] resulted from desirable characteristics and qualities and the ability to influence employee performance. A good leader exhibits qualities such as providing employee support, two-way communication, knowledge of problem-solving, effective decision-making skills, interpersonal behaviors, empathy for subordinates, and providing solutions. Leadership is an essential feature of employee productivity as noted by Osundina and Owoeye [5] to direct employees to set and reach goals and objectives of the organization; therefore, it helps to develop teamwork and integrate individual goals and group productivity. However, management cannot develop leaders, as argued by Peter Drucker [6], it can only establish the environment necessary for the development of potential leadership traits.

2. Theory X and Theory Y

The term leadership was only coined in the 1970s [7], referring to the Theory X and Theory Y understanding of leadership effectiveness. These two theories, both developed by Douglas McGregor [4], used these insights to build two opposed managerial scenarios. Theory Y assumes that effective managerial leadership refers to the kind of direction a leader can give to a group of employees to enable the group to achieve goals [4]. Good leadership is measured by what qualities it possesses and how effective it is in the performance of the job. The measure of leadership effectiveness is the extent to which the group leader does the job and achieves the required goals and satisfaction achieved by employees [4]. Productivity is an overall measure of the ability to produce a good service [5]. However, Theory X leadership views the employees as "lazy," unmotivated, and in need of an intimidating person to coerce them into working. Theory Y is perceiving the employer as highly driven and self-motivated. Theory X is a style of leadership in which the employee is subjected to strict control and monitoring [8]. This type of leadership is more prevalent in management, which is more representative of the current workforce [9], especially to those employees who do not want to take responsibility [7]. This style of leadership views the organization as a chain of demand, with employees either being punished or rewarded for their efforts. In this chapter, Theory X is evaluated from a micromanagement standpoint [10] to identify and investigate two essential indicators for "leader" and "ship"—trust and staff turnover, which is the ability to lead the ship. Or would poor leadership cause personnel to abandon ship? We determined that self-ethnographic case studies are appropriate for demonstrating the victim's experience with micromanagement.

3. Micromanagement

Micromanagement is classified as a "disease" [10]. This leader is what Roosevelt would see as "meddling" [1]. This "disease" has been observed in the workplace, and several studies have examined its impact on the workforce. Symptoms include the following:

3.1 Emotional manipulation

Machiavellianism is a context-specific domain characterized by a belief in manipulation to achieve work-related goals when necessary. Managers who are comfortable manipulating others are known as Machiavellians. The primary premise of the organizational Machiavellian is that they will only use manipulative and dishonest practices when it benefits them. These managers are not necessarily vengeful or brutal, but they may be quite charming and sympathetic when their objectives are served [11].

Leaders may use manipulation methods to inspire trust and confidence in others. While it can be used for benign purposes, it can also be used to commit malicious acts. Managers intimidated by manipulative techniques abstain from modern and convincing techniques. All these rhetorical strategies such as "storytelling, scenario planning, or emotional appeals" can be used to benefit the organization [12]. However, manipulation of others is an unethical and unprofessional strategy to influence others, as in the findings by Auvinen et al. [13]. The authors gathered data for their qualitative study using thematic interviews, which featured anecdotes presented by managers to influence their employees. The authors identified four types of manipulative storytelling:

3.1.1 Humor

Humor has traditionally been related to a sense of superiority, rapid changes in situations, and the coexistence of opposites such as pleasantness and unpleasantness, joy and misery, power, and pointlessness. Additionally, humor typically combines the aspects of drama, as it is frequently associated with strong emotions. The humorous narrative has educational and moral implications. Through the story, employees are taught to cherish their working conditions. False information is the type of manipulation used in this case since the management exaggerates irrelevant and unfamiliar circumstances out of context [12].

3.1.2 Pseudo-participative manipulation

The management gives the false appearance that the subordinate shares their thoughts and concerns through pseudo-participative manipulation. As a result, participation is fictitious and unidirectional. The stories portray a predetermined strategy for meeting and guiding persons through the instillation of a misguided perception of free will.

3.1.3 Pseudo-empathetic

This idea is closely tied to power and the ability to manipulate other people's emotions and is known as the capacity to sense and understand another person's sentiments. Although Lidow [12] are discussing pseudo-empathy, they are not denying that genuine and sincere empathy can manifest as well. Pseudo-emphatic manipulation is frequently associated with consequence-based ethics, in which managers deceive employees to terminate them. Managers make a concerted effort to mitigate the repercussions of termination. Additionally, this strategy carries a cost, which includes pseudo-empathetic subordinate management. Managers are viewed as immoral by virtue ethics due to their seeming lack of empathy and self-interest. The actual reason leaders do not exercise control over their subordinates is to absolve themselves of culpability if something goes wrong. Additionally, it provides managers with a means of survival in the intensely unpleasant circumstance of dismissals [12].

3.1.4 Subjective manipulation

The phrase subjective manipulation describes the situation in which employees are encouraged to notice and report only the positive happenings in their workplace. The panoptic narrative is subjective manipulation since the story can only be perceived one way [12].

However, emotional manipulation techniques gone wrong might spark "gaslighting" [14]. Gaslighting is a form of control that uses authority to manipulate employees into feeling as though they are reliant on their manager for their employment [15]. Manipulative leaders are deceitful.

3.2 Obsessive control/overparenting

Control is the mechanism put in place to guarantee that employees act in the best interests of the organization, and a system of controls must be designed to guard against undesirable behavior and to encourage desirable activity. Control systems, on the other hand, may cause managers to treat their subordinates as if they were children [11]. The author asserts that this kind of management requires compliance and over-policing of personnel. Machiavellianism is a term that refers to this obsessive control [11]. According to the authors, Machiavellianism's optimal strategy for exercising power is to "tell the people what they want to hear."

3.3 Bullying

Bullying is one of the micromanagement practices in the workplace [16]. Bullying in the workplace has gained international attention as a relevant research topic [17–19]. Bullying creates a hostile working environment [20]. The author indicates that bullying consists of several activities such as mocking and criticism with the objective of producing anxiety or stress [20]. Bullying may also include giving unfair workloads, personal insults, and prohibiting professional development opportunities [21].

These micromanagement practices can be damaging to the organization and frequently contribute to high employee turnover. As is frequently the case, senior management is unaware of the reasons behind their companies' high employee turnover, which is a result of ineffective line manager leadership styles [22]. The following symptoms should raise alarm, as they suggest that the employee is considering leaving the organization.

3.4 Lack of delegation

Micromanagers are unaccustomed to delegation [20], while Kivimäki et al. [21] assert that micromanagers struggle with delegation. Effective leaders understand that distributing work does not imply relinquishing control. This means they are allowing themselves more time to devote to tasks that require their focus and attention while also contributing to the organization's professional development by diversifying the skill sets of others [23].

The following part outlines the methodology employed and gives actual evidence to support the theoretical assumptions made previously.

4. Methods

The study is qualitative in nature, with data acquired through interviews with "victims" of poor leadership. Ethnographic studies are the most effective method for correctly portraying bad leadership [24, 25], and the stories are typically delivered by someone who has personally experienced bad leadership.

The following is a self-ethnographic narrative about the subjective manipulation, control, and bullying of four people. The participants were all employed by large corporations with between 5000 and 12,000 employees. The setting is fictious and we used pseudo-names to protect the identity of the participants.

"The mother" better known as the controller, bully or Pseudo-participative manipulator

Anna worked for a multinational corporation that had a positive global image and was frequently referred to as one of the most prominent organizations in terms of research output. Anna had joined the company shortly after graduating and was one of the company's youngest employees at the time. Anna described Mary, her manager, as someone who cared about her and her well-being. She frequently informed them that her door was always open and that she believes in transparency. Anna was content to work under Mary's supervision, whom she frequently addressed as "the mother" and her employees as "children." She always asked Anna about her family and their health, showing an interest in the life of her staff. During her staff meetings, Mary routinely used the phrase "today I'm going to smack you on the wrists." That day had come for Anna when she tried to get hold of Mary during a crisis at work. It was a Saturday, and Anna called Mary several times, but she did not respond to her call. Not finding Mary, Anna called another manager to seek advice on how to resolve the situation. This manager phoned Mary, who immediately responded to the other manager's call, informing her about the lurking crisis. Mary was so upset with Anna phoned another manager to resolve the problem, claiming that she oversteps boundaries and had no right to call another manager. Never, did she acknowledge Anna's calls to her. The now-friendly "mother" turned vengeful, making Anna's life at work intolerable. Anna was compelled to resign because she was unable to deal with Mary's mood swings, her disregard for Anna's input, or her refusal to sign Anna's leave request.

"You got fired" better known as the bully

Toni, Lily, Greg, Marvin, Dylan, Daisy, and Bobby were all managers in a well-known international organization, and their senior boss was "You got fired." Toni dreaded Wednesday manager meetings because she never knew who his next victim would be. "You got fired" made a habit of picking out one manager based on their performance and weekly reviews and insulting them to the point of tears. Toni had seen adult men cry at those talks. "You've got fired," threatened to fire managers. Toni could no longer manage the stress, as she developed bad leadership skills and the staff covertly referring to her as "Miranda Priestley," a character from Lauren Weisberger's novel The Devil Wears Prada. Toni's staff, on the other hand, was unaware of the added pressure to perform that "You Got Fired" imposed on managers and that they may be fired at any time. Toni became emotional and held pointless staff meetings whenever she was in a foul mood, which was generally after the weekly manager meeting. She ceased smiling and being friendly and began sending emails to her staff at 3 a.m., becoming enraged when they did not instantly respond to her emails. She was rapidly establishing a hostile workplace climate. Not only did she strike out at her staff, but also at her family. Toni eventually resigned from her work due to the stress and verbal abuse associated with "You got fired."

"The Selective responder" or the emotional manipulator

The selective responder, the line manager who ignores your emails. Even emails you submit with suggestions for improvement go unanswered. That was the situation with Dolly, a charming young woman in her late twenties. She consistently obtained the most favorable assessment comments from the "Selective responder," yet her correspondence with the "Selective responder" was ignored. Dolly indicated that she wanted to speak with the "Selective responder" about her current duty, and she had summoned all her bravery to send an email requesting a meeting to address her position. She saw the "Selective responder" daily, either going by their office or the staff area, but she was never informed that they had received her email or intended to discuss the concern with her. Interestingly, when Dolly went around the office to see if anyone else was having trouble with "Selective responder" and if anyone else had gotten a response to their emails. At least three of her colleagues said that they never had to wait more than a few minutes for a response. This prompted Dolly to inquire as to what was wrong with her, as she was now suffering feelings of self-doubt, and whether the "Selective responder's" nonresponse indicated that the "Selective responder" had a personal vendetta against her. Weeks passed into months, and she attempted one final time to send a follow-up email requesting a meeting. At the time, she felt as though she was merely a "worker" who added no value and that the "Selective responder" lacked the civility to acknowledge her email as a matter of ordinary courtesy. Dolly resigned a year later, and she never got the meeting she had worked up the courage to ask.

"You cannot take initiative" better known as a controller and bully

Barry was continually told how to conduct his job by his manager. Even though this manager had no prior knowledge of the job, he received daily guidance on how he should do his duties. Barry was so frustrated with his manager that he felt compelled to agree with whatever this manager advised him, even if it made no practical sense. Additionally, the manager used to speak to Barry in a childlike manner, with slow tones and plenty of emphases. While his line manager was the cause of Barry's anxiety, another manager would approach him and request that he create online content for her, even though she never acknowledged Barry's presence at work. She would only greet him when she needs a workplace favor. Barry is still employed by the company, but he maintains an unusually low profile.

5. Discussion

Self-ethnographic narratives about micromanagement in the workplace revealed a tendency for viable control, bullying, and manipulation as fear tactics. Anna's workplace "mother" became angry and vindictive after Anna attempted to contact another manager during a crisis. She accuses Anna of crossing her limits, but she never recognizes the phone calls on the Saturday following the incident. Rather than praising Anna for being proactive in averting a potential crisis and contacting another manager on her level, she treated her as an adversary. Simultaneously, Anna became depressed and terrified that the incident would result in her termination. Although Anna spent another year in the same department, she resigned because she knew the bullying would continue if she stayed another year at the company.

Toni and her coworkers were bullied at work and were terrified that their names would be announced as the person with the lowest performance during the weekly staff meeting. Additionally, "You got fired" implied that he may terminate the managers' employment at any time. Toni had treated her department's workers similarly harshly because of this tension, but she recognized that she was beginning to change and decided to step away from this stressful work environment.

Dolly was sure that her manager is pleased with her work since she had received good scores on her performance appraisals. However, Dolly that always had a positive impression of her manager slowly turned to self-doubt and negative feelings against her colleagues.

Barry was not only manipulated but also controlled by another manager. He was asked to do work favors even though the other manager never noticed his existence.

The damaging actions created by the micromanagement disease drove educated and experienced employees to reconsider their position in the organization and depart. Three of the participants, except Barry, did not leave the company; instead, they left their manager. The findings indicate that the leaders were unable to "lead" the "ship."

6. Connecting micromanagement to trust and high staff turnover

Micromanagers often display a lack of trust in their coworkers [26]. The reason for this is that they want to control the situation alone. However, failure to delegate also means that there is no mutual trust between the supervisor and the subordinates. According to Mineo [27], trust acts as the binding agent for leaders to their followers, and this promotes leadership and organizational success. The author argues that true success is not reached through a single event, but rather as the cumulative outcome of numerous investments made over time. Managers must reciprocate trust, and delegating is one approach micromanagers can use to demonstrate their confidence in the staff [28].

High staff turnover is the result of bad leadership. Managers that act as bullies and refuse to accept the viewpoints of their subordinates are the reason why good employees jump the ship. Employees might exhibit signs that they are preparing to abandon ship. They would become withdrawn, would still do their job, but will become disengaged [29].

Micromanagement presents itself in several ways, including manipulation, control, bullying, and a lack of delegation, as demonstrated in this chapter. Additionally, each of these symptoms is associated with two indicators: The manager lacks trust in their subordinate, and micromanagement might result in high employee turnover. On the other side, micromanagement does have a cost. Investments in recruiting new staff, compensating them reasonably, and training them may prove to be costly in the long run if the issue of micromanagement is not addressed. While micromanagers can be advantageous in that they exhibit a manager's dedication to their job and organization, they must be controlled properly to avoid being viewed as a disease. Managers who receive enough training will be able to switch easily between manager and subordinate.

7. Conclusion

Organizations exist within unique environments that seek good leadership styles in order to build and uplift employees and company goals. To achieve this, organizations should ensure that suitable leadership training is provided. Theory X and Theory Y are contrasting theories in view of employee performance, and the relevance of Theory Y is based on technological innovation and changes affected in a modern organization where leaders following the Theory Y leadership style value their contributions and commitments to the organization and view these as a positive impact on work performance and organizational performance. It is evident that within an organization that McGregor's Theory Y, which is an open management system as well as changing leadership, is used within an organizational setting to ensure success for employees and the organization.

Instead of abandoning Theory X with its limited assumptions, it is important for leaders to consider the needs of employees, develop teamwork, encourage a spirit of participation, consider multidisciplinary teams [30], and change low morale to high morale as suggested by Theory Y according to McGregor [31].

Acknowledgements

Dain Luke Adams is acknowledged for his assistance with the literature search.

Conflict of interest

The authors declare no conflict of interest.

Author details

Lindall Elaine Adams[1*], Marion Williams[2,3] and Ibrahim Al Zaabi[4]

1 Institute of Applied Technology, Abu Dhabi, United Arab Emirates

2 University of Limpopo, South Africa

3 University of Antwerp, Antwerp, Belgium

4 University of Cordoba, Córdoba, Spain

*Address all correspondence to: lindallelaine@gmail.com

References

[1] Three Critical Leadership Lessons from the Roosevelts [Internet]. Managementisajourney.com. Available from: https://managementisajourney.com/three-critical-leadership-lessons-from-the-roosevelts/ [Accessed: 12 September 2021]

[2] Yildirim E. Concept of leadership in the ancient history and its effects on the Middle East. Sociology and Anthropology. 2016;**4**(8):710-718

[3] Ishaya J. Presentation on Influence of Leadership Pattern and Style on Employee—[PPTX PowerPoint] [Internet]. Vdocuments.mx. 2016. Available from: https://vdocuments.mx/presentation-on-influence-of-leadership-pattern-and-style-on-employee.html [Accessed: 13 September 2021]

[4] Folarin KD. Leadership Styles, Organizational Performance and Effectiveness among Sub-Saharan African Employees [Internet]. Ijseas.com. Available from: http://ijseas.com/volume7/v7i6/IJSEAS202106128.pdf [Accessed: 13 September 2021]

[5] Osundina KS, Owoeye J. Role of Leadership in Enhancing Workers Productivity in an Organization in College of Health Technology, Offa, Kwara State [Internet]. 2020;6(2):18-37. Available from: https://www.ijaar.org/articles/Volume6-Number2/Social-Management-Sciences/ijaar-sms-v5n12-dec19-p29.pdf [Accessed: 13 September 2021]

[6] Druker P. British Library [Internet]. Available from: https://www.bl.uk/people/peter-drucker [Accessed: 13 September 2021]

[7] Morse JJ, Lorsch JW. Beyond Theory Y. Harv Bus Rev [Internet]. 1970;**48**(3). Available from: https://hbr.org/1970/05/beyond-theory-y [Accessed: 13 September 2021]

[8] Aydin OT. The Impact of Theory X, Theory Y and Theory Z on Research Performance: An Empirical Study from a Turkish University. 2012;**1**(5):24-31. Available from: http://www.managementjournal.info/index.php/IJAME [Accessed: 13 September 2021]

[9] Bobic MP. A kind word for Theory X: Or why so many newfangled management techniques quickly fail. Journal of Public Administration Research and Theory. 2003;**13**(3):239-264

[10] White RD. The Micromanagement Disease: Symptoms, Diagnosis, and Cure. 2010. Available from: https://homepages.se.edu/cvonbergen/files/2012/12/The-Micromanagement-Disease_Symptoms-Diagnosis-and-Cure.pdf [Accessed: 13 September 2021]

[11] Kessler SR, Bandelli AC, Spector PE, Borman WC, Nelson CE, Penney LM. Re-examining Machiavelli: A three-dimensional model of Machiavellianism in the workplace. Journal of Applied Social Psychology. 2010;**40**(8):1868-1896

[12] Lidow D. Understanding How Good Leadership Requires Great Manipulation. Forbes Magazine [Internet]. 2019. Available from: https://www.forbes.com/sites/dereklidow/2019/11/17/understanding-how-good-leadership-requires-great-manipulation/ [Accessed: 13 September 2021]

[13] Auvinen TP, Lämsä A-M, Sintonen T, Takala T. Leadership manipulation and ethics in storytelling. Journal of Business Ethics. 2013;**116**(2):415-431

[14] Neilson K. Gaslighting at Work: How do You Manage It?—HRM Online [Internet]. Com.au. 2019. Available from: https://www.hrmonline.com.au/how-tos/

gaslighting-at-work-how-do-you-manage-it/ [Accessed: 13 September 2021]

[15] Michael J. How to Extinguish Gaslighting in the Workplace. Forbes Magazine [Internet]. 2020. Available from: https://www.forbes.com/sites/forbescoachescouncil/2021/12/28/how-to-extinguish-gaslighting-in-the-workplace/ [Accessed: 13 September 2021]

[16] Kurter HL. Is Micromanaging a Form of Bullying? Here are 3 Things You Should Know. Forbes Magazine [Internet]. 2021. Available from: https://www.forbes.com/sites/heidilynnekurter/2021/06/29/is-micromanaging-a-form-of-bullying-here-are-3-things-you-should-know/ [Accessed: 13 September 2021]

[17] Chan CMH, Wong JE, Yeap LLL, Wee LH, Jamil NA, Swarna NY. Workplace bullying and psychological distress of employees across socioeconomic strata: A cross-sectional study. BMC Public Health. 2019;**19**(Suppl 4):608

[18] Giorgi G, Perminienė M, Montani F, Fiz-Perez J, Mucci N, Arcangeli G. Detrimental effects of workplace bullying: Impediment of self-management competence via psychological distress. Frontiers in Psychology. 2016;7:60

[19] Samnani A-K, Singh P. 20 Years of workplace bullying research: A review of the antecedents and consequences of bullying in the workplace. Aggression and Violent Behavior. 2012;**17**(6): 581-589

[20] Akella D. Workplace bullying: Not a manager's right? SAGE Open. 2016;**6**(1):215824401662939

[21] Kivimäki M, Elovainio M, Vahtera J. Workplace bullying and sickness absence in hospital staff. Occupational and Environmental Medicine. 2000;**57**(10):656-660

[22] Allen T. How Bad Bosses Compel Good Employees to Leave. Forbes Magazine [Internet]. 2019. Available from: https://www.forbes.com/sites/terinaallen/2019/09/21/how-bad-bosses-compel-good-employees-to-leave/ [Accessed: 13 September 2021]

[23] Marcine Johnson V. Delegating: Why bother? Delegating is as beneficial to you as it is to your team. To be a strong leader, delegation skills are important to have. Not only will delegating allow you to grow, but it will also help your team succeed and grow with you. Don't allow excuses to get in your way of becoming a great leader. Strategic Finance. 2013;**94**(8):19-21

[24] Deckers J. The value of autoethnography in leadership studies, and its pitfalls. Philosophy of Management. 2021;**20**(1):75-91

[25] Moments M. Autoethnographic Methods for Leadership Research [Internet]. Ila-net.org. Available from: http://www.ila-net.org/files/resourcerewind/2015-Method-Moment-Autoethnographic-Methods-for-Leadership-Research-Ngunjiri-Hernandez-Chang.pdf [Accessed: 13 September 2021]

[26] Remote Managers Are Having Trust Issues. Harvard Business Review [Internet]. 2020. Available from: https://hbr.org/2020/07/remote-managers-are-having-trust-issues [Accessed: 13 September 2021]

[27] Mineo DL. The Importance of Trust in Leadership [Internet]. Eric.ed.gov. Available from: https://files.eric.ed.gov/fulltext/EJ1038828.pdf [Accessed: 13 September 2021]

[28] The Neuroscience of Trust. Harvard Business Review [Internet]. 2017. Available from: https://hbr.org/2017/01/

the-neuroscience-of-trust [Accessed: 13 September 2021]

[29] Micromanage at Your Peril. Harvard Business Review [Internet]. 2008. Available from: https://hbr.org/2008/02/micromanage-at-your-peril [Accessed: 13 September 2021]

[30] Heller NA. The Application of Management and Leadership Theory to Healthcare [Internet]. Ijrbmnet.com. Available from: http://ijrbmnet.com/uploades/volumes/1613401080.pdf [Accessed: 13 September 2021]

[31] Switcheducation.com. Available from: https://switcheducation.com/wp-content/uploads/2017/06/SEB_LYO_McGregor_Thinker.pdf [Accessed: 13 September 2021]

Chapter 3

Humane Leadership in Islamic Approaches

Mohd Faridh Hafez Mhd Omar

Abstract

A leadership style that meets the interests thus ensures the sustainable development of humanity would be a key factor in the current disruptive world. Leadership in Islam prioritizes human values and that becomes a founding principle as stated in the Qur'an and the *hadith* of the Prophet Muhammad (peace be upon him). Using a descriptive method from previous studies, this study found that three issues would make the country a failed state. Prior to that, a leadership that values humanity is identified as a new approach that deserves attention as it was shown successfully through the leadership of Prophet Muhammad (peace be upon him). Such approaches were proven in the following events: 1) to make peace between communities; 2) recognizing the right to life and prohibiting murder; 3) no coercion in religion and social problems; and 4) *da'wah* activities which are inviting to goodness and forbidding evils. This study concludes that humane leadership that incorporates with fundamental principles of Islam while upholding the universal values of humanity should lead a new narrative in the current disruptive world.

Keywords: humane leadership, Prophet Muhammad, the Islamic approaches

1. Introduction

Islam views leadership as the most important element that would drive organizations or states forward. Good leadership has a great responsibility in ensuring that the governance of the organization or state meets and preserves the rights of civil society with the guidance outlined by Islam in terms of policies and approaches. Trust from the public is the only pillar that deserves attention to build a sustainable development where the benefit of society is the main concern of leaders. This is because, leadership according to Islam has two direct relationships at one time, namely obeying the ruling of Allah (SWT) and fulfilling the interests of the society at large. Explaining further about the two relationships as Allah (SWT) recorded in surah Ali-Imran: 103, Samsudin [1] stated that this verse can be a stimulating factor in increasing motivation and subsequently has a greater impact on leadership performance.

However, these two elements seem increasingly neglected in today's leadership setting despite both are proven as unseparated coin in solving human crisis [2]. Even worse when the term "Islamic leadership" is only fluent on the lips but increasingly vague in implementation at all levels of organization and state administration. Muhammad [3] found the Islamic leadership system, especially in the political system in Malaysia, has caused various wrong perceptions that lead to suspicion and scare toward Islamic leadership. As Malaysian political development has formed upon the dualism of Islamism-nationalism and conservative-progressive and always colored by the religion which is Islam, thus these splits were not at all surprising given the fact that the battle between these two schools of taught has been ongoing since the early 1900s [4]. In the global scene, failure in coordinating the ideology of political Islam has contributed to the rise of terrorism and violent extremism [5] thus affected the narrative to Islam as a religion of peace and security.

As a result, leadership with Islamic values that uphold the principles of divinity and recognize human relations is seen as failing to create sustainable development within the Muslim society as well as the society as a whole. Therefore, the depravity of evils in society, as well as the occurrence of leadership crisis on its understanding and application, has become causes to the deficit of trust in bringing peace and preserving human values, although Islam is recognized a peaceful religion. Analyzing reality where appreciation on values-based leadership is important yet not overwhelming, Islam is consistently seen very much intact in defining the meaning, concept, and impact of leadership toward the development of society as well as the state.

However, as these issues might influence the notion of humanistic values in the long run, it could worsen the true understanding of Islamic leadership and ultimately also affects human development, economic justice, and national well-being after Islamic leadership, and Muslim leaders were seen as a leading cause to global crisis. Therefore, this paper's objective will explain in detail the concept of Islamic leadership that has had evolved since the time of Prophet Muhammad (peace be upon him) where human values work as focal point in his leadership in sustaining peace and security within the society. Bringing current crises in today's leadership that deprived the values of humanity need great attention to be solved by Islamic leadership approaches.

2. Islamic leadership according to previous and contemporary Muslim scholars

Scholars in the past have discovered various definitions to explain the meaning of Islamic leadership. Imam al-Mawardi's (d. 422H) definition on the term has been referred by many scholars after him, as he said "Islamic leadership is a task to replace the prophetic duty in preserving the religion (Islam) and managing worldly life." Such a novel definition of al-Mawardi's was repeated in the classical works of Muslim scholars like al-Ramli (Nihayah al-Muhtaj fi Syarh al-Minhaj and Ibn al-Azraq (Badai 'al-Silk fi Tabai' al-Malik) [3].

In addition to that, Ibn Khaldun is also one of the scholars who unraveled the basic definition of Islamic leadership in his magnum opus *al-Muqaddimah*. Muhammad [3] says Ibn Khaldun defined leadership has the same responsibility as the caliph where it should lead all human beings to live according to *Shāri 'ah* for the balanced well-being in both this world and the hereafter. This is because every command set by Allah (SWT) in this world is measured by God's acceptance and mercy. Instead of calling for doing good and stopping evils, thus as a caliph, the vital role should be played is ensuring the implementation of religious teachings in daily life. In fact, it should transcend into diverse community that celebrates diversity and differences within commonalities. Hence, the definition of a leader explained by Ibn Khaldun has emphasized on the religious aspect as an undeniable guiding principle in the humanistic management and administration of the country.

In addition to that, Muhammad [3] has elaborated another definition of Islamic leadership from the point of view of other scholars such as Rashid Rida, Ibn al-Azraq al-Qalqasyandi, and al-Juwayni. In his summary, it can be understood that all these scholars translate Islamic leadership by including the administration task with the interest of public is at top priority. Preservation of Islam and ensuring the implementation of *maqasid Syariah* (the highest objectives of Islam) must be advocated, while the welfare of the society in social, economic, education, and politic are developed justly and peacefully. Muhammad [3] then summarizes al-Juwayni's view with the following statement:

> *"Leadership must be an 'exemplary leadership', which has comprehensive approaches in preserving public matters in accordance to religion by prioritizing perseverance of national security, the interests of the people, overcoming malpractices with da'wah (calling to goodness) with discussions and dialog as a tool for helping the oppressed, ensuring that those who have the right get their rights, also ensuring that those rights are not taken away by any party [including the government or leaders]."*

The definition of Islamic leadership has evolved and been broadened over the centuries. This is important to counter Moten's [6] examination as he said leadership from an Islamic perspective which has so far been neglected or misrepresented because it is studied based on European experiences. Responding to this, Gazi [7] emphasizes the pivotal to examine the root of why the concept of leadership in Islam is different from the West. Thus, the views of contemporary Islamic scholars on the definition the term deserves to be discussed.

For example, Beekun and Badawi [8] view leadership in Islam as a basic two-way relationship between an individual and Allah (SWT) directly. The existence of a relationship between two individuals which in turn is translated in the aspect of leadership is upon their faith in Allah (SWT). So leaders had responsibilities to achieve the high-end demand of leadership. Apart from that, leadership in Islam is also referred to as a noble moral activity and communication process toward achieving a common goal [9]. Thus, leaders are distinguished from followers in terms of knowledge, commitment to the teachings of Islam and holding higher moral values. Altalib [10] and Chowdhury [11] shared the view of Islamic leadership combining the process of volunteerism in inspiring and mentoring followers to achieve the vision together.

Leadership or *al-Qiyadah* is generally associated with *al-Siyasah, al-Siyadah, al-Imamah, al-'Umara', alRi'ayah, al-Wilayah, al-Ri'asah, and al-Khilafah*. All these words are defined as leadership. Thus, leadership in Arabic language covers a wide area and is not limited to state or racial (group) leadership but extends to leadership in the fields of knowledge, worship as well as custody and guardianship of a trust [12]. Leadership is the influence exerted by an individual in a situation directed toward achieving specific objectives, mission, and vision [13].

Upon that understanding, leaders are warned that they cannot imply autocratic leadership but must act humanely in leading a state or an organization. In many Islamic works, explained leadership in Islam is a trust that binds the leader from abuse of power or deviance in making the decision. Instead, the leader is responsible for providing guidance, preserving, and fulfilling the rights or demands of the followers fairly and justly [14]. As leadership in Islam is a combination of relationships – with human beings and Allah (SWT), Gazi [7] asserted that Islamic leadership is to lead achieve and compete to be ahead of others to seek the measure of Allah and success in this life and hereafter. Therefore, Kader [15] emphasizes that the focus of Islamic leadership is to promote good deeds in the name of Allah (SWT), the Muslim community, and mankind as a whole.

Therefore, it is clear that previous and contemporary Muslim scholars have similar perspectives on the meaning of "Islamic leadership" and its impactful toward societal development. In fact, their statements are complemented, although they come from different centuries while maintaining the fundamental, preserving *maqasid syari 'ah*, promoting goodness, and forbidding evils which are basic values of humanity that must be attended by leaders. In other words, this concept reflects that the Islamic notions of *tajdīd* (renewal) and *islāh* (reform) are basic goals for Muslim leaders to attain [16]. The leaders who promote these two concepts are the people who occupy themselves in the things conducive to goods, not the things conducive to evil or bad in the light of Islamic essences. Upon these notions, Malik, Safarudin, and Mat [17] acclaimed that putting the best leaders to lead the country will justify Islamic leadership attributes in places.

3. Values of humanity in the leadership of Prophet Muhammad (peace be upon him)

Prophet Muhammad (peace be upon him) was the best role model in all aspects of life, including leadership. His leadership ability had a great impact on Meccan people both before and during his appointment as the Messenger of Allah (SWT). Prophet Muhammad's leadership received extensive acknowledgment from many researchers mainly the West despite they have different views on his personality [9]. For instance, Hart [18] in his book "The 100: A ranking of most influential persons in history" listed the Prophet Muhammad (peace be upon him) in the top place in the 100 influential leaders throughout human history.

Prophet Muhammad's leadership style can be referred to the Al-Qur'an and *hadith*. From these two main sources, there are three principles that form the leadership framework of Prophet Muhammad (peace be upon him): the element of *Tauhid*, the element of *ibadah* (obedience to the Shariah or the law of Allah), and the element of *akhlaq* (the personality of the Prophet Muhammad (peace be upon him) on a daily basis). It is believed that the goal of leadership highlighted by the Prophet Muhammad (peace be upon him) either before he was appointed as the Messenger of God or after is only to elevate the human's dignity to deify Allah (SWT) by obeying the *shariah* as enshrined in the Qur'an and *hadith* thus make the Prophet Muhammad (peace be upon him) as an example to follow. Each of these elements is explained by Allah (SWT) in the Qur'an through verse 70 of surah *al-Isra'*, verse 4 of surah *al-Tīn*, and verse 52 of surah al-Zāriyyāt. It can be concluded that these three principles show that the value of humanity is the main focus in the Prophet Muhammad's leadership style. This leadership style is the key to get true happiness for human beings in this world and the hereafter.

Discussing this matter further, Abbasi et al. [19] explained value and accountability that created by the creation of man are two basic things that are emphasized by Allah (SWT) in the Qur'an many *hadith* of the Prophet Muhammad (peace be upon him).

In surah al-Isra', verse 13 and 14 says.

> *We have bound every human's destiny to their neck.*[1] *And on the Day of Judgment, We will bring forth to each "person" a record which they will find laid open (13). And it will be said, "Read your record. You 'alone' are sufficient this Day to take account of yourself."*

Meanwhile, the *hadith* of the Prophet Muhammad (peace be upon him), Ibn Umar said, he heard from Nabi Muhammad (peace be upon him) who says:

> *"Everyone of you is a guardian and answerable with regard to his trus"" (al-Bukhari: 212).*

Syahansyah [20] highlights four values of humanity that can be learned from the character of the Prophet Muhammad (peace be upon him) thus shaping his leadership style. First, the peaceful agreement between races and tribes is the backbone of the leadership of the Prophet Muhammad (peace be upon him) in Medina which he was refusing to continue the tradition of ignorant practices that are fond for fighting or war. Explaining this matter further, verse 107 in surah *al-Anbiya* emphasizes as "*We did not send you, O Muhammad except as a mercy for all the worlds*" is a special declaration from Allah (SWT) to the Prophet Muhammad (peace be upon him) who is responsible to ensure prosperity and mercy to all creatures created by Allah (SWT).

Elaborating further the definition of "*rahmatan lil- 'ālamīn*" generally means loving and caring. Ar-Raghib al-Ashfahani (d. 502H) described the word *al-rahmah* as *al-riqqah* (gentleness) or *al-ihsān* (virtue) or *al-khayr* (goodness) and *al-ni'mah* (enjoyment). Therefore, Syahansyah [20] explained this word is *musytarak*, which is an indication to use the meaning of the word that tied or determined with something else after it.

In addition, *al-Imam Ibn Jawziy* gave 16 literal meanings to describe the meaning of mercy based on the al-Quran [21]. The 16 meanings are (1) heaven, (2) Islam, (3) faith, (4) prophethood, (5) the Quran, (6) rain (*al-matar*), (7) sustenance, (8) pleasure, (9) health (*afiya*), (10) bestowal (*al-minnah*), (11) delicacy (*al-riqqah*), (12) forgiveness (*al-maghfirah*), (13) vastness (*al-si' ah*), (14) love (*al-mawaddah*), (15) maintenance (*al-'ismah*), and (16) light (*al-shams*). So in general, most of the meanings expressed by Ibn al-Jawzi describe the nature of love and mercy brought by Allah and His Messenger in this worldly life until the day of judgment (*akhirah*). Therefore, it is very clear that the value of humanity through peace and avoiding conflict in leadership is very important to every Muslim leaders as has been shown by the Prophet Muhammad (peace be upon him).

Secondly, Islam consistently prohibits the killing of any individual. This stance is a value that must be considered in leadership while realizing any leader holds the power to start a war or can give an order to take anyone's soul without clear justification. The consequence of killing any individual and its prohibition was reminded by Allah (SWT) in surah *al-Maidah* verse 32 which means:

> *"That is why We ordained for the Children of Israel that whoever takes a life—unless as a punishment for murder or mischief in the land—it will be as if they killed all of humanity; and whoever saves a life, it will be as if they saved all of humanity. ⸢Although⸣ Our messengers already came to them with clear proofs, many of them still transgressed afterwards through the land."*

The above-mentioned verse clearly forbids one person to kill another individual. Not only that, taking away (killing) the life of human beings, is considered the same as killing humanity as a whole. Islam never teaches to kill anybody and never made emotional be a justification or motive in any action. Killing here means taking the one's right to live. While living in the world is necessary to be accountable to Allah (SWT). Peace in Islam becomes something that cannot be negotiated with anything else. Even so, war is allowed to take place if to obtain peace and to defend the right of territorial sovereignty by fulfilling the conditions as prescribed in the Al-Quran and *hadith*.

Preserving life is one of the five objectives of *al-maqāsid al-syar'iyyah*. Imam al-Syatibi explained that the preservation of life or *hifz al-nafs* is the second most important thing that needs to be preserved after religion (*hifz al-din*) [22]. In line with that goal, Islam was revealed with the aim of elevating and preserving human values based on compassion and community [23]. It is understandable that the objective of preserving life has to do with the protection and implementation of the universal principle of human rights, namely the right to life (Al-Isra: 31–33). In another surah, the Qur'an also emphasizes the importance of providing protection to the weak and oppressed (Al-Balad: 12–16). Thus, it is very clear that the principle of preserving life also includes the following understanding; everyone has the right to life, has the right to live, and improve the standard of living, everyone also has the right to live in peace and well-being physically and mentally, and everyone has the right to feel safe and secure from the threat of violence and destruction. Arummi [23] concludes that all the aspects mentioned include the guarantee of safety of life, limbs, and also human dignity.

The third that become a pillar of values of humanity in the leadership of the Prophet Muhammad (peace be upon him) is there is no compulsion in religion. Syahansyah [20] refers to the whole understanding of surah *al-Kāfirūn* verses 1 to 6 which is the basis of understanding there is no compulsion in religion and also social problems. Syahansyah explained that this surah is a proposition on no coercion in all matters related to individual life including in the question of governance of life affairs where each individual is given the freedom to choose what is best for himself.

According to Friedmann [24], no compulsion in religion in Islam is a trait of tolerance inherited since the early days of Islam. Although the people of Mecca and Madinah were not forced to choose Islam, but what happened was that a group of Muslims who believed in Allah (SWT) and the Prophet Muhammad (peace be upon him) were forced to leave Islam while in Mecca before the Hijrah. Such incidents happened on Bilal bin Rabah, Ammar bin Yasar, and several other companions of the Prophet Muhammad (peace be upon him), and this shows that tolerance did not exist among the Quraish people in Mecca ([24], p. 103). Having said that, al-Qur'an is a proof of the implementation of tolerance without coercion in religion, thus the *Sahīfah Madīnah* treaty made by the Prophet Muhammad (peace be upon him) immediately after leading the city of Madinah proves that the Islamic leadership recognizes peaceful coexistence where indirectly rejects racism and preserving equality as well as guaranteeing the right to freedom of religious choice [25].

Sahīfah Madīnah signed in 622 AD between the Prophet Muhammad (peace be upon him) and the leaders of the Arab tribes in Medina was considered to be the earliest document of statehood in the history of human civilization [25]. In addition, the agreement reached in the *Sahīfah Madīnah* is also recognized as a guiding model of coexistence in the diversity of society's different races and cultures in this modern era [26]. The *Sahīfah of Madīnah* has 47 articles, and the following are the things that need to be agreed upon while respecting the principle of no religious compulsion:

i. brotherhood treaty between the Muhajirin (those who migrated to Madinah from Mecca) and the Ansar (the people of Madinah);

ii. the safety of non-Muslims living in Muslim neighborhoods in Medina;

iii. a public declaration that Medina was a Muslim territory;

iv. acknowledging the Quran and *Hadith* are the two main sources in Islam;

v. Prophet Muhammad is the head of state;

vi. Cooperation of all Muslim or non-Muslim residents to defend Madinah from enemy attacks.

It is very clear that the leadership style led by the Prophet Muhammad (peace be upon him) has the highest interest of values in humanity. With the *Sahīfah of Madīnah* as an example, it shows that the Muslim population must respect and treat the non-Muslims with good consideration and generosity. In a situation where the non-Muslims does not do any harm or become a threat to the Muslim population, then tolerance should be shown. This matter is explained by Allah (SWT) in surah *Al-Mumtahanah*, verse 8:

> *Allah does not forbid you from dealing kindly and fairly with those who have neither fought nor driven you out of your homes. Surely Allah loves those who are fair.*

Fourth, the value of humanity that can be emulated from the personality of the Prophet Muhammad (peace be upon him) is from the command to call to Islam (*da'wah*) with three basic principles: wisdom, good advice, and debating or discussing politely and kindly. These three basic principles are based on verse 125 of surah *al-Nahl*:

> *"Invite ˹all˺ to the Way of your Lord with wisdom and kind advice, and only debate with them in the best manner. Surely your Lord ˹alone˺ knows best who has strayed from His Way and who is ˹rightly˺ guided."*

Da'wah aims to invite people to obey Allah (SWT) in accordance with the Qur'anic mission as mentioned in surah *al-Zāriyyāt* verse 56. This verse emphasizes that the duty and responsibility of human beings are to serve Allah by following all His commands and abandoning all His prohibitions. Therefore, the implementation of *da'wah* which is the task inherited from all prophets must be used methods or approaches that are appropriate to the target group so that it does not become a slander to religion. This is important in ensuring the effectiveness of *da'wah* and its development continues effectively. The importance of proper approaches and methods in doing *da'wah* is due to the nature of Islamic *da'wah* assured human life by ensuring eternal goodness in the hereafter [27].

Da'wah is one of the noblest acts that entail a high reward. *Da'wah* is one of the means to propagate Islam to others. This is unanimously agreed in Islam and the Qur'an itself which absolutely go against compulsion in religion. People need to be convinced the truth that Islam brings to mankind. According to Račius [28], the word "*da 'wah*" in the Qur'ān has three primary meanings, namely (1) worshiping God or idols, 2) addressing, asking, and calling (God, idols, and people), and (3) inviting to religion (Islam or other). The first two meanings of "*da 'wah*," worshiping and calling, are frequent in the Qur'ān, for example, in 2:186, 3:38, 6:40, 11:22, 11:106, 19:48, 19:91, 22:12, 72:18, and others. Meanwhile in the last meaning, the Qur'ān urged the Prophet Muḥammad to appeal to pagan Arabs and (occasionally) Jews and Christians, for example, in 12:108, 13:36, 16:125, 23:73, 40:10, 41:33, and 70:17.

Ismatullah [29] explains the method of *da'wah* from verse 125 of surah *al-Nahl* where Hamka states that this verse is a basic guide to the prophets in conveying the message of Islam so that people have straight path toward Allah (SWT). The word wisdom in this verse carries various interpretations among scholars. For example, commentators such as Imam Fakhrul al-Radzi explained the word *al-Hikmah* in the verse is the basic approach in inviting people to do goodness effectively. It should be based on the revelation of the Qur'an and refer to the *sunnah* of the Prophet Muhammad (peace be upon him), and it must be based on true religious understanding in ensuring that the target group understands the essence of what is to be conveyed [30]. Meanwhile, Wahbah al-Zuhailiy thinks that the wisdom (*al-Hikmah*) in the verse has been bestowed on a chosen and pious servant such as Luqman al-Hakim, as a great gift from Allah (SWT). This attribute was given to justify the deep understanding and intelligence level anyone had in considering the best decision to make ([31], p. 2024). Furthermore, wisdom can also be referred as a noble attribute that describes activity of *da'wah*. Thus, the wisdom in *da'wah* includes any behavior and manners, speech, community service, and leadership [32]. So it is clear here that the element of wisdom is important in the management of humanity which is not limited to religious questions but also covers the welfare of society.

The second element in the same verse is *mau 'izah al-hasanah* or a good advice. In conveying the message of *da'wah* through the method of good advice is important. This is because human beings have soft heart and instinct; hence, good speech and advice are more easily to be accepted than hurtful messages and feelings [33]. In this regard, Hamka in his tafsir Tafsir al-Azhar explains that the element of good advices should start from the home where education and teaching from parents in the home have a direct impact on *da'wah* activities outside the house and on the various target of *da'wah* [29].

In addition, there are many examples of good advice used by the Prophet Muhammad (peace be upon him) in conveying the message of Islam in Mecca and Madinah. Abdul Fattah Abu Ghuddah [34] explained that the method of giving good advice shown by the Prophet Muhammad (peace be upon him) has a positive effect where the noble values are successfully normalized among his companions and family members and then show that his leadership style has high human values [17]. In the meantime, Mohamad et al. also listed the important elements that must be present in conveying good advice, namely gradual delivery, contextual, be exemplary, repetitive methods, direct communication, metaphorical methods, and stories ([17], pp. 7–15). For example, when the Prophet (peace be upon him) spoke about something, he would repeat the matter three times so that those who heard the matter could understand it well, as narrated in Sahih al-Bukhari, meaning:

> *"From Anas bin Malik, and Prophet (peace be upon him) says; verily whenever Prophet (peace be upon him) spoke, he will repeat it three times so that people can understand" (no.94, Sahih al-Bukhari).*

Having good discussions or giving good arguments has an intrinsic human value that defines the relationship with leadership style. It is worth to note from the mentioned verse, Don [33] through Fu'ad Ifram al-Bustani explains the meaning of "*mujadalah*" is a method of debate with politeness and proficient in the issues discussed where the purpose is only to reveal the truth. Zin [35] emphasizes that the arguments must be reasonable, appealing to reason and refrain from indulging in polemics, sophistry, and controversy. Elaborating further on this, he points out that "one should adopt a comprehensive method to convince the addressee which includes: arguments and appeal to his feeling; condemnation of evils and deviations as well as repugnance to all that lies embedded in the human nature, warning of the consequence of evil; soundness of argument, excellence of guidance and righteous deed." Another point mentioned is that "admonition should be administered in such a manner as to show sincere concern for the welfare of the addressee."

The goal of having a good debate for truth is also recorded in surah *al-Ankabut* verse 46 which means:

> *"Do not argue with the People of the Book unless gracefully, except with those of them who act wrongfully. And say, "We believe in what has been revealed to us and what was revealed to you. Our God and your God is 'only' One. And to Him we 'fully' submit."*

well as public and private organizations. Yet, the world today faces a crisis of trust at all levels of organizational and national leadership. A report from the Edelman Trust Barometer shows from 2016 to 2020, four sectors: governments, business organizations, NGOs, and the media, which are facing a crisis of public confidence despite the growing global economic sector. In addition, the same report also states that clerics are in the same group as politicians and businessmen, who have the lowest "believe" scores compared to the media and NGO activists. This crisis of trust stems from the public view that these three groups are not convinced that they are able to solve the problems they face, including managing the country out of the global crisis. Although most studies state that the ability to manage the economy is the biggest factor influencing public trust, the ability to lead by focusing on the well-being of human values also contributes to increased levels of trust in leaders. If this matter is not given priority, then slowly the value of humanity will erode from the compass of leadership and will eventually collapse the social system as a whole [38].

Corruption has had a major contribution to the collapse of human values in the current leadership setting. The worse of corruption can bring down a strong civilization, and rebuilding a destroyed civilization needs time. The Corruption Perceptions Index 2021 report states that since January 2020, the global has not only faced a health and economic crisis due to the COVID-19 pandemic but also faced a protracted corruption crisis. According to CPI 2021 spokesperson Delia Ferreira Rubio, "the crime of corruption is the only problem unsuccessfully solved by most countries compared to health problems." Apart from that, the failure to manage the crime of corruption is because there is no precise definition to describe the meaning of "corruption" [39]. On that basis, some of the corruption cases that occur involve the top leadership of a country. This means that the human values glorified by Allah (SWT) are not respected by leaders, thus willingly involve in corruption. On that basis, to stop one from involving corruption needs a proper planning. For example, in Indonesia, coworkers and leaders are the main factors that contribute to a person engaging in corruption and at the same time these two groups are also the main indicators in ensuring that corrupt practices do not occur [40].

Generally, researcher views corruption is a domestic crime in any country. It is a local cultural phenomenon that depends on the level of understanding and cultural values of the society [41]. Thus, in modern perspective, a person who is not involved in corruption is not able to justify another person who is involved in a crime of corruption because he or she has different values of belief and point of view. However, in the Islamic point of view, corruption is a major crime that can damage the whole system and structure of a prosperous society, thus demean human dignity [42]. Human dignity held high position in Islam and has direct connection to leadership. Azra [43] explains that Islam places great emphasis on the concept of *akhlāq al-karīmah* or moral par excellence. In this regard, Islam strongly opposes all types of activities that violate the values of human dignity such as corruption, theft, and robbery which can result injustice to others.

Of equal importance, abuse of power is also a problem in today's leadership. Many reports state that world leaders from both the Western and the Islamic world are involved in abuses of power. Noam Chomsky in his book Failed State states that a leader who fails to preserve his citizens from violence and destruction can be considered a failed state ([44], p. xi). Not only that, for the leader of a country who abuses his power and commits violence or brings harm to another country, is also categorized as a failed country. This is because, every life has the right to live in peace and prosperity as enshrined in the declaration of human rights (UNDHR). Therefore, the power in the hands of leaders should be used in preserving universal human values and rights as prescribed by law (international and local). Take the example from Muslim world where many were associated with the act of abuse of power in their leadership. In fact, abuse of power has originated from a misinterpretation of religion and leadership concepts that Willy, Karwur, and Karouw [45] found as a major cause to violent extremism and terrorism that happened in Iraq and Pakistan.

Having said that, abuse of power can occur anywhere including at the highest levels of the nation and also in the workplace in small organizations. Based on 20 years of study, Dacher Keltner [46] stated that the workplace or company/organization is the easiest place for abuse of power to occur without being noticed by the individual involved. This is because, within an organization, a person has the authority or can be empowered due to promotion or change of department based on the job performance. Yet, having such power has slowly made him or her irritable, unethical, and selfish which eventually at last engages in abuse of power. To Dacher Keltner, this situation is called "the power paradox" and it is just as dangerous as the country's leaders abusing power for personal gain. In other words, the abuse of power can erode the value of humanity in oneself and fail to respect the value of humanity in others. On that basis, one good example made by Manuela Priesemuth as she launched the "Time's up for toxic workplace" campaign and accordingly this campaign was expanded to the election of national leaders who openly abused power to the public.

Concurrent to these crises in today's leadership that obstructed the development of global society, at times Muslim population is expected to rise to 2.2 billion by 2030, Shadi Hamid [47] argues Islam and Muslim readiness in reshaping the world outside the Arab world play a major role in governance, law, and politics. He further emphasizes the exceptionalism of Islam in the leadership manifestation that can be played by Muslim leaders in a value-neutral sense in response to twentieth- and twenty-first-century challenges. Such notion has firstly been analyzed by Sardar's *Islamic Futures: The Shape of Ideas to Come* as the future is controllable and common societal desires and goals have influenced in shaping future Islamic resurgence and realization [48]. Realizing that, Hasan [49] reminds that the *ummah* is in dire need a new breed of leaders who committed to lead Muslim societies and nations out of valley of despair and indignity to a better future civilization of Islam. Inspired by the Prophetic model of leadership, the future leaders that Muslim must produce shall embed the following characters: high moral integrity, *taqwā*, and deep spiritual and moral awareness (*ihsān*) of Divine omnipresence and omniscience. In fact, Rafiki [50] had done great work by simplifying 56 leadership attributes from Quranic verses that celebrate the value of humanity. These can be a future consideration in determining Islamic leadership approaches toward humane leadership framework.

5. Conclusion

The concept of Islamic leadership is built on principles and concerns for human values. From the discussion of the literature, it shows that Islamic leadership is blended with human development in an integrated manner with an emphasis on four values that can be emulated from the leadership of the Prophet Muhammad (peace be upon him). The elements of humanity found in the leadership of the Prophet Muhammad (peace be upon him) are peace between communities, recognizing the right to life and prohibiting murder, no coercion in religion and social problems, and the practice of da'wah calling to good and forbidding evil.

Nonetheless, today's leadership is seen not to adhere in elevating the dignity of human values in their leadership style. The problems of corruption, abuse of power, and deficits of trust in leaders both at the national and organizational levels are becoming a global trend today [51]. The involvement of key national leaders in corruption and misuse of power for personal gain has slowly resulted in the country's development being disrupted and had bad impact on the well-being of civil society. Therefore, the Muslim community firmly rejects leadership that ignores and debunks the basics of human values as highlighted by the Prophet Muhammad (peace be upon him) where such examples can be referred in the Qur'an and *hadith*.

To sum up, it can be concluded that the future of balanced society lies on a leadership style based on human values which are embodied in the basic principles as outlined by Islam. This is not optional to Muslim leaders except agreeing to practice Islamic leadership within these frameworks and making them a policy in the administrative and leadership approach. With that application of human values, it would definitely elevate "human leadership" as a new approach of human development in a comprehensive and holistic manner now rather to wait in the future.

Author details

Mohd Faridh Hafez Mhd Omar
Universiti Sains Islam, Malaysia

*Address all correspondence to: faridhomar@usim.edu.my

References

[1] Samsudin NH. The application of Habluminallah and Habluminannas in the work motivation of the management. International Journal of Academic Research in Business and Social Sciences. 2018;**8**(5):1148-1157

[2] Ishak AK, Razak HA, Jamaludin N. Keeping public servants' mental health intact during and post COVID-19 pandemic through the Islamic Mental Health Model. In: Modeling Economic Growth in Contemporary Malaysia. Bingley: Emerald Publishing Limited; 2021

[3] Muhammad S. Kepimpinan Islam: Satu Agenda Pembangunan Ummah. Jurnal Usuluddin. 1997;**6**:131-148

[4] Jan WSW. Islamism in Malaysian politics: The splintering of the Islamic Party of Malaysia (PAS) and the spread of progressive ideas. ICR Journal. 2018;**9**(4):128-153

[5] Mamud YA, Agyeno O. Islamism and social movement framework in global politics. Africa Insight. 2019;**49**(2): 32-40

[6] Moten AR. Leadership in the West and the Islamic world: A comparative analysis. World Applied Sciences Journal. 2011;**15**(3):339-349

[7] Gazi MAI. Islamic perspective of leadership in management; Foundation, traits and principles. International Journal of Management and Accounting. 2020;**2**(1):1-9

[8] Beekun RI, Badawi JA. Leadership: An Islamic Perspective. Maryland: Amana Beltsville; 1999

[9] Al-Sarhi NS, Salleh LM, Mohamed ZA, Amini AA. The West and Islam perspective of leadership. International Affairs and Global Strategy. 2014;**18**:42-56

[10] Altalib H. Training Guide for Islamic Workers. Virginia: International Institute of Islamic Thought (IIIT); 1991

[11] Chowdhury N. Leadership strategies and global unity for the 21st century: An Islamic perspective. In: Leadership & Unity in Islam. San Jose: Writers Club Press; 2002

[12] Kelawa AMA. Kepimpinan wanita dalam Islam: kedudukannya dalam syariah. Bangi: Penerbit Universiti Kebangsaan Malaysia; 1999

[13] Mohd Yusof A. Kepimpinan. Kuala Lumpur: Dewan Bahasa dan Pustaka; 1990

[14] Ahmad K, Ogunsola O. An empirical assessment of Islamic leadership principles. International Journal of Commerce and Management. 2011;**21**(3):291-318

[15] Kader A. Islamic leadership and personality from man to mankind. Al-Ittihad. 1973;**10**(1):9-10

[16] Abdullah AA, Esa M. Towards holistic concept of leadership in Islam for sustainable development community. International Journal of Social Policy and Society (IJSPS). 2015:**27**-49

[17] Mohamad N, Majid MA, Nasir BM. Pendekatan Dakwah dalam Kaedah Pengajaran Kepada Muallaf. Wardah. 2018;**19**(01):1-17

[18] Hart MH. The 100: A Ranking of the Most Influential Persons in History. Canada: Citadel; 1992

[19] Abbasi AS, Rehman KU, Bibi A. Islamic leadership model an accountability perspective. World Applied Sciences Journal. 2010;**9**(3):230-238

[20] Syahansyah Z. Telaah Nilai Kemanusiaan dan Perdamaian dalam

Perspektif Rahmatan lil Alamin. Rahmatan Lil Alamin: Journal Of Peace Education And Islamic Studies. 2018;**1**(1):1-1

[21] Azmi AS, Ismail MY. Konsep Rahmatan Lil Alamin Dalam Hadith: Penerokaan Makna Serta Aplikasi Di Malaysia. Journal of Hadith Studies. 2018;**3**(1):1-13

[22] Abdelgafar BI. Public Policy: Beyond Traditional Jurisprudence: A Maqasid Approach. United States: International Institute of Islamic Thought (IIIT); 2018

[23] Arummi A. Hifzh An-Nafsas Instrument of Maqāshid A'sy-Syarī'ah to Revive the Human Values (Perspective of Fiqh Priority). In: Proceeding International Conference on Middle East and Southeast Asia (ICoMS). Indonesia: Universitas Sebelas Maret Surakarta; 2016. pp. 89-90

[24] Friedmann Y. Tolerance and Coercion in Islam: Interfaith Relations in the Muslim Tradition. Cambridge: Cambridge University Press; 2003

[25] Nor MRM. Protecting non-Muslim: Its implementation during early Muslim rule of Islamicjerusalem. Al-Bayan: Journal of Qur'an and Hadith Studies. 2011;**9**(1):209-249

[26] Ibrahim Z. Islam and pluralism. American Journal of Islam and Society. 2010;**27**(4):i-vi

[27] Don AG, Puteh A. Pengurusan Dakwah: Analisis Pendekatan KeMalaysiaan. Al-Hikmah. 2010;**2**:97-106

[28] Račius E. The Multiple Nature of the Islamic Da'wah [Academic Dissertation]. Helsinki, Finland: University of Helsinki, Faculty of Arts, Institute of Asian and African Studies, Arabic and Islamic Studies and Vilnius University, Institute of International Relations and Political Science; 2004 Available from: http://ethesis.helsinki.fi/julkaisut/hum/aasia/vk/racius/themulti.pdf

[29] Ismatullah AM. Metode Dakwah dalam Al-Qur'an (Studi Penafsiran Hamka terhadap QS. An-Nahl: 125). Jurnal Lentera. 2015;**IXX**(2):155-169

[30] Al-Radzi Fakhru al-Din. Tafsīr al-Fakhr al-Radzī al-Musytahar bi al-Tafsīr wa Mafātihī al-Ghaib. Beirut: Dar al-Fikr; 1994

[31] Al-Zuhaili W. Tafsir Al-Munir Fi Al-'Aqidah wa Asy-Syari'ah wa al-Manhaj. Dimasyq: Dar al-Fikri; 1998

[32] Yasin R, Abdullah MRT, Ghani SA, Shahril MI, Ali SKS. Pendekatan hikmah dalam pembentukan perpaduan masyarakat berbilang kaum di Malaysia. The Malaysian Journal of Social Administration. 2015;**11**(1):29-44

[33] Don AG. Relevansi dan Aplikasi Ayat 125, Surah al-Nahl dalam Konteks Dakwah Serantau. Al-Hikmah. 2010;**2**:127-134

[34] Ghuddah AFA. Rasulullah Pendidik Terulung, 40 Teknik Rasulullah Mengajar. Negeri Sembilan: al-Azhar Media; 2009

[35] Zin AM. Islamic Da'wah (Mission): The Definition, Conception and Foundation. Kuala Lumpur: Pustaka Antara; 1995

[36] Ulwan AN. Silsilah Madrasah al-Du'at. Al-Qahirah: Dar Al-Salam; 2001

[37] Fukuyama F. The Great Disruption Human Nature and the Reconstitution of Social Order. United Kingdom: Profile Books; 2017

[38] Zinchenko V. Humanistic values and enlightenment strategies of global society in the potential of the sustainable

development of democracy. American Research Journal of Humanities and Social Sciences. 2018;**4**(1):1-13

[39] Sanusi A, Ismail SHS. Analisis Strategi Membanteras Rasuah Menurut Islam. Online Journal of Research in Islamic Studies. 2016;**3**(2):33-51

[40] Silitonga MS, van Duijn M, Heyse L, Wittek R. Setting a good example? The effect of leader and peer behavior on corruption among Indonesian senior civil servants. Public Administration Review. 2019;**79**(4):565-579

[41] Melgar N, Rossi M, Smith TW. The perception of corruption. International Journal of Public Opinion Research. 2010;**22**(1):120-131

[42] Ismail SHS, Ab Rahman A, Zain MIM. Pengukuhan nilai dan profesionalisme di kalangan penjawat awam ke arah efektif governan di Malaysia. Jurnal Syariah. 2009;**17**(3):559-592

[43] Azra A. Islam, corruption, good governance, and civil society: The Indonesian experience. Islam and Civilisational Renewal (ICR). 2010;**2**(1):109-125

[44] Chomsky N. Failed States: The Abuse of Power and the Assault on Democracy. New York: Metropolitan Books; 2007

[45] Willy W, Karwur BS, Karouw YW. Phenomences of violence on the name of religion towards terrorism acts. International Journal of Social, Policy And Law. 2021;**2**(3):92-101

[46] Keltner D. Don't Let Power Corrupt You. Boston, MA, USA: Harvard Business Review; 2016. Available from: https://hbr.org/2016/10/dont-let-power-corrupt-you [Accessed: October 10, 2021]

[47] Hamid S. Islamic Exceptionalism: How the Struggle Over Islam is Reshaping the World. New York: St. Martin's Press; 2016

[48] Sardar Z. Islamic Futures: The Shape of Ideas to Come. United Kingdom: Mansell Publishing Limited; 1985

[49] Hasan K. The Muslim Ummah in Dire Need for a New Breed of Leaders. IIUM; 2021. pp. 1-32. Available from: https://www.iium.edu.my/media/70298/THE%20MUSLIM%20UMMAH%20IN%20DIRE%20NEED%20FOR%20A%20NEW%20BREED%20OF%20LEADERS.pdf [Accessed: February 2, 2022]

[50] Rafiki A. Islamic leadership: Comparisons and qualities. In: Franco M, editor. Digital Leadership - A New Leadership Style for the 21st Century. London: IntechOpen; 2020. DOI: 10.5772/intechopen.90151

[51] Ries TE. 2021 Edelman Trust Barometer Global Report. New York: Edelman Trust Institute; 2021

Section 2

Leadership and Innovation and SMEs

And from surah *al-Fussilat* verse 34:

> *"Good and evil cannot be equal. Respond ˹to evil˺ with what is best, then the one you are in a feud with will be like a close friend."*

Based on above three keywords – wisdom, good advice, and good argument - the priority is to bring rational dialog and discussion with all parties. Thus, it is important for a leader to have these skills to debate or discuss with facts and evidences in revealing the truth so that none is persecuted at the end of discussion. Abdullah Nasih Ulwan [36] stressed that it is important for the preacher (*da'wah* activist) owned two strengths in debating or arguing which can help them to convey the true message and then be accepted with an open heart. The two strengths are satisfactory strength (*quwwah al-iqnaiyyah*) and factual strength (*quwwah al-hujjah*). In Syed Qutb's view, these two strengths belong only to the prophets and some of the *da'wah* scholars and activists only because the mission is to elevate the rank of *da'i* and quality them to the degree of *al- 'azīm* [33].

Based on the discussion through the descriptive method of literature review, it can be understood that the leadership style of the Prophet Muhammad (peace be upon him) when in Mecca and Madinah has signified the values of humanity as requirements to meet the basic human nature as the best creation (Al-Quran, Al-Tīn: 4). So many explanations are shown in the Qur'an and the hadiths of the Prophet Muhammad (peace be upon him) regarding the value of humanity which is the cornerstone in leading people toward goodness and abandoning evil for the sake of eternal prosperity in the hereafter.

Even so, the world today faces leadership problems that stem from a misunderstanding of evaluating the human aspect in human beings. The next discussion will discuss some of the current problems that stem from leadership styles that do not give priority to the humanitarian aspect. Failure to prioritize human values in leadership has the potential to jeopardize the development of the global society and further destroy the civilization of a country.

4. Crisis of human values in today's leadership

The exemplary leadership inherited by the Prophet Muhammad (peace be upon him) is to strengthen the practice of Islamic teachings that elevate the human dignity in this world and in the hereafter. It is appropriate to Muslim leaders today to pay attention to the advancement of society by values-based development. This is because the value of humanity that already exists in each individual, without limiting on one's background of race, religion, culture, and language, is the key to the successful development of civilization as well as a state.

Francis Fukuyama in his book The Great Disruption explains that the strength of civilization and the development of a country depend on the paradigm shift of human values (humanity) on the changes that are happening globally in various sectors such as economic, social, information, and political leadership structure. Assessing these factors, he asserts that social law and universally shared moral values do not lie in individual choice; instead, it also depends on the social system and the strength of the leadership structure ([37], p. 85). Therefore, he also thinks that the value of humanity in an uncertain global environment will be determined by the political factors of power compared to the values that exist in religion ([37], p. 126).

For example, "trust" is the most important value that binds togetherness between civil society and leaders or administrators within the national structure as

Chapter 4

Strengthening Innovative Leadership in the Turbulent Environment

Iffah Budiningsih and Tjiptogoro Dinarjo Soehari

Abstract

Recently, in the Digital Transformation era that is trigger by technology, Industry 4.0 is a transformation process that leads to company changes that disrupt and affect all business processes. In the current transformation phase, leaders must have the ability to manage digital transformation processes and new digital organizations that are emerging which are changing in a volatile (turbulent) business environment. The discussion in this chapter book includes a content analysis of several leadership characters that are very influential in anticipating turbulent environmental changes, which include: leadership in the turbulent era, innovative leadership, leadership with high integrity, leadership with high EQ. The dynamics of the external environment such as economic, political, social, cultural, scientific, and technological changes very rapidly which will have an impact on the business environment: customers, suppliers, competitors, investors, government/law, and interest groups. The external environmental turbulence must be anticipated by all institutions by strengthening leadership so that leaders and their followers can create innovative products, processes, collaborations, communication, and have emotional intelligence that can capture the substance of the problem objectively and arouse the spirit of participation of all parties. Another very basic thing is a leader who has strong integrity, which is trustworthy, honest, moral, and has the credibility to produce solutions to various business problems so that in the end it produces excellent performance according to stakeholder expectations. Leaders need to proactively manage change through strengthening innovative ideas, creating new things as the key to creating a prime competitive advantage for the company. The leader is a figure who must be able to continuously adapt to the dynamics of the rapid development of the environment and market, supported by human resources, superior organization, and the right systems and procedures to achieve organizational goals.

Keywords: leadership, innovation, integrity, emotional intelligence (EQ)

1. Introduction

The rapid development and rapid spread of digital technology and especially industry 4.0. significantly changing business processes, business models, customer relationships, and operations leading to destructive changes in all business structures. Digital transformation management is a huge challenge for organizations today. Strong leadership is of paramount importance to an organization/institution/company, both profit-oriented and non-profit-oriented, to face the rapidly changing environment to produce a competitive advantage in crises that might hit the organization/institution/company. Types of leadership are many: e.g., transactional leadership, managerial leadership and, transformational leadership. In application, one does not always refer to one of the concepts. Therefore, the present paper will not discuss further the concept of leadership. Rather, it focuses on discussing how to strengthen the leadership to solve problems that might occur due to rapid environmental changes or turbulence. Such as the industrial revolution 4.0, namely the existence of technology disruption which implies a new culture, such as human-machine communication; connection: global village; smart robots; internet of things; 3D Printers; driverless cars, big data; online/virtual education. This has the impact that many jobs involve science, technology, engineering, and math skills, the internet of things, lifelong learning. In [1] Leadership characteristics 4.0 include: (a) responsive leadership; (b) swarm leadership; (c) learning and innovation leadership; (d) open leadership; (e) agile leadership; (f) participatory leadership; (g) leadership networking; (h) trust leadership; (i) digital leadership; and (j) collaborative leadership.

The strategic policy to cope with a turbulent change of environment requires a strong leader with innovative ability, high integrity, and high emotional intelligence. Creativity and innovation are regarded as essential to have to compete. Such are not easy aspects to learn, as they are related to several matters: (a) product innovation to generate new products as well as process innovation for more efficient and effective production activities to generate lower prices with better quality; (b) communication innovation with the elements of business such as supplier, distributor, regulator; (c) collaboration innovation with customers, distributors, suppliers, regulator, and involved community members. The results of research by [2] explain that developing creativity (innovation) in organizations requires the level of emotional intelligence of the leader, and this supports previous research, namely that there is a positive influence between the emotional intelligence of the leader and the level of creativity of his subordinates. A leader is also required to have strong integrity as the figure that upholds honesty, openness, objectivity, not abusing power and authority, and upholds the important values of the organization/company. The main role of a leader is to lead one's subordinates towards the objectives of an organization/company that is responsive to a dynamic change of environment. According to [3] leader integrity is important because it plays an important role in the decision process used by followers when deciding who they will follow, whom they will trust, to whom they will be loyal and committed, and ultimately to who they will appear. The importance of a leader's integrity can lie in its positive influence on the leadership process and the positive organizational outcomes it achieves. Perspective leadership is employee-centered leadership, that is, there is consistency between words and actions, increases follower trust, and helps in predicting behavior to follow.

Leaders who lack integrity will not provide a basis for followers to infer consistency between their actions and words. According to [4] explains that the possibility of a leader being able to perform effectively. They are two important things that need to be tested, the first: integrity as a core executive in the context of the overall personality; the second: active participation of leaders using a wide range of possibilities to provide solutions to various conditions and challenges. Based on the findings of [5], integrity is the most important character strength for the performance of top-level executives, but what is interesting from this finding is that it has nothing to do with the performance of middle-level managers. The irony of this statement can provide insight into why there are ethical failures on the part of managers when they are promoted to executive leadership? This may happen because managers generally focus their work on a technical level that prioritizes hard skills, so they may often lack the integrity to perform effectively at a higher level. The ability to handle problems is a key component of personality that adds to predictive accuracy about how a leader may perform under a leadership role especially when the future conditions of the business are unpredictable. In a turbulent work environment, high integrity leaders offer stability by providing clear positive values for followers to identify which can encourage followers' willingness to promote a good organizational image and also to adapt to dynamic changes and take initiatives to increase effectiveness. Overall organizational activities.

Moreover, a leader must also have a high level of emotional intelligence as the figure that is capable of managing the emotions of oneself and other people, grasping a piece of clear and objective information, guiding the thoughts and actions of other people, coordinating resources, and acting as motivator and catalyst to achieve organizational success. That said, the achievement of organizational objectives benefits from a leader who has high emotional intelligence. According to [6] explaining that over the last two decades, emotional intelligence has become a point of concern, especially related to leadership. Empirical findings have confirmed that the EQ dimension is more necessary to achieve leadership effectiveness with successful coping with stress in the workplace than IQ. Several previous studies revealed that emotional intelligence is significant in social situations, IQ is very important in cognitive tasks; Undoubtedly, IQ is an important and key element of leadership, but research shows that emotional intelligence (EQ) is more important for leaders in different contexts, namely to be able to be more successful and be able to cope with stress in the workplace. A leader who does not have sufficient emotional intelligence will have wider consequences, namely resulting in lower employee engagement and higher turnover rates. While it is possible to excel in technical work, if a leader cannot communicate effectively with his team or subordinates or collaborate with others, his technical skills will be neglected.

In [7] opine that the phenomenon of a turbulent environment approves the idea that employees must have a sense of belonging to the organization/company; employees must also bear multiple roles as a leader for oneself as well as a businessperson. That being mentioned, every employee is demanded to have optimal managerial and entrepreneurship competence as the strategic element of organizational success. The role of a leader is to mobilize all resources to achieve the objectives. In [8] Points out that in a business strategy, the essential aspect is to offer better values to the customer in comparison with the competitors, in the form of a product/service that has the lowest cost and is sustainable; however, at present, there are competitors from all over the world that can provide optimal service to the customers, that said, the single strategy of price competitiveness may not be as strategic as it was used to be but has to combine with other strategies. To formulate an effective strategy, a leader must be informed of all information all over the world and analyze the correlation with organizational needs and the resources owned to provide a fast and appropriate response on the business condition. No leader can guide the company to be competitive without understanding the commercial, social, economic, political, and technological impact in a global scope. Strategy in an organization is the main factor for a leader to observe one's scope globally as well as to observe the needs of the organization to operate effectively and efficiently to develop competitiveness. A company's strategy involves the decision to make regarding the prioritized business to be focused on and what business is to be abandoned. The analysis encourages the leader to mobilize all resources to innovate in the product, process, organization, communication, and collaboration effectively and efficiently; such conduct must be supported by a leadership that has high integrity and emotional intelligence to develop competitiveness.

The discussion in this chapter book includes a content analysis of several leadership characters that are very influential in anticipating turbulent environmental changes, which include: introduction, leadership in the turbulent era, innovative leadership, leadership with high integrity, leadership with high EQ. Some of the dominant leadership characters are suspected in the era of turbulent environmental change to be predictors of successful leadership. The writing of this article is a literature study using the content analysis method. The limitation of this chapter book is that it only partially discusses leadership characteristics that can anticipate turbulent environmental changes, namely: innovative leadership, leadership with integrity, and high emotional intelligence.

2. Leadership in the turbulence environment

In [9] point out that environment consists of internal, industrial, and societal environment. The internal environment comprises internal factors in an organization/company, viz.: human resources, organization, organizational culture, and others. Meanwhile, industrial or business environment consists of stakeholders, suppliers, employee/labor unions, competitors, trade associations, communities, creditors, customers, special interest groups, working partners, and others, while societal environment relates to ideology, politics, economy, social, culture, security, and science and technology of a country. Moreover, a turbulent environment is an environment that undergoes a change that might disrupt the activities of an organization/company. In [10] argues that when turbulence occurs, a leader must make assumptions, create new norms, values, and work procedures in facing the disruption. A turbulent environment can lead to a new organizational culture that might result in negative emotions if the elements of the organization are unprepared to face the turbulent environment. The turbulent period requires an increased intensity of learning of the occurring problems, the impacts, and how to manage the negative impact that might occur. According to [11] when a turbulent organizational environment changes, due to changes in technology and new values, the emergence of sustainable innovation will be able to provide sustainability benefits or generate profits within the organization.

A turbulent environment could also lead to a high level of anxiety; therefore, a strong motivator to lower the anxiety as well as to learn the possible outcomes. This also requires the care and knowledge sharing towards fellow organization members regarding management of anxiety that might occur to manage the turbulence in the environment. This shows that a leader must be creative and innovative in conducting a situational analysis with strong assumption, high integrity, and high emotional intelligence to acquire the aspiration of the subordinates as well as to interact with the subordinates to tackle the changes in the environment. Turbulence is commonly unique/specific; therefore, the management must consider the aspects of turbulence. For instance, the monetary turbulence in 1997 was managed by applying a much-interest rate. Regarding this, a question might appear: will the next turbulence be managed by the same method? The answer to the question is uncertain since the demands of the environment have changed from the problems of the number of money supply and the principle of currency demand vs. supply to other demands. One example is the balance of industry or the advancements in the real sector, in which cost leadership is the main strategy that requires a minim-interest rate. The reason is that the real sector and monetary sector are becoming closely related and require a strong integration in the policies in both sectors as an innovative policy. According to [2] in the past two decades, acquisition and divestment activities were strategic activities for business leaders who were expected to increase productivity, increase efficiency, increase innovation and market share, but several research results showed a failure to achieve this goal because it is contrary to belief and tends to harm the organization because it inhibits creativity and innovation.

A leader's quality is reflected in one's ability to conduct an in-depth assumption regarding the main issues related to the external environment. A leader's assumption is also reflected in the turbulence regarding internal integration. The best moment to easily observe the internal condition of an organization/company is when a conflict occurs between the employees. There are many elements of organizational culture that are related to hierarchy, authority, and power that can influence the behavior of employees; that said, the resolution of the conflict must always be re-established and evaluated by referring to the common consensus. It is a challenge for the leader to test the truth of one's assumptions in front of one's subordinate. A leader may emphasize that one is not the best one by showing tolerant behavior and encourage the subordinates when in an argument to think about whether or not to obey him/her. In a turbulent environment, innovation becomes essential; it is stimulated by the ability to identify, grasp, and utilize any opportunity. Innovation does not only relate to creating new products, opening a new market, but also establishing communication and collaboration, offering new solutions in giving service, and developing an organization/company. An organization/company must always continue to be productive and competitive; regarding this, it depends on human resources that can create innovative and sustainable ideas. Therefore, a leader of an organization requires to be able to inspire and motivate one's subordinates.

A leader must feel dependent on one's subordinate to know what is the best; one must also request to the subordinate not to obey him/her if they feel that they are right. Regardless, the subordinates might not fully obey the concept due to the factors of authority and power that are embedded within a leader. In this regard, the leader is demanded to be creative, innovative, have strong integrity (credible, trustworthy, intelligent, and insightful), as well as having the high emotional intelligence to communicate and integrate the subordinate's potentials.

3. Innovative leadership

Creativity goes along with innovation; that said, innovation requires creativity, as it is the main factor of innovative behavior [12]. In [13] elaborate that the complexity of innovative behavior involves three processes: (a) recognition of problems and formulation or adoption of new solutions and ideas; (b) formulation of alternatives to express the solution/idea, establishing legitimacy and seeking support from internal and external elements of the organization; and (c) creation of prototype or model to be tested. Further, [14] argues that innovative behavior serves as a grounding for an individual to achieve a maximum outcome in organizational work. This is because innovation significantly contributes to the enhancement of the competitiveness of an organization by which drives the institution to act differently beyond its limit. With that being said, an innovative person tries through his or her limitation to optimize new ideas and concepts, resulting in a better product and service. Another study by [13] shows that organization of learning, knowledge-sharing, and organizational commitment simultaneously contribute 62% to the achievement of innovative behavior in employees; in this regard, the three factors are regarded as a dominant factor to predict and strengthen the innovative behavior of employees.

Moreover, [14] explain that entrepreneurship leadership and creativity are the dominant factors of innovative behavior. Technically, entrepreneurship leadership is the ability to coordinate one's subordinates to create new ideas that orientate towards the future, indicated with the efforts of:

- finding out the opportunity to develop business;
- performing optimum efforts to survive and develop one's business
- conducting changes that are relevant to the changing dynamics of business demands;
- mobilizing resources effectively and efficiently that orientates towards the results;
- committed to taking business risks; and
- being motivated and persistent in innovating for a better solution.

As a dominant factor of innovation, creativity is the capability of turning imaginative ideas to generate new products/services. A person with high creativity is indicated with characteristics as follows:

- openness in creating;
- freedom of expression;
- continuous exploration of new ideas;
- high flexibility in creating;
- in favor of originality of ideas;
- ability to elaborate on new ideas.

Innovative behavior is commonly directed to discover, produce, introduce, and apply new "products", either regarding ideas, solutions, or beneficial technology for human activity to indicate the effort to seek for the opportunity, develop ideas, and search for support to implement new ideas. Strong leadership influences the innovation of an organization/company [15]. In line with that, according to [16] the leadership has a strong influence on the innovation ability of a micro-enterprise business.

Process innovation is the factor that can reduce production cost; this is in line with the business strategy of price competitiveness that is applicable in facing a sharply competitive market in such a digital era. Companies that fail to innovate will suffer from difficulties when the prices fall while the fixed cost is un-reducible; they will also find it difficult to position the differential competitiveness on the products/services generated, resulting in drawing the product back from the market. In [17] opine that creativity and IT training significantly influence the innovative behavior of the employees. Such a notion indicates that a leader should support the development of the employees' creativity to encourage innovative behavior. Further, [18] elaborate that the function of a leader is to move the organization so that that all individuals are free to realize their motivation potential to achieve the organizational objectives. There are main variables of a leader's level of effectiveness:

- A leadership that meets the expectation, needs, and competence of one's subordinates;

- an organization with an appropriate structure that supports both the interest of its members and itself in a balanced way;
- strong, harmonious, united, and peaceful interaction between the leader and one's subordinates

For a leader, innovation and communication are essential to encourage the participation and collaboration of the subordinates, either internally or externally. In [19] point out that communication to promote the participation of other parties requires considering these aspects:

First: To be successful,

- use simple means of communication that reaches the feeling, not complex, and not too technical;
- prepare oneself to formulate a relevant matter of communication to the subordinates' feelings;
- clarify to the subordinates' anxiety, confusion, anger, and disbelief.
- ensure that the channel of communication and messages is clear from disruption so that important messages are delivered with ease and received clearly by the subordinates;
- make use of technology that supports fast and easy communication with a large and trustworthy scope of communication.

Second: Causes of failure:

- Unclear and interrupted communication;
- Only uses the transfer of information in expressing and solving any problems;
- Sparks a cynical behavior due to the inconsistency of a leader (not conducting what was previously said).

In [20] indicates that communication is an essential aspect for a leader to achieve the expected performance; that said, these aspects are of significance to consider:

- suggesting and influencing other people, either internally or externally;
- giving instruction or direction to other people;
- preparing written means of communication: report, letter correspondence, email, and others;
- giving presentation;
- negotiation and partaking in a debate or discussion;
- providing technical advice or support.

In [20] points out the positive and negative indicators of the variable of communication.

Positive indicator of communication:

- speaking and writing clearly and effectively;
- listening thoroughly to other people, interpreting the contents of the message from other people carefully, and providing an appropriate response;
- asking questions to clarify and showing interest in a two-way communication setting;
- composing words, intonation, style, and format to adjust with the audience;
- showing openness in sharing information and maintaining the transfer of information.

Negative indicator of communication:

- unconfident in communicating;
- compose an unclear or too long piece of writing without focusing on a single message;
- use non-proper words;
- tend to stick to one style of communication that is unsure of its appropriateness;
- tend to lose the attention from readers/audience;
- tend to lose focus and linkages from one topic to another;
- lack of positive feedback from other people as an indicator of the effectiveness of communication;
- holding down information without proper reasoning.

About relation to collaboration, [20] indicate that a strong collaboration requires strong teamwork from each member of the organization/company; the aspects are:

- always cooperating with the team in all activities;
- providing support to each other;
- dividing responsibility in making decisions and compensating the risks;
- motivation for contributing to each other;
- establishing new teams if needed;

- collaborating with colleagues between work units, departments, or divisions;
- forming and developing team culture or standard behavior to be applied in team collaboration:

Moreover, [20] points out the positive and negative indicators of the variable of collaboration.

Positive indicator of collaboration:

- collaborating to cooperate with colleagues to realize organizational goals;
- requesting input from other people by showing a willingness to appreciate the ideas and experiences of the person as the manifestation of determination to learn from the person.
- putting team agenda before personal agenda;
- building cooperation towards the objectives of the work unit/team that orientate towards the members of the team.
- supporting and acting according to the final agreement of the team, despite that the decision might not suit the leader's position;
- appreciating the work achievement of the team and accepting the common responsibility of the team's slackness.

Negative indicator of collaboration:

- rarely provides support to the colleagues;
- tend to work alone;
- emphasize on personal goals achievement;
- refrain from showing attention towards the ideas and inputs from other people;
- tend to act alone;
- showing indications to ignore or disrupt the decisions of the majority;
- take personal advantages on team achievement and break free from responsibility for the team's lack.

Strategy in an organization is the main factor for a leader to observe one's scope globally as well as to observe the needs of the organization to operate effectively and efficiently to develop competitiveness. A company's strategy involves the decision to make regarding the prioritized business to be focused on and what business is to be abandoned. The analysis encourages the leader to mobilize all resources to innovate in the product, process, organization, communication, and collaboration effectively and efficiently; such conduct must be supported by a leadership that has high integrity and emotional intelligence to develop competitiveness.

4. The leadership that has high integrity

The term "integrity" derives from English, which means complete and thorough. According to [21] integrity means thinking, saying, behaving/acting properly and correctly, and upholding the code of ethics and moral principles. In other words, someone's actions are always consistent with the existing values and codes of ethics. According to [3] integrity is one of the main attributes of a great leader and the concept of consistency of actions, values, methods, measures, principles, expectations, and results; or in other words a deep commitment to doing the right thing for the right reasons, regardless of the circumstances. In [22] Propose indicators of integrity, which involves:

- honesty;
- consistency between words and actions;
- obeyance towards rules and ethics of organization/community;
- uphold commitments and principles that one believes to be true;
- be responsible for one's actions, decisions, and the risks that might follow;
- one's quality to gain respect from others;
- wisdom to differ between righteous and wrong conducts and encouragement to other people to conduct similar things.

Generally, people with high integrity are reliable, trustworthy, uphold moral principles, and consistent in realizing the characteristics into one's daily activities without the feeling of shame to express what s/he believes. Commonly, a person with high integrity possesses the traits of intelligence, honest, resilience, trustworthiness, responsible, have self-control, and loyal. Integrity is an absolute requirement for a leader to run the organization effectively and efficiently to achieve the organization's vision and missions. That said, competence, insight, quick and accurate decision-making, as well as uphold ethics and morality are required so that the success achieved is not solely for personal and organizational purposes but also integrated as all stakeholders' success. Integrity can also be referred to as the commitment to accomplish a task correctly and ethically by upholding the values and norms that apply in the business environment without coercion to achieve optimum performance.

Integrity also correlates with credibility and trust; a leader with high integrity is supposed to be credible, trustworthy, and have a strong analytical ability to decide whether something is right or wrong, staying true to one's principles, maintain confidentiality, encourage ethics when discussing business and work, as well as maintaining a commitment to conduct a follow-up on the agreed matters. Credibility comprises two essential aspects, i.e., skills and trust [23]. A leader will be left behind by one's subordinates if they lose trust towards the leader and assume that the leader:

- is incapable of providing solutions to problems that occur,
- is immoral.

- is inconsistent with one's promises,
- betrays the company,
- no, commit to strive for the interest of members and the organization.

According to [24] Propose that to develop trust with the subordinates is to maintain the trust level. Moreover, to build trust is to:

- ensure that all words said will be followed up by actions and avoid the impression of unclearness that can lead to hesitation in the subordinates,
- conduct actions that go with the values of the organization,
- Discuss with the subordinates if encountering any difficulties with one of the subordinates,
- express ideas that represent the interest of the organization, particularly when discussing sensitive issues; be a good listener that can grasp the problems expressed by the subordinates,
- express ideas as based on personal perspective, despite the ideas, maybe different with majority perspective,
- avoid expressions and actions that give the impression of the "yes man".
- maintain the big idea and the main objectives; strive to direct the discussion towards the topic,
- be responsible for one's actions and the aftermath of the actions,
- be sportive and not blame others, focus on the efforts to improve or resolve any problem.

According to [4] A leader who is strong in this element will be aware of their emotions, motivations, and weaknesses. They have an open heart to receive input from various sources. They gather what they know about themselves and their situation to gain a deep understanding of the possibilities that are open to them. Meanwhile, leaders who have low integrative capacity have poor focus, blinding them to information that is inconsistent with their understanding of their limited worldview. If they have little awareness of their motivations and moods, they will tend to misunderstand the motivations of others as well. They tend to deal with events one at a time, fail to see the relationship between them all, and are unable to extrapolate them into the future. In the world of work, a concrete manifestation of integrity is a good performance. Integrity and skill go hand in hand, which leads to better performance. In the absence of competence or skills, it is difficult to demonstrate integrity itself, and conversely, competence or skills without integrity will be difficult to form good performance. Integrity truly manifests itself through the success achieved by utilizing abilities and skills.

The previous aspects are the example of alternative actions to build trust in one's subordinates. In [20] argued that integrity is a core value that must be applied by all staff regardless of the nature of their role to work honestly, openly, objectively in applying the values adopted by the institution for all staff. Moreover, [20] points out the positive and negative indicators of the variable of integrity.

Positive indicator of integrity:

- consistently upholding the principles in a charter of guidelines of an institution
- applying the values of objective neutrality, fairness, honesty, and uphold truth in accomplishing the daily tasks,
- carrying out one's tasks without personal intentions; prioritizing the accomplishment of tasks above personal gains,
- making decisions based on objective and rational reasoning and resisting inappropriate political pressure,
- not abusing power or authority,
- always upholding the interests of the organization in every decision making even though the one has to make unpopular decisions,
- responding quickly when unprofessional or unethical behavior occurs.

Negative indicator of integrity:

- Interpreting principles and ethics carelessly without proper consideration,
- seeking personal gain,
- compromising too easily when faced with pressure,
- being subjective to specific issues related to individual or group problems,
- being unreliable,
- potentially conducting dishonest acts.

In regards to integrity, [25] the key in carrying out the task of creating stability requires credibility and trust. That said, it is impossible to create stability without the trust gained from all stakeholders. Further, [25] also adds that the strategic characters that a leader must possess, include:

- risk-taking;
- innovate and improve to accomplish duties;
- ability to analyze, such as to remodel something to make something more useful to achieve a better goal;
- ability and courage to make decisions in situations where other people may not be able to think clearly.

A breakthrough to change or fix problems on a large scale and fundamentally is not a short-term oriented process; rather, it is a whole optimal process to understand the reasonings. It is not revolutionary, but it prefers a discourse of deep discussion and reflection. As elaborated by Abdullah, the essential values of character and behavior to develop to improve the performance of an organization/company, include competence, integrity, transparency, accountability, and togetherness. To realize these values, several elements are needed:

Organization:

- have the will and ability to adapt to changes in vision and mission
- have high performance based on core values and strategic values
- always be proactive, visionary, and adapt the outward-looking organizational approach

Human resources:

- have a proportional portion of character, integrity, and competence
- take the lead in finding solutions to the moral and intellectual problems of the nation

A leader's integrity must be proven with one's ability to formulate the appropriate policies. In [19] argues that the formulation of the appropriate policies requires people who have strong competence and integrity as well as the ability to maintain and develop professionalism, such as:

- devote commitment to the task/work, idealism for work, and do not work just to earn.
- grow and develop professionalism in the individual's self
- master every issue of one's responsibility as a whole; find links within one issue and another that might occur, analyze the profit, loss, and risk of each problem.
- understand the intention of stakeholders and adjust one's duties and needs, as based on the stakeholders' intention,
- develop the organization the required competencies

The integrity of a leader must be equipped with attributes that support it. The summary of leadership attributes, as proposed by [26] are as follows:

a. Determining the direction of the organization, with dimensions as follows:

   - Dimension: Understanding what is happening on the output, with indicators of (a) showing strong customer orientation; (b) thinking deeply and look carefully at the new possibilities that will emerge; (c) possessing the vision, skills, and resources needed to build networks outside of their home base; (d) utilizing resources for process innovation that can increase customer productivity; (e) consistently clarifying the clarity of organizational direction, and; (f) demonstrating full responsibility towards the environment without any compromise.

- Dimension: Focusing on the future, with indicators of (a) showing confidence in the vision; (b) being able to explain easily to make the other party understand the organization vision, mission, and strategy; (c) being able to carry out mission quests appropriately; (d) taking action based on the inspiration of core values and beliefs; (e) defining, shaping, and utilizing core values; (f) visualizing the business through the customer's perspective; (g) seizing the future through the involvement of careful observation, technology, future outlook, the flexibility of the concept, vision, strategic alignment, and by enhancing the image of the institution; (h) using strategic thinking.

- Dimension: Turning the vision into action, with indicators of (a) aligning performance with the vision; (b) inspiring a shared vision; (c) asking others to seize for the future; (d) transforming strategies into tangible results; (e) inspiring the will for togetherness; (f) creating a conducive condition for success.

b. Mobilizing individual commitment, with dimensions as follows:

- Dimension: Building cooperative relationships, with indicators of (a) Carrying out the process of loving people; (b) Being able to work alone or with other people; (c) bearing a cheerful, supportive, and encouraging role rather than just judging, criticizing, and evaluating; (d) fostering cooperation by promoting common goals and building trust.

- Dimension: Sharing of power, with indicators of (a) showing good faith and ability to share power and control; (b) listening more than speaking; (c) having good faith and the ability to involve others and to gain support with their participation; (d) using force with dignity; (e) empowering and engaging subordinates; (f) empowering others to do their best; (g) strengthening others by sharing strengths and information; (h) using a variety of different approaches to get the best out of each person; (i) creating opportunities for everyone to put all the maximum effort and best of their skills for optimal teamwork results.

- Dimension: Managing attention, with indicators of (a) managing energy and changing one's physical appearance; (b) using appropriate language to touch someone's heart; and (c) evoking emotions, such as: generating confidence when frightened; gaining reassurance when in doubt, taking action when in doubt, gaining strength when weak, gaining skill when floundering helplessly, cultivating courage when feeling afraid, arousing optimism when feeling pessimistic and cynical, as well as gaining confidence that the future will be better.

c. Generate organizational capability, with dimensions:

- Dimension: Building organizational infrastructure, with indicators of (a) demonstrating the ability to unite formal leadership, resources, and unite activities harmoniously across various project clusters; (b) establishing the ad hoc leadership required by each cluster of projects; (c) aligning and ensuring the harmony between the organization and its strategy; (d) actively communicating information to all employees; (e) being fully committed to the long-term strategy by building an institution that can generate added value; (f) providing the necessary impetus and resources for continuous progress; (g) creating enthusiasm for all parties to support the achievement of business targets/goals.

- Dimension: Utilizing diversity, with indicators of (a) showing tolerance for differences but zero tolerance for performance, standards, and values; (b) being not afraid of the forces below him; (c) integrating cultural, sector, and disciplinary differences; (d) resolving conflicts diplomatically and finding common causes; (e) advocating partnership and collaboration as preferred styles of behavior; (f) fully utilizing the skills of people, regardless of race, gender, ethnic origin, or culture.

- Dimension: Deploy team; with indicators of (a) building teams to manage their projects; (b) cross-developing teams and bringing the best form from one place to another; (c) selecting the best available team members' talents; (d) providing specific and frequent feedback that can help improve team performance; (e) supporting the team even when they fail; (f) building or creating culture; (g) maintaining culture; (h) having skills in analyzing cultural assumptions; (i) serving as a catalyst and manager of cultural change; (j) consciously promoting a clearly articulated and highly engaging culture.

- Dimension: Making changes, with indicators of (a) realizing change and working as change agents; (b) demonstrating emotional reinforcement to manage anxiety caused by change; (c) serving as a catalyst and manager of strategic change; (d) seeking opportunities by complaining and challenging the status quo; (e) trying and taking risks; (f) learning from mistakes/failures and successes; (g) constantly looking for more straightforward methods to provide customers with better goods and services; (h) seeking opportunities in change is better than avoiding change; (i) undertaking change initiatives despite reactions in the form of pressure from external parties; (j) vigorously questioning the status quo; (k) using other inputs and ideas as triggers for change.

d.Demonstrates personal character, with dimensions:

- Dimension: Living the values by practicing what is being expressed, with indicators of (a) living the values of the work unit; (b) conducting self-reflection to test his comfort; (c) leading by example.

- Dimension: Possessing and creating a positive self-image, with indicators: (a) having confidence as well as humility in oneself; (b) exhibiting an extraordinary degree of perception and insight into the realities of the world and groups or unit members; (c) demonstrating an extraordinary level of motivation to enable group members to overcome learning difficulties and create changes

- Dimension: Possessing cognitive abilities and personal attractiveness, with indicators of (a) having open-mindedness and partnership relationships; (b) receiving information from outside the existing frame of mind; (c) imagining something new, with the possibility of leaving the standard print; (d) looking for opportunities to learn; (e) acting with integrity; (f) seeking for broad business knowledge; (g) training one's insight by seeing things from various perspectives; (h) learning from mistakes; (i) being open to criticism; (j) possessing the willingness to learn science on one's own, thinking through problems in new ways, and trying new things; (k) finding one's challenges to move forward; (l) dealing effectively with complex, ambiguous, and contradictory situations; (m) looking for consideration of alternatives that may be contradictory.

Further, [26] summarize the dimensions of the survey results on Leadership Effectiveness as follows:

- Dimension: Vision, with indicators of (a) creating and communicating a clear, simple, customer-focused vision as the direction of the organization; (b) thinking ahead, imagining a challenge, spreading ideas far ahead; (c) inspiring and energizing other people/parties to hold a firm commitment to the vision, grasping a hint of thoughts, and guiding by example; (d) updating the vision to better support the acceleration of changes that will have an impact on business performance if the changes are of necessities.

- Dimension: Customer/focus on quality, with indicators of (a) listening to customers and setting them as a top priority to generate customer satisfaction, including internal customers; (b) inspiring and showing enthusiasm to perform the best in all sectors; (c) striving to optimally commit to meet quality standards for goods and services produced; (d) serving customers with a mindset and creativity as a good server.

- Dimension: Integrity, with indicators of (a) maintaining a strong commitment to honesty and truth in every behavior; (b) realizing a commitment to take responsibility for one's own mistakes; (c) implementing full compliance company policy to realize its commitment to compliance with ethical behavior; (d) taking action and behaving consistently the rules, gaining trust from other people.

- Dimension: Accountability/commitment, with indicators of (a) aggressively setting and fulfilling commitments to achieve business goals; (b) showing enthusiasm and confidence to stand firm with his beliefs, ideas, and co-workers; (c) being fair and compassionate but is willing to make tough decisions; (d) showing firmness without compromise on one's responsibilities to prevent environmental damage.

- Dimension: Communication (efforts to influence), with indicators of (a) communicating openly, honestly, clearly, completely, and inconsistently inviting responses that allow different opinions; (b) listening effectively and looking for new ideas; (c) using facts and sound reasoning to influence and persuade; (d) breaking down barriers and building smooth cooperation between teams, functions, and strata/levels.

- Dimension: A shared sense of ownership (without boundaries), with indicators of (a) being confident to share information without traditional boundaries and open to new ideas; (b) encouraging/promoting a shared sense of ownership of the team's vision and goals/goals; (c) trusting others, being eager to take risks, and valuing freedom of behavior; (d) diligently practicing listening to others, being open to ideas originating from any places.

- Dimension: Team building and empowerment, with indicators of (a) selecting talents of members, providing coaching and input or feedback to develop the potential of team members as optimally as possible; (b) delegating the necessary authority to all task forces, empowering the team to carry out their duties effectively and efficiently, especially for core personnel; (c) recognizing and rewarding achievements, creating a positive, conducive and comfortable work environment; (d) fully utilizing the differences of team members (culture, ethnicity, and gender) to achieve business success.

- Dimension: Knowledge, expertise, and intellectuality, with indicators of (a) possessing the willingness to share functional, structural, and technical knowledge and skills; (b) demonstrating one's broad business knowledge/understanding, having cross-functional and cross-cultural perspectives; (c) being able to make decisions with limited data by fully applying one's intellectual abilities; (d) being able to quickly sort out which information is important and which is not important, understanding the essential matters from complex problems to be able to initiate action.

- Dimension: Initiative and fast response, with indicators of (a) creating real and positive change, viewing change as an opportunity; (b) anticipating problems and finding a better way to take action more effectively; (c) rejecting/avoiding/eliminating "bureaucracy" and striving for brevity, simplicity, and clarity; (d) understanding and utilizing speed as a competitive advantage.

- Dimension: Global thinking framework, with indicators of (a) showing strong global awareness/sensitivity and being comfortable in building diverse/global teams; (b) developing values and promoting the full use of global diversity and employment; (c) taking into accounts all global consequences of any decision making, proactively seeking global knowledge; (d) treating everyone with dignity, trust, and respect.

Further, [27] suggests that indicators of effective leadership in an era of dynamic and rapid environmental change are: (a) be able to move subordinates; (b) challenge the subordinates to produce outstanding innovations; (c) have charisma and use it effectively and efficiently; (d) encourage and facilitate subordinates to think rationally and be able to overcome all problems that arise in carrying out their duties; (e) create a proper working climate so that the subordinates feel like an integral part of their leader.

The integrity of the leader plays a very important role in preventing corruption in an organization/institution/company. In [28] explained the results of their research in a government institution that the integrity of the leader plays an important role in its function as a perpetrator of corruption prevention because it has the potential to weaken the prevention of corruption if it is not accompanied by strengthening organizational culture, internal control, and competence in preventing corruption. The programs that need attention to support the prevention of corruption are developing and strengthening leadership in an integrated manner regarding organizational culture, internal control, competence, and leadership as an instrument for preventing corruption. All these aspects in an integrated manner have a significant influence on preventing corruption. Without an increase in organizational culture, internal control, competence, and integrated leadership, corruption prevention tends to be ineffective.

5. Leadership that has high emotional intelligence

According to Goleman in [29] suggests that emotional intelligence is a person's ability to motivate oneself to:

- Able to deal with the pressure that can lead to frustration;
- Able to control the will from within his heart not to exaggerate his pleasures;
- Able to control his mood and keep it so that the stress that weighs on him does not interfere with the ability to think to produce the best solution;
- Respect and care for others;
- Always draw closer to God Almighty.

The research results of [30] show that EQ is the most decisive predictor of a leader's successful performance in the workplace. Several other studies have shown that there is a positive relationship between leaders' EQ levels and employee satisfaction, retention, performance, and income. In a later article in the Harvard Business Review, Goleman wrote that it is very important for leaders to have a high EQ to be successful; but that doesn't mean IQ and technical skills are irrelevant, they are both entry-level requirements for executive positions. Hard skills tend to correlate with IQ, while soft skills have an association with Emotional Intelligence [31]. It is argued that hard skill approaches are less significant to success attainment in workplaces. Currently, some companies are in high demand for prospective employees who are competent in soft skills, although they have low hard skills; however, companies expect that the candidates' hard skills can be improved through training. Hard skill improvement is not that complex compared to shaping a person's character to meet the needs of a company or organization. Although hard skills are one of the important keys in workplaces, soft skills significantly determine the success of employees.

In general, Emotional Intelligence is a skill of a person to understand his or her emotion and other people's emotion, resulting in adaptability. This notion correlates with soft skill concepts, where it is regarded as a characteristic of an individual that allows him or her to interact, socialize, and collaborate with others. The skills are essential for a leader to lead his or her subordinates. For instance, teachers are a leader in their small community at a school. Having high Emotional Intelligence will help teachers direct their students, especially in the current situation where all learning activities are online-based and the absence of emotional bonds between teachers and students is inevitable. Teachers' presence, especially in elementary schools, is of paramount importance, since no technology or educational platform can replace teachers. Online learning oftentimes hinders the teachers from monitoring their students' progress. This condition further emphasizes the significance of forming emotional bonds between teachers and students. This is crucial, specifically for elementary school teachers and pre-school teachers. Similarly, having high Emotional Intelligence contribute to the way a leader in a workplace-copes with their subordinates' problems, ranging from the problems to comprehend vision, mission, and strategies of a company, limitations of systems and procedures, limited work hours, facilities, and working tools, and conflicts among workers. Leaders with high Emotional Intelligence can help their subordinates in providing coaching and counseling sessions to motivate their fellow workers and encourage them to formulate solutions. In [32] mentions several abilities that a leader should possess before providing training to his or her subordinates:

- Abilities to listen and comprehend the opinion of subordinates
- Abilities to monitor and identify potentials of subordinates

- Abilities to provide impactful feedbacks
- Verbal and written communication

In [27] proposes several aspects of Emotional Intelligence in a leader.

- Demonstrating empathy
- Considerate (to the surrounding and its dynamics)
- Able to distinguish common interests and self-interests
- Able to encourage and challenge their subordinates to come up with innovation and solutions to multidimensional crises

In [33] mention Leaders should have the high Emotional Intelligence to understand the characteristics of their subordinates, thus allowing them to identify and balance the needs of themselves and their subordinates in terms of cognition, action, and decision. Emotion is a short, strong reaction encompassing joy, excitement, surprise, anger, sadness, despair, disappointment in responding to an event or someone. A person's feeling affects the performance of an individual or a group. On that ground, a competent leader should be able to manage the emotion of all team members. Leaders can help promote a positive atmosphere to the team by

- showing enthusiasm
- inspiring subordinates through motivational speeches, and
- expressing optimism and confidence amid problems

Emotional Intelligence enhancement for subordinates needs to be performed through emotional contagion. This process occurs when the leader transfers and influences all subordinates or when a subordinate motivates other fellows. In some cases, expressing negative emotions, such as expressing anger and disappointment, can help leaders cope with irresponsible employees by criticizing inappropriate behavior. Nevertheless, the leaders should apply the approach with precaution.

In [33] describe the term "Emotional Intelligence" is the ability of oneself to understand and express his or her emotion, allowing the individual to take advantage and manage his or her emotion and other people's emotion. Emotional Intelligence can affect the change in an organization. Further, Emotional Intelligence controls the emotional reaction of employees towards job insecurity and the way the employees cope with stressful situations. Emotional Intelligence involves the process of emotional regulation to control anxiety and other negative emotional reactions to result in positive emotions. Negative emotions are detrimental to the performance of employees. On that ground, emotion regulation and control are required to manage positive emotions at workplaces.

Almost all people have different skills in comprehending other people's emotions by their facial expressions, although seven types of universal emotion can be identified from seeing other people's faces regardless of race, culture, ethnicities, ages, sexes, and religions. Those emotions may cover joy, sadness, fear, surprise, anger, humiliation, and disgust. Understanding other people's emotions are central to the communication process, establishing and building relationships, negotiating, collaborating, and many other managerial tasks. Effective communicators need to recognize emotions by seeing facial expressions. Reports have revealed that Emotional Intelligence, including identifying emotions from facial expressions, can be trained. For successful managers, Emotional Intelligence skills required for managing their subordinates involve:

- Understand what people think and feel
- Able to persuade and motivate team members
- Problem-solving skills
- Cooperative

In [33] argue that leaders need to take into account their subordinates' feelings and respect their opinions; these are among the aspects of Emotional Intelligence. Leader-subordinate relationships are seen from mutual trust and respect and two-way communication. When implementing the approach of initiating structure behavior, leaders are urged to explain the responsibilities of the subordinates and everything that the leaders expect from them. Leaders are also demanded to develop communication channels and determining which methods are applicable to succeed in workplaces. Three adaptive abilities are integral to Emotional Intelligence [34, 35].

a. Ability to evaluate and express emotions of oneself and others (verbal and non-verbal);

b. Ability to control the emotions of oneself and others;

c. Ability to utilize emotion in solving problems and in decision-making processes (e.g., flexible planning, creative thinking, giving attention, and non-directive motivation).

6. Summary

In the coming days, leadership seems to move toward a teaching organization in which it functions to foresee changes and diverse knowledge, skills, and abilities of human resources and enhance an institution's performance. The momentum of the institution determines the success of an institution in the competitive, globalized era to change or adapt to its business or industrial environment. A leader is demanded to be responsible for directing every attempt to cope with issues and ensure the vision's clarity. Further, a leader is required to conceptualize an organizational climate that promotes the employees' independence and, at the same time, the employees aware of their responsibility. Involvement in strategic planning processes will cultivate the sense of belonging of employees. To further optimize the motivational process, one should consider the implementation of innovative leadership. This type of leadership effectively encourages employees, specifically in turbulent conditions; it focuses on products, processes, organization, communication, and collaboration. Provided in **Figure 1** are the approaches to strengthen innovative leadership for survival solutions in turbulent situations. The contribution of the above discussion is expected to provide a reference for designing curriculum and training of leadership and guideline for similar studies.

6.1 Innovation

Charisma is essential for a leader to direct his or her subordinates in coping with turbulent situations. Further, charismatic leaders can facilitate their team members to reason in formulating solutions. Below are the tasks of leaders in dealing with problematic atmospheres.

- Observing and monitoring threats and seizing opportunities to come up with new products, processes, organizations, communication systems, and collaboration to maintain and develop the current market, as well as open new market.
- Establishing communication and collaboration to market new products and services to the internal parties to grow markets and get support (in the form of material supplies and new technologies) to the external parties. Opening new markets, developing the current market, and finding the right investors to create conducive atmospheres for the business.
- Developing organizations through producing creative human resources with their sustainable innovation and new cultures to advance the competitiveness of the business.
- Inspiring and motivating involved parties to keep innovating in every aspect, ranging from products, processes, organizations, communication, and collaboration to support business strategy implementations.
- Determining the direction of all activities to find, produce, introduce, and implement innovations.
- Following up on findings of potential innovations by elaborating development ideas and finding solutions to create new products that meet market demands.
- Finding potential technologies to actualize innovation in products, processes, and organizations that fit market demands.
- Continuously develop innovative ideas that support the success of business strategy implementations, including cost leadership, differentiation, and focus on creating competitive advantage.
- Continuously inclined to take risks and motivated to find innovative solutions in implementing business strategies to attain the business's goals.
- Demonstrating openness in creative innovation and respecting freedom of expression.
- Developing a well-structured organization that is following the interests of stakeholders in a balanced way and encouraging a culture of innovation.
- Promoting harmonious interaction between leaders and subordinates

6.2 Integrity

Leaders with integrity can deal with problems, build trust, and integrate all interests of stakeholders by upholding morals and ethics. Provided below are the aspects of integrity that a leader should possess.

- Having credibility, i.e., strong analytical skills to determine right and wrong, being steadfast, keeping information confidential, encouraging ethical behavior when discussing business and work issues, and committing to follow up on what has been agreed upon.
- Being reliable, i.e., able to provide solutions and committed to pursuing the interests of team members and organizations.
- Demonstrating honesty to prevent ambiguity and doubt and performing tasks according to the organizational values.
- Being responsible for everything the leader has made, demonstrating sportsmanlike conduct, and focusing on everything that can be done for improvement.
- Being objective and rational, prevent inappropriate political tensions and power abuses.
- Acting quickly to cope with unprofessional or unethical issues, prioritizing the interests of the organization in every decision-making even though the leaders have to make unpopular decisions.
- Cultivating professionalism by analyzing and accomplishing tasks as a whole and examining the possible profit and loss in every problem.
- Understanding the intention of stakeholders and adjusting their duties and needs, developing the organization according to the required competencies, constantly improving knowledge, experience, and skills for better task execution.
- Embracing the future through careful observation of the dynamics of the business environment, business operations, technology, views of the future, concept flexibility, strategic alignment, and strategic thinking to achieve strategic goals.
- Preventing corruption through an integrated leadership capacity enhancement that covers the aspect of organizational culture, internal control, competence, and leadership as an instrument for preventing corruption.

6.3 Emotional intelligence

Emotional Intelligence is central to coping with turbulent situations. The following are the significance of Emotional Intelligence in workplaces.

- Emotional Intelligence enables a person to deal with pressure, manage emotion, and maintain the ability to produce the best solution, thus allowing the individual to be innovative.
- Emotional Intelligence enables a person to appreciate and pay attention to others and to grow closer to God in keeping the best performance and spreading positivity for all.
- Emotional Intelligence enables a person to interact, socialize, collaborate, and contribute to others.
- Emotional Intelligence cultivates the ability to formulate solutions by providing coaching and counseling.

- Emotional Intelligence motivates a person to devote to task completion, listen to other people's opinions, and observe the behavior and potential of others, ensuring the best work outputs.

- Emotional Intelligence instills empathy for others, thus enabling an individual to be aware of the surroundings and to collaborate with others in overcoming crises.

- Emotional Intelligence helps leaders to motivate and instill self-confidence in their subordinates.

- Emotional Intelligence helps leaders to have better management of emotions of themselves and others through emotional contagion.

- Emotional Intelligence helps leaders to persuade and motivate others to formulate solutions and form collaboration.

- Emotional Intelligence enables leaders to develop communication channels and determining which methods are applicable to succeed in workplaces.

6.4 Policies and measurements in facing turbulent environment

- Demonstrating integrity to build trust in the internal and external environment.

- Conducting intensive communication and negotiation to promote the participation of internal and external parties.

- Protecting and empowering the internal resources of the business sector to be able to contribute optimally.

- Collaborating with the internal and external environment.

- Strictly implementing the institutional reform program by developing democratization and decentralization.

- Developing and applying the concept of Emotional Intelligence, i.e., patience and persistence in dealing with a turbulent environment.

- Empowering internal resources for the development of strategic productivity.

- Establishing policies that support the business operation the dynamics of the environment to overcome turbulence.

- Developing various approaches in formulating policies for the operation of the business or organization.

- Establishing anti-corruption divisions.

The Diagram of Innovative Leadership Strengthening for Survival Solution in Turbulent Environment (**Figure 1**).

Turbulence Environment. By Soehari (2021).

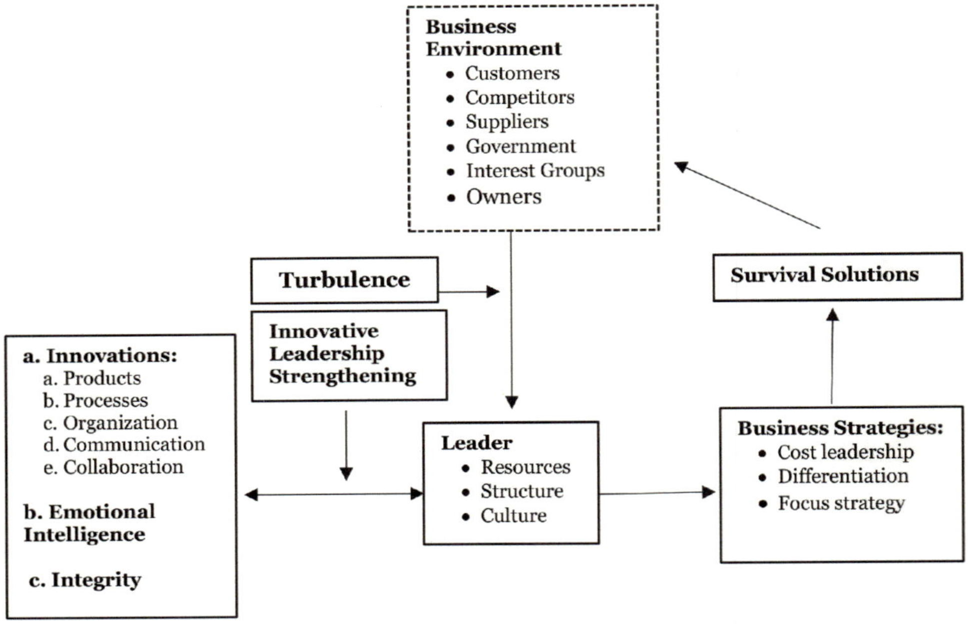

Figure 1.
The Diagram of Innovative Leadership Strengthening for Survival Solution in.

Author details

Iffah Budiningsih[1]* and Tjiptogoro Dinarjo Soehari[2]

1 As-Syafi'iyah Islamic University, Jakarta, Indonesia

2 Mercu Buana University, Jakarta, Indonesia

*Address all correspondence to: iffah_budiningsih@uia.ac.id

References

[1] Guzmána VE, Muschardb B, Mateus Gerolamoa M, Kohlb H, Rozenfelda H. Characteristics and Skills of Leadership in the Context of Industry 4.0. *Procedia Manufacturing*. 2020; 43: 543-550.

[2] Guo, J., Gonzales, R., Dilley, A.E. Creativity and Leadership in Organizations: A Literature Review. *Creativity. Theories – Research – Applications*. 2016; 3 (1): 127-151. DOI: 10.1515/ctra-2016-0010.

[3] Karthikeyan C. A Meta Analytical Study on Leadership Integrity: A leadership Ethics Perspective. *International Journal of Management, IT & Engineering*. 2017; 7 (4): 240-263.

[4] Gea A. Personal Integrity and leadership. *Humaniora*. 2016; Vol. 7 No. 3, pp: 359-369

[5] Gentry WA, Cullen KL, and Altma DG. The Irony of Integrity: A Study of the Character Strengths of Leaders, *Center for Creative Leadership*. 2016.

[6] Bashir NA. Leadership Connection to Emotional Intelligence and Stress at Workplace. *Journal of Management Research*. 2017; 9 (1): 43-51. http://dx.doi.org/10.5296/jmr.v9i1.9338.

[7] Soehari TD, Budiningsih I. Competitive Advantage Leadership in the Ultra-Modern Era. In: M. Franco (Ed), Digital Leadership: A New Leadership Style for the 21st Century (pp. 37-55). London: Intechopen; 2020. p. 37-55. DOI: 10.5772/intechopen.77615.

[8] Holbeche L. Aligning Human Resources and Business Strategy. USA: Elsevier Butterworth Heinemann. 2004. 461.

[9] Wheelen TL, Hunger JD. Strategic Management and Business Policy. Tenth Edition. Pearson International Edition. New Jersey: Pearson Education, Inc. 2006. 405 p.

[10] Schein. HE. Organizational Culture and Leadership. Fourth Edition. San Francisco: Jossey-Bass; 2010. 436 p.

[11] Johannessen JA and Skaalsvik H. Innovative leadership in organizations: the road to innovation performance. *Problems and Perspectives in Management*. 2014; 12 (2): 139-152.

[12] Budiningsih I, Sukamto H, Mujiani S. Dominant Determinant Characteristics of Innovative Behavior of New Entrepreneur Candidates. Management Sciences Letters (MSL). 2021; 11(Issue 5): 1813 -1820. DOI: 10.5267/j.msl.2021.1.022.

[13] Fauzia S, Budiningsih I, Djaelani A, Ahmad M. Dominant Factors Affecting the Behavior of Innovative Employees. Polish Journal of Management Studies/ (PJMS). 2017; 15 (1):32-40. DOI: 10.17512/pjms.2017.16.1.03

[14] Budiningsih I, Soehari TD, Leonard J. Dominant Factors Influence the Behavior to Produce Innovative Products. David Publishing. Chine-USA Business Review. 2018; 17(9): 453-461. DOI:10.17265/1537-1514/2018.09.002.

[15] Prihantoro AN, Soehari TD. The Effect of Creativity, Leadership and Organizational Culture on Organizational Innovation the Education and Training Center of the Ministry of Communication and Informatics. International Journal of Innovative Science and Research Technology. 2020; 5(5): 1742-1753. https://ijisrt.com/assets/upload/files/IJISRT20MAY958.pdf.

[16] Soehari TD, Budiningsih I, Sari A. Strengthening of Micro Business Innovation. Journal of Business and

Economics Review. 2019; 4(3): 131-138). DOI: 10.35609/jber. 2019.4.3(2)

[17] Budiningsih I, Soehari TD, Hidayati RN. Technology Training and Creativity for Strengthening Employees Innovative Behaviors. Journal of Business and Social Science Review. 2019; 8(3): 162-169. DOI: 10.35609/jber.2019. 4.3920.

[18] Soehari TD, Budiningsih I, Mirza. Managerial Leadership for Competitive Advantage University. International Journal of Applied Business and Economic Research. 2017; 15(24): 1-11.

[19] Kotter PJ, Cohen SD. The Heart of Change. Deloitte: Consulting LLC; 2008. 250 p.

[20] United Nation. UN Competency Development-Practical Guide. New York: United Nations Office of Human Resources Management. 2010. 186 p.

[21] Sujiyanto S. Pengaruh Integritas dan Loyalitas Pegawai terhadap Kebijakan Pimpinan dan Dampaknya terhadap Kinerja di lingkungan Dinas Komunikasi dan Informatika Kota Batu (The Influence of Integrity and Employee Loyalty on Leadership Policy and Its Impact on Performance in the Communication and Informatics Office of Batu City). Jurnal Ilmu Manajemen (JIMMU). 2017; 2 (2): 65-84. http://riset.unisma.ac.id/index.php/jimmu/article/view/991/1029.

[22] Rejeki DPS, Heridiansyah J. Memahami Sebuah Konsep Integritas (Understanding a Concept of Integrity). Jurnal STIE Semarang. 2013; 5 (3): 1-14.

[23] Huges RL, Ginnett RC, Curphy GJ. Leadership: Enhancing the Lessons of Experience. New York: McGraw-Hill. 2012.624 p.

[24] Robinson DG, Robinson JC. Strategic Business Partner. San Fransisco: Berrett-Koehler Publishers, Inc. 2005. 624 p. 238 p.

[25] Abdullah B. dkk. Membangun Karakter Sebuah Bank Sentral. Jakara: Bank Indonesia. 2005. 293 p.

[26] Ulrich D, Zenger, Smallwood N. Result Based Leadership. Boston: Harvard Business School Press. 1999. 234 p.

[27] Soekarnoputri SMPD. The Leadership of President Megawati in the Era of Multidimensional Crisis, 2001-2004. Jurnal Pertahanan dan Bela Negara. 2021; 11(4): 49-66. http://jurnal.idu.ac.id/index.php/JPBH/article/view/1211/476

[28] Soehari TD, Budiningsih. Model of Bureaucratic Corruption Prevention. International Journal of Asian Social Science. 2020; 10(10): 638-646. DOI: 10.18488/journal.1.2020.1010.638.646.

[29] Bahyudi, Soehari TD. The Impact of Leadership and Culture of Organization to Emotional Intelligence by Training of PT XYZ. Akademika. 2020; 9(1): 17-32. DOI: 10.34005/akademika. v9i01.751

[30] Vann, Valerie, Sparks, Betsy, Baker, Cassandra. A Study of Emotional Intelligence and Self-Leadership. *SAM Advanced Management Journal*. 2018; 82(3):18-28.

[31] Budiningsih I, Soehari TD, Marlison. Hard Skill Versus Soft Skill dalam Pencapaian Kinerja karyawan Proyek Infrastruktur MASS Rapid Transit (MRT) Jakarta (Hard Skill Versus Soft Skill in Achieving Employee Performance of MASS Rapid Transit Jakarta Infrastructure Project). Akademika. 2020; 9 (2):29-42. DOI: 10.34005/akademika. v9i02.895.

[32] Walton J. Strategic Human Resources Development. England: Pearson Education Limited. 1999. 614 p.

[33] Yulk G. Leadership in Organizations. Eighth Edition. England: Pearson Education Limited. 2013. 524 p.

[34] Griffin RW, Phillips JM, Gully SM. Organizational Behavior Managing People and Organization. Twelfth Edition.Boston: Cengage Learning. 2017. 608 p.

[35] Budiningsih I, Soehari T D, Casriyanti. The Strengthening of Teachers' Eq in Facing Various Changes in the Educational Environment. Global Journal of Human- Social Science: Linguistic & Education. 2021; 21 (Issue 5): 33-39. DOI: https://doi.org/10.34257/GJHSSGVOL21IS5PG33

Chapter 5

Optimizing Innovative Leadership and Followership

Neil E. Grunberg, Erin S. Barry, Michael Morrow-Fox and Maureen Metcalf

Abstract

Leadership and followership development are increasingly recognized as important in all fields of the workforce. The Innovative Leadership Model helps leaders increase self-understanding and optimize the performance of organizations by focusing on Leader Type, Developmental Perspective, Resilience, Situational Analysis, and Leadership Behaviors and Mindsets. The Leader-Follower Framework identifies key elements – Character, Competence, Communication, Context – to guide the development of individual leaders and followers across four psychosocial levels – Personal, Interpersonal, Team, Organizational. Each of these approaches has value and has been applied in various settings and contexts. The present chapter offers a new insight relevant to leadership by combining these two perspectives and their component elements. Understanding and developing each of these elements will optimize effective leadership and followership in a wide range of situations and settings.

Keywords: innovative leadership, leader type, developmental perspective, resilience, situational analysis, leadership behaviors and mindsets, leader-follower framework, character, competence, communication, context, personal, interpersonal, team, organizational

1. Introduction

Development of individuals as leaders is important in all fields of the workforce. Within teams, in addition to the diversity of the individual team members (including leaders and followers), uniqueness of team members, individual goals, communication styles, differing leadership and followership styles, and so on introduce challenges to true teamwork and must all be considered to optimize goal achievement of individuals, teams, and organizations [1–3].

Leadership influences individuals, teams, and groups by enhancing behaviors (actions), cognitions (perceptions, thoughts, beliefs), and motivations (reasons behaviors and cognitions) to achieve common goals. Leaders are aspirational, inspirational, provide resources, and remove barriers to optimize the success of followers, organizations, and the people served by organizations. Leaders must continuously attend to and align all elements of the systems within which they operate to adapt and respond to changes from within and outside the system. Followership refers to the actions of individuals who are not in leadership roles. Followers are members of a team or group who contribute (or not) to the team; align (or not) with the vision of the leader, and adapt (or not) to the situations and to other members of the team. Effective followers are essential to achieve goals and can influence all members of the team, including their leaders [4–9].

Day [10] distinguishes between leaders and leadership, such that "leader" refers to human capital and intrapersonal knowledge, skills, abilities, attitudes, and attributes, and "leadership" refers to social capital, interpersonal relationships, and organization culture. The same distinction can be made for followers and followership.

Innovative leaders engage their intentions and actions with those of their followers within the organization's culture and systems to reach the organization's objectives and goals and those of the people it serves. Innovative leaders consider and serve the interests of the organization and its members. Leaders influence followers, teams, and the whole organization. Followers can influence leaders, other followers, teams, and the entire organization. Innovative leaders and followers adapt and develop themselves and their organizations to optimize effectiveness within changing environments or context (physical, psychological, social) [11, 12].

There are many different models and approaches for leader and leadership development. Some focus on the development of leaders [9, 10, 13–19] and followers [20–28] *per se*, whereas others focus on leadership and followership in practice or on the organizational or systems levels [29–32]. There is value to both levels of development to achieve optimal performance of individuals within organizations and systems.

Recently, we have merged two models to address all of these needs for health care leadership [12]. The Innovative Leadership Model helps leaders increase self-understanding and optimize the performance of organizations by focusing on Leader Type, Development Perspective, Resilience, Situational Analysis, and Leadership Behaviors and Mindsets. The Innovative Leadership Model focuses on development perspective and growth of individuals to serve organizations and systems. The Leader-Follower Framework identifies key elements – Character, Competence, Communication, Context – to guide the development of individual leaders and followers across four psychosocial levels – Personal, Interpersonal, Team, Organizational [5, 7]. The Leader-Follower Framework focuses on the elements relevant to meaningfully development and performance of individual leaders and followers. The inclusion of key aspects of these two models may offer a valuable new insight into optimizing. Each of these approaches has value and has been applied in various settings and contexts. The present chapter offers new insights into how integrating these approaches can optimize innovative leadership and followership in a wide range of situations and settings.

2. Innovative leadership and followership

Leadership impacts people strategically and tactically, effecting change in intentions, actions, cultures, and systems to move organizations forward in ways that improve the lives of the people it serves while considering the interests of the organization's members and stakeholders. Innovation refers to novel ideas, processes, and advancements that contribute to and shape organizations and people. Meaningful leadership and innovation are inextricably connected. Merging leadership with innovation encourages and, perhaps, demands transformational personal and organizational growth [33, 34]. **Table 1** presents contrasts between traditional leadership and innovative leadership.

Innovative leadership and followership mean that leaders and followers influence and contribute by engaging personal intention/character and action/competence/communication with the organization's culture, systems, and context. Innovative leadership and followership can improve organizations and the lives of the people it serves by considering the interests, needs, and goals of the organizational members and stakeholders. Innovative leaders consistently deliver results using [35–37]:

Traditional Leadership	Innovative Leadership
The leader is guided primarily by the desire for personal success and peripherally by the organizational success	The leader is humbly guided by a more altruistic vision of success based on both performance and the value of the organization's positive impact
The leader decides in a "command and control" style; the leader has all the answers	The leader leverages the team for answers as part of the decision-making process
The leader picks a direction in "black/white" manner; tends to stay the course dogmatically	The leader perceives and behaves like a scientist: continually experimenting, measuring, and testing for improvement and exploring new models and approaches
The leader focuses on being technically correct and in charge	The leader is continually learning and developing self and others
The leader manages people to perform by being autocratic and controlling	The leader motivates people to perform through strategic focus, mentoring and coaching, emotional and social intelligence
The leader tends to the numbers and primarily utilizes quantitative measures that drive those numbers	The leader pays attention to performance, customer satisfaction, employee engagement, community impact, and cultural cohesion

Table 1.
Traditional vs. innovative leadership [11, 12].

- Strategic approaches that inspire individual intentions and goals and organizational vision and culture;
- Tactical approaches that influence individuals' actions and organizations' systems and processes;
- Holistic approaches that align individual intentions and actions with organizational cultures and systems.

Innovative followers embrace, embody, and contribute to all three of these approaches.

2.1 The value of innovative leadership and followership

Innovating/elevating leadership and followership means to successfully adapt in ways that allow optimal performance, even within the changes and complexity of an organization or system. Conceptually, individuals integrate ideas and perspectives from many leadership and followership principles and concepts, and from developmental, communications, and systems theories [38, 39]. Innovative leaders and followers recognize and critically examine themselves and their organizations' cultures and systems during various circumstances. It is valuable for individuals to focus on the needs and mission of the organization, system, and cultures to which they contribute. In addition, individuals should recognize how they contribute to something larger than themselves.

2.2 Defining what innovative leaders and followers do

Innovative leaders utilize their advanced developmental capability to facilitate transformational ideas and approaches that enable innovation [33, 34, 36]. They are aware of and focus on others and the organizations/systems in which they operate. Behaviors of developmentally mature innovate leaders and followers who grow developmentally and in organizational effectiveness include (**Table 2**):

Innovative Leaders	Innovative Followers
Articulate clear vision	Embrace and contribute to vision
Connect vision with attainable actions	Connect vision with attainable actions
Develop themselves and followers	Develop themselves and other teammates
Are resilient and navigate complexity, uncertainty, and stress	Are resilient and navigate complexity, uncertainty, and stress
Communicate effectively, sending and receiving information, verbally and nonverbally	Communicate effectively sending and receiving, verbally and nonverbally
Build effective teams by helping followers participate and grow	Contribute to their teams
Communicate roles for all team members clearly	Understand their roles and the roles of others
Create a culture of fairness, respect and recognition	Ability to impact individuals, teams, and systems to create a fair and engaging organization
Develop a culture of safety	Embody a culture of safety
Cultivate alliances and partnerships	Cultivate alliances and partnerships
Anticipate and effectively respond to challenges and opportunities	Anticipate and effectively respond to challenges and opportunities
Develop robust and resilient solutions	Apply robust and resilient solutions
Measure, learn, and adapt	Learn and adapt
Grow personally and developmentally to evolve perceptions and meaning-making capabilities	Grow personally and developmentally to evolve perceptions and meaning-making capabilities

Table 2.
Behaviors of innovative leaders and followers.

3. Merging innovative leadership and the leader-follower framework: New insights

To optimize innovative leadership and followership, we offer the merging of two conceptual models. The "Innovative Leadership Model" [11, 12] and the "Leader-Follower Framework" [5–7] complement each other and overlap with a differing depth of emphasis on essential leadership and followership elements and processes. Together they provide new insights into a broadly inclusive structure to develop optimal leadership and followership. These two approaches recently have been applied together to optimize the development of innovative leaders in health care [12, 40]. Yet, they also can be applied more broadly to enhance the innovative leader and follower development in all settings.

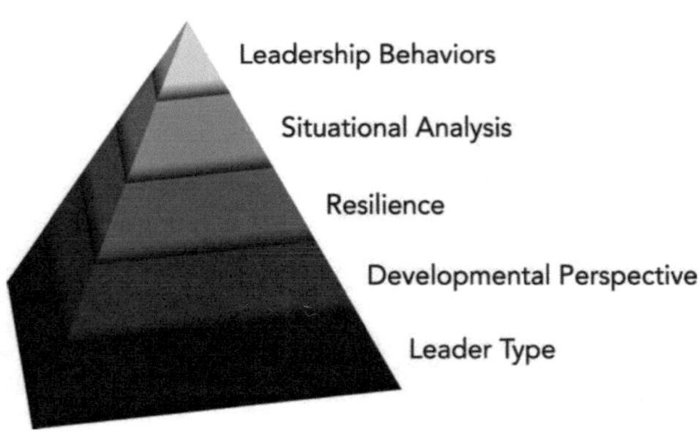

Figure 1.
Overview of the innovative leadership model.

The Innovative Leadership Model is a five-element roadmap to becoming an innovative leader [11, 12]. The elements of the Innovative Leadership Model are (**Figure 1**):

- Leader Type
- Developmental Perspective
- Resilience
- Situational Analysis
- Leadership Behaviors and Mindsets

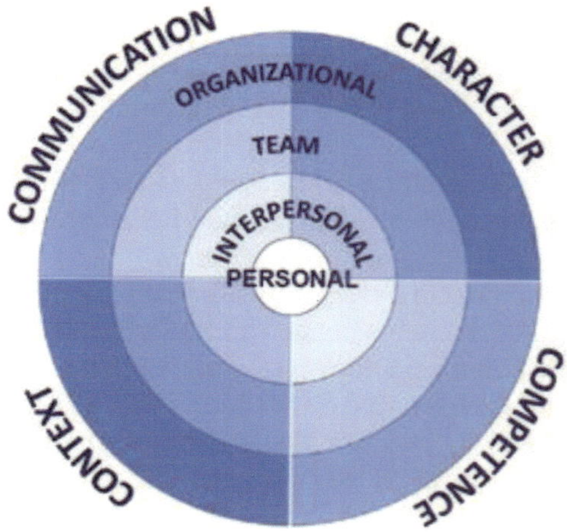

Figure 2.
The leader-follower framework.

The Leader-Follower Framework [5, 7] includes four "C" elements:

- Character
- Competence
- Context
- Communication

that apply across four psychosocial levels:

- Personal
- Interpersonal
- Team
- Organizational

The Innovative Leadership Model and Leader-Follower Framework are valuable to develop both as leaders and as followers. To be an effective leader, you also must be willing and able to develop followers. It is essential for leaders and followers to understand, develop, and know when and how to lead and follow (**Figure 2**).

3.1 Elements of innovative leadership

The Innovative Leadership Model [11, 12] focuses on:

- Developmental maturity – developing the advancing meaning-making capacity to easily and intuitively identify complexity, approach others without ego, embrace both tactical and strategic concerns, and embrace transformation (i.e., capabilities to execute highly effective Competence and Communication at the Interpersonal, Team, and Organizational psychosocial levels)

- Self-understanding – the inner process including Character and outer behaviors including Competence and Communication (i.e., three of the C's of the Leader-Follower Framework at the Personal psychosocial level)

- Understanding organizational culture and systems (i.e., Context within the Leader-Follower Framework at the Organizational psychosocial level)

The Innovative Leadership model addresses: Leader Type, Developmental Perspective, Resilience, Situational Analysis, and Leadership Behaviors and Mindsets.

Leader Type refers to the core predispositions, traits, and attitudes of each person. These attributes influence who we are as a leader, our responses to stress, and how other people (including followers) experience our leadership. There are several valuable tools to help describe our Leader Type: Enneagram [41]; Myers Briggs Type Indicator (MBTI) [42, 43]; Revised NEO Personality Inventory (NEO-PI-R) [44]; True Colors [45]; Big Five Personality Test [46]. The DISC Profile [47] and StrengthFinder 2.0 [48] provide additional, useful information relevant to Leader Type.

Self-awareness is the practice of engaging in self-reflection and achieving clarity of insight. Internal self-awareness refers to our own understanding of ourselves, whereas external self-awareness refers to understanding how others perceive and understand us. Self-understanding, understanding how others perceive us, and the extent to which perceptions about ourselves are accurate and compatible with others' perceptions play a pivotal role in our effectiveness and leader-follower relationships. Self-aware individuals possess high levels of emotional intelligence; self-regulate behaviors, cognitions, and emotions more effectively depending on the situation; and continually evaluate their impact on others [49–53]. These attributes allow self-aware individuals to become more versatile, adaptive, and may perform better. The ability to use deep self-reflection relies on developing self-understanding and self-awareness, features of emotional intelligence. Self-understanding and self-awareness allow us to expand our perspective and to understand others better. A clearer understanding of ourselves and others can help build interpersonal, team, and organizational effectiveness. Feedback from trusted colleagues, family members, and friends in psychologically safe contexts is extremely valuable to develop self-awareness. Leader Type is an aspect of Character.

Developmental Perspective or Developmental "Maturity" refers to stages of personal development that include perspectives, experiences, and capabilities to make the meaning necessary to execute change initiatives [35, 36], solutions to complex problems [54, 55], and organizational transformations [38, 56]. Developmental Perspectives affect how we view our roles, how we interact with other people, and how we solve problems. In other words, this perspective can be described as "meaning-making," or how we make sense of experiences using the Leadership Maturity Framework (LMF). The LMF considers cognitive complexity, emotional competence, and behavior and holds that we can progress through maturity levels as we learn and evolve. Moreover, more mature or evolved individuals are more effective at leading complex organizations in times of change. In contrast, individuals at an earlier level of developmental maturity rely on rules to make decisions and determine appropriate courses of action, whereas individuals at later stages use their values to guide decision-making and to determine what actions to take.

Developmental growth occurs as other capabilities expand in our lives. By understanding and building upon our Leader Type and Character, we can continue to grow, increasing access to and capacity for additional skills and capabilities. That is, we can develop our capacity to build beyond the basic skills we have now by moving through more progressive stages. The successful individual has a broad repertoire of mindsets and behaviors and can select the most appropriate ones depending on the context.

Resilience reveals how much disturbance we can withstand before breaking [57] and also refers to the ability to adapt to change while continuing to be both fluid in approach and driven toward attaining strategic goals [58]. Addressing and strengthening resilience is critical to manage stress and increase capacity to function in stressful environments and situations.

Innovative leaders and followers must adapt to volatile, uncertain, complex, and ambiguous (VUCA) situations and demands while maintaining physical, psychological, and emotional health to have the resilience essential for success. They must build and sustain flexibility, adaptability, and focus; regain balance after disorienting situations; and be able to support and inspire others. Resilience can inspire and positively impact others.

Resilience requires physical and psychological health, a clear sense of life purpose, emotional intelligence, and strong supportive relationships. For most people, enhancing resilience requires personal change. Our view of resilience has four categories: maintaining physical well-being, managing thinking, working from the heart, and harnessing the power of connection. These categories are interlinked and all must be present and in balance to create long-term resilience. Maintaining resilience is essential to success. Improved resilience is accompanied by clearer thinking and greater positive interactions with others. Investing in resilience supports the entire organization's effectiveness [12]. Resilience is a transcendent leadership Competence.

Situational Analysis involves understanding and adapting to Context; aligning and balancing self, individual action, organizational culture, and organizational systems; and performing to achieve the best outcomes [12]. This multi-pronged approach provides a complete and accurate view of events and context to create alignment across the Innovative Leadership Model on an ongoing basis. Understanding an organization's culture and systems is essential to determine how to adapt our behaviors. We must understand the context and adjust to the situation and to the organization's mission and goals.

In addition, innovative leaders and followers communicate with teammates and stakeholders relevant to the mission and goals of an organization. Effective communication requires "making meaning" of what is happening based on context, translated into words that senders and receivers mutually understand. We sense, receive, and convey messages verbally and non-verbally. Situational analysis allows us to make more informed decisions, and also helps to optimize performance within oneself, teams, and the broader organization.

Leadership Behaviors and Mindsets refer to leadership knowledge, skills, and attitudes and the resulting behaviors [12] or Competence and mindset or meaning making. The mindsets inform effective behaviors. These behaviors are essential and measurable because they are the objective actions that leaders and followers take to impact organizational success. Effective behaviors of leaders and followers determine individual and team performance, team cohesiveness, individual and team morale, and organizational success. Conversely, ineffective behaviors of leaders and followers lead to poor performance, poor cohesiveness, poor morale, and organizational dysfunction or failure.

Knowledge of the key concepts described in the Innovative Leadership Model and associated skills and practice result in effective leadership behaviors and mindsets – the objective actions that leaders take to impact individual, team, and organizational success. Knowledge and practice of these same concepts result in effective followership behaviors. These behaviors align with the idea of developmental maturity and specify critical behaviors and mindsets associated with the most effective leaders in complex and dynamic situations. Therefore, it is important to understand the critical leadership and followership behaviors relevant to you and your organization. With this understanding, you can determine where you excel and where you need to refine your skills.

It also is relevant to consider and to develop your mindset to exercise effective leadership and followership behaviors. **Table 3** lists seven mindsets and associated behaviors that effective leaders and followers put into action regularly [12, 59].

3.2 Leader-follower framework

To develop as innovative leaders and followers, it is helpful to reflect upon, consider, and continuously develop Character, Competence, Context, and Communication across the four psychosocial levels – Personal, Interpersonal, Team, and Organizational [5–7].

Character is the "who" of leaders and followers. It includes all aspects of who we are psychologically (self-awareness, honesty, integrity, trustworthiness, reliability, personality, values, biases, leader type, developmental maturity, resilience) and physically (demographics and physical attributes). Self-awareness includes internal self-awareness (i.e., our own awareness of the many aspects of our Character) and external self-awareness (i.e., our awareness of how others including peers, followers, supervisors, stakeholders, friends, strangers, family members, perceive us and all aspects of our Character and the extent to which the perceptions of ourselves and others are consistent or inconsistent). Understanding oneself is essential to innovative and effective leadership.

Competence is the "what" of leadership and followership. It includes what we know and do concerning role-specific knowledge and skills relevant to our specific role or job (e.g., as a parent, administrator, health care professional, attorney, entrepreneur, teacher, carpenter, artist, athlete, etc.). Competence also includes transcendent knowledge and skills relevant to all roles and positions (e.g., critical thinking, problem-solving, motivating others, emotional intelligence, conflict resolution). The leadership and followership behaviors described above are examples of the practice and execution of competence. Leader type, resilience, and developmental maturity all impact ability to exercise the behaviors associated with successful leadership and followership. Competence reflects knowledge, skills, and applications.

Context is the "when" and "where" of leadership and followership. It refers to when and where leadership and followership occurs, physically (i.e., time of day, climate, nutritional state, tiredness), psychologically (i.e., behavioral health, biases), socially (i.e., size of the group, group dynamics), culturally (i.e., cultural values, practices, attitudes, beliefs), and situationally (i.e., what's happening around us as well as stress). Context is the meta-framework that contains the individual and the organization at any point in time. The leader must consider the entire context and apply Situational Analysis to make decisions while being able to align

Examples of Innovative Mindsets and Behaviors	
Professionally humble	*Cares most about team's and organization's success* • Commits to the team and organizational mission • Cares most about the organization's success • Gives credit to others • Puts principles and values ahead of personal gain
Unwavering commitment to the right action	*Is unstoppable and unflappable when on a mission* • Commits fully, drives hard, and focuses. • Stays the course when under pressure • Changes course when a better approach emerges
A 360-degree thinker	*Takes a systems view – understanding context and interconnectedness of systems when making critical decisions* • Understands the relevant systems, constraints, near term, long term, and secondary impacts of strategy and decisions • Balances interests of multiple stakeholders • Commits to continuous learning and building learning systems • Understands cross-organizational impact and interconnections across multiple complex systems • Thinks in terms of systems, constraints, perceptions, and context when making decisions
Intellectually versatile	*Develops interests, expertise, and curiosity beyond the job and organization making them life-long learners.* • Interested and involved with areas beyond comfort zones • Considers ecosystem, including industry-wide activities, political developments, and the international landscape • Uses external interests to make contributions
Highly authentic and reflective	*Focuses on individual behaviors to enhance team and organization successes* • Commits to personal growth and development • Helps others to grow and develop • Open to feedback and non-defensive • Seeks out discussions and feedback • Manages emotions • Maintains perspective under stress • Confronts challenging situations • Continually looks for ways to enable the organization to improve its ability to meet its mission efficiently and effectively
Inspires followership/team work with others	*Connects with people at all levels of the organization* • Diffuses conflict without avoiding the sources of conflict • Creates psychologically safe spaces and puts people at ease • Relates to a broad range of people • Connects projects to individual talents and goals • Provides resources and removes barriers for followers to succeed • Provides feedback to others that supports recipient's' growth and development

Examples of Innovative Mindsets and Behaviors	
Innately collaborative	*Welcomes collaboration in a quest for novel solutions that serve the highest outcome for all involved* • Seeks input and values diverse points of view • Synthesizes multiple perspectives into new solutions • Creates solutions to problems by developing new approaches • Understands that input from multiple stakeholders with diverse perspectives is required to achieve the best results

Table 3.
Examples of innovative Mindsets and Behaviors [12, 59].

all elements of individuals and the organization on an ongoing basis. Followers also should be aware of and work to align elements of individuals and the organization to optimize performance.

Communication is the "how" of leadership and followership. It includes sending and receiving information verbally (oral and written) and non-verbally (body language, facial expressions, paralanguage). Communication is separated from competence because it is such a key component of successful leadership and followership behaviors. It is critical to recognize that the purpose of communication is to achieve understanding. Moreover, the key to effective reception of communications as leaders and as followers is embedded in the word "listen"; that is, rearranging the letters spells "silent" – how we should listen to others to truly hear what is being said.

Leadership and followership operate at four psychosocial Levels:

Personal refers to the individual and focuses on self-awareness (internal and external), knowledge and skills appropriate for one's role, effective communication, and appropriate situational awareness. Unless we understand and work to develop all leadership aspects of ourselves, we will be in no position to be innovative or effective for others. Focusing on personal development is particularly important of early stages of Developmental Maturity.

Interpersonal refers to dyadic relationships, such as leader-follower, supervisor-supervisee, teacher-student, athlete-coach, parent–child, spouse-spouse. Interpersonal focuses on working and communicating effectively and respectfully with other individuals in all situations, understanding the other individual, knowing how one is perceived, and applying appropriate knowledge and skills in relationships with others. It is important to adapt to each individual with whom we interact to optimize innovative leadership and followership.

Team refers to a small group of people with complementary skills who are committed to common goals. Teams build shared values, trust, and cohesiveness, work together, communicate effectively in various situations, understand team dynamics, and respond appropriately. Optimizing team performance and relationships among all members of the team poses a substantial challenge because it requires understanding and interacting with every individual in that group and with all combinations of members of this group.

Organizational refers to large groups, institutions, and systems. It focuses on vision and mission and understanding systems, processes, and various cultures. Innovative and effective leadership at the organizational level requires advanced Development Perspective. In addition, leadership and followership at the organizational level requires consideration of the needs and goals of the large group, system, and culture, rather than on the individual members of the group.

4. Relating the leader-follower framework to the innovative leadership model

Leader Type: It is important to recognize and understand "who" you are, "what" you do, "when and where" you do it, and "how" you do it. "Who" you are, including core values, attitudes, beliefs, and the relevance of your demographics (including age, gender, physical characteristics) that contribute to your experiences and how others respond to you, is **Character** in a broad sense. "What" you do, including role-specific actions and behaviors as well as transcendent behaviors (including decision making, problem-solving, conflict resolution, emotional intelligence) is **Competence**. "When and where" you lead (**Context**) refers to physical, psychological, social, cultural, and situational aspects. "How" you do it focuses on **Communication**, both sending and receiving. Effective leader style (e.g., authentic, democratic, servant, transactional, transformational) depends and should adapt based on all of these "C" elements. Effective follower style (e.g., along dimensions of commitment to the team and mission, alignment with the leader's vision) also depends on adapting all four of the "C" elements.

Developmental Maturity: Developmental maturity level influences the breadth of perspective, mindset, meaning-making capability, and focus both as a leader and follower. In the early development stages, the focus is on our own, or "**Personal**," growth and expertise. Interactions with other individuals (including team members, peers, supervisors, patients, etc.) and how to optimize those dyadic relationships are "**Interpersonal**." As leaders and followers expand and increase their developmental perspectives, they widen their perspectives and interactions and become more effective working with small groups of people who work together for common goals and interact at the "**Team**" level. Broadening developmental maturity to focus on large groups, organizations, systems, and cultures is required at the "**Organizational**" level.

Resilience: The extent to which one can adapt to various physical, psychological, socio-cultural, and economic stressors (**Context**) and maintain focus and performance (i.e., resilience) depends on **Character**, **Competence**, and **Communication**. Resilience also depends on "**Context**" – physical, psychological, and social environments and factors that are inside and outside us, including physical and psychological well-being, the situations we face, and the extent to which we can adapt, continue, and grow.

Situational Analysis: This fourth element applies who we are (**Character**), what we do (**Competence**), and how we do it (**Communication**) in various situations, influenced by organizational culture and systems. i.e., when and where (**Context**).

Leadership Behaviors and Mindsets: The fifth element includes our mindsets and actions – that is, what (**Competence**) and how (**Communication**) – and are related to who (**Character**), what (**Competence**), when and where (**Context**).

5. Putting it all together

- Innovative leadership and followership are optimized when elements of the Innovative Leadership Model and the Leader-Follower Framework are understood and applied.

- Innovative leaders and followers develop internal and external self-awareness of their leader and follower types; stage of developmental maturity; level of resilience; value of situational analysis; leadership and followership behaviors.

- Innovative leader and follower development depends on the four "C" elements of leadership and the four psychosocial levels of interaction.

- Innovative leaders and followers develop mindsets, awareness, and maturity; behave in ways that reflect these ways of thinking; and update organizational cultures, systems, and processes to continue evolving. Innovative leaders and followers are open to novel, new, and creative ways to develop themselves and others.

- Innovative leaders and followers attend to the development or change of themselves, their behaviors, the culture, systems, and processes concurrently and ensure they continually align all elements during ongoing changes.

- Leaders and followers evolve in maturity stages throughout the course of their careers. They learn to behave in ways that optimize effective outcomes, considering themselves, others, and situations. Each stage of developmental maturity advances the individual's capacities to deal with VUCA environments.

6. Conclusions

In the book, *Innovative leadership for health care* [12], we developed a conceptual structure for merging the Innovative Leadership Model and the Leader-Follower Framework to health care. This structure can be applied more broadly to leadership and followership. The section below summarizes the major points of this structure relevant to individuals, teams, and organizations.

6.1 Know thyself

Both the Innovative Leadership Model and the Leader-Follower Framework emphasize the importance of self-awareness. **Leader Type** refers to core predispositions and attitudes. **Character** is more extensive than Leader Type and also includes physical and psychological makeup. Understanding our Leader Type and Character allow us to leverage strengths and help guide our development planning. These concepts also can be used to better understand and develop ourselves and others as followers and to recognize that there are times and situations when we each should lead and when we each should follow.

6.2 Develop your capabilities

Developmental Perspective and Maturity refer to psychological and emotional capabilities to influence less defensively, more strategically, more inclusively, and more sustainably. We each need to continually develop our knowledge and skills – **Competence** includes role-specific knowledge and skills as well as and general knowledge and skills that transcend particular roles. Additionally, **Resilience** is an ongoing practice that facilitates maintaining balance, energy, and perspective when adapting to challenges while learning, growing, and persisting. Combining advanced developmental maturity, a high degree of competence, and strong resilience allows us to influence our team members **(Interpersonal)**, **Teams**, **Organizations**, and communities powerfully, productively, and innovatively.

6.3 Evaluate your influence

Situational Analysis is the process of aligning context and desired results by evaluating the self, actions, systems, and cultures. **Context** delves into the situation deeper by being aware of the physical, psychological, social, and cultural environments around us. Context occurs across four psychosocial levels: **Personal** contexts which are psychological and biological aspects; **Interpersonal** contexts which are dyadic relationships and interactions; **Team** contexts which are small groups with common goals; and **Organizational** contexts which include larger groups, institutions, and systems.

6.4 Execute your influence

Leader Behaviors are the observable skills and actions (Competence). One of the most essential behaviors individuals execute to influence outcomes is **Communication**. Communication includes sending and receiving information, verbally and nonverbally, and must emphasize understanding to contribute optimally to achieve goals.

Combining the Innovative Leadership Model and the Leader-Follower Framework perspectives and their component elements provides new insights for leader and follower development. Understanding and developing each of these elements will optimize effective leadership and followership in a wide range of situations and settings.

Conflict of interest

The authors declare no conflict of interest.

Disclaimer

The opinions and assertions contained herein are the sole ones of the authors and are not to be construed as reflecting the views of the Uniformed Services University of the Health Sciences or the Department of Defense.

Author details

Neil E. Grunberg[1*], Erin S. Barry[1], Michael Morrow-Fox[2] and Maureen Metcalf[2]

1 Department of Military and Emergency Medicine, Uniformed Services University of the Health Sciences, Bethesda, MD, USA

2 Innovative Leadership Institute, Columbus, OH, USA

*Address all correspondence to: neil.grunberg@usuhs.edu

References

[1] Gordon J. Are you a real team? 2013 [Available from: http://www.jongordon.com/positive-tip-a-real-team.html.

[2] Hackman JR. Leading Teams: Setting the stage for great performances. Boston, MA: Harvard Business School Publishing Corporation; 2002.

[3] Katzenbach JR, Smith DK. The Wisdom of Teams. New York, NY: HarperBusiness; 1999 May 1, 2019.

[4] Ahearn B. Influence people: Powerful everyday opportunities to persuade that are lasting and ethical. Westerville, OH: Influence People, LLC; 2019.

[5] Barry ES, Grunberg NE. A conceptual framework to guide leader and follower education, development, and assessment. Journal of Leadership, Accountability, and Ethics. 2020;17(1): 127-134.

[6] Callahan CW, Grunberg NE. Military Medical Leadership. In: O'Connor FG, Schoomaker EB, Smith DC, editors. Fundamentals of Military Medicine. San Antonio, TX: Borden Institute; 2019. p. 51-66.

[7] Grunberg NE, Barry ES, Callahan C, Kleber HG, McManigle JE, Schoomaker EB. A conceptual framework for leader and leadership education and development. International Journal of Leadership in Education. 2018:1-7.

[8] Heifetz RA, Linsky M, Grashow A. The practice of adaptive leadership: Tools and tactics for changing your organization and the world. Cambridge, MA: Harvard Business Press; 2009.

[9] Northouse PG. Leadership: Theory and practice. 8th ed. Los Angeles, CA: Sage Publications; 2018.

[10] Day DV. Leadership development: A review in context. The Leadership Quarterly. 2001;11(4):581-613.

[11] Metcalf M, Palmer M. Innovative leadership fieldbook. Teaneck, NJ: Integral Publishers, LLC; 2011.

[12] Metcalf M, Barry ES, Blakaj DM, Fitzpatrick S, Morrow-Fox M, Grunberg NE. Innovative Leadership for Health Care. Teaneck, NJ: Integral Publishers, LLC; 2021.

[13] Day DV. Integrative perspectives on longitudinal investigations of leader development: From childhood through adulthood. The Leadership Quarterly. 2011;22(3):561-571.

[14] Egorov M, Verdorfer AP, Peus C. Taming the emotional dog: Moral intuition and ethically-oriented leader development. Journal of Business Ethics. 2019;160(3):817-834.

[15] Kwok N, Shen W, Brown DJ. I can, I am: Differential predictors of leader efficacy and identity trajectories in leader development. The Leadership Quarterly. 2020:101422.

[16] Liu Z, Venkatesh S, Murphy SE, Riggio RE. Leader development across the lifespan: A dynamic experiences-grounded approach. The Leadership Quarterly. 2020:101382.

[17] Steele AR, Day DV. The role of self-attention in leader development. Journal of Leadership Studies. 2018;12(2):17-32.

[18] Riggio RE, Lee J. Emotional and interpersonal competencies and leader development. Human Resource Management Review. 2007;17(4): 418-426.

[19] Rupprecht S, Falke P, Kohls N, Tamdjidi C, Wittmann M, Kersemaekers W. Mindful leader development: How leaders experience the effects of mindfulness training on leader capabilities. Frontiers in psychology. 2019;10:1081.

[20] Chaleff I. The courageous follower: Standing up to & for our leaders: Berrett-Koehler Publishers; 2009.

[21] Chaleff I. In praise of followership style assessments. Journal of Leadership Studies. 2016;10(3):45-48.

[22] Gobble MM. The value of followership. Research-Technology Management. 2017;60(4):59-63.

[23] Kellerman B. Followership: How followers are creating change and changing leaders. Boston, MA: Harvard Business School Press Boston; 2008.

[24] Kellerman B. The future of followership. Strategy & Leadership. 2019.

[25] Riggio RE. Why Followership? New Directions for Student Leadership. 2020;2020(167):15-22.

[26] Siangchokyoo N, Klinger RL, Campion ED. Follower transformation as the linchpin of transformational leadership theory: A systematic review and future research agenda. The Leadership Quarterly. 2020;31(1): 101341.

[27] Uhl-Bien M, Riggio RE, Lowe KB, Carsten MK. Followership theory: A review and research agenda. The leadership quarterly. 2014;25(1):83-104.

[28] Woolley L, Caza A, Levy L. Authentic leadership and follower development: Psychological capital, positive work climate, and gender. Journal of Leadership & Organizational Studies. 2011;18(4):438-448.

[29] Busari AH, Khan SN, Abdullah SM, Mughal YH. Transformational leadership style, followership, and factors of employees' reactions towards organizational change. Journal of Asia Business Studies. 2019.

[30] Griffith JA, Baur JE, Buckley MR. Creating comprehensive leadership pipelines: Applying the real options approach to organizational leadership development. Human Resource Management Review. 2019;29(3):305-315.

[31] Litano ML, Major DA. Facilitating a whole-life approach to career development: The role of organizational leadership. Journal of Career Development. 2016;43(1):52-65.

[32] Ruben BD, Gigliotti RA. Communication: Sine qua non of organizational leadership theory and practice. International Journal of Business Communication. 2017;54(1):12-30.

[33] Morrow-Fox M, Metcalf M. Business Agility. Integral Leadership Review. 2020;20(1):78-80.

[34] Schoemaker PH, Heaton S, Teece D. Innovation, dynamic capabilities, and leadership. California Management Review. 2018;61(1):15-42.

[35] Boiral O, Raineri N, Talbot D. Managers' citizenship behaviors for the environment: A developmental perspective. Journal of Business Ethics. 2016;149(2):395-409.

[36] Brandt E, Kjellström S, Andersson AC. Transformational change by a post-conventional leader. Leadership & Organization Development Journal. 2019;40(4):457-471.

[37] McEwen CA, Schmidt JD. Leadership and the corporate sustainability challenge: Mindsets in action. SSRN Electronic Journal. 2007:1-49.

[38] Braks A. Leadership coaching leads to later stage development. Integral Review. 2020;16(1):332-356.

[39] Rant MB. Sustainable development goals (SDGs), leadership, and sadhguru: Self-transformation becoming the aim of leadership development. The International Journal of Management Education. 2020;18(3):1-11.

[40] Morrow-Fox M, Barry ES, Grunberg NE, Metcalf M. The innovative health care leader. Academia Letters. 2021;Article 116:1-5.

[41] Howe-Murphy R. Deep Coaching: Using the Enneagram as a Catalyst for Profound Change. El Granada, CA: Enneagram Press; 2007.

[42] Myers IB. The Myers-Briggs Type Indicator: Manual. Palo Alto, CA: Consulting Psychologists Press, Inc.; 1962.

[43] The Myers & Briggs Foundation. MBTI Basics 2018 [Available from: https://www.myersbriggs.org/my-mbti-personality-type/mbti-basics/home.htm?bhcp=1.

[44] Costa PT. NEO Personality Inventory-Revised (NEO PI-R). Odessa, FL: Psychological Assessment Resources; 1992.

[45] True Colors. True Colors: The Four Color Personalities 2021 [June 20, 2021]. Available from: https://truecolorsintl.com/the-four-color-personalities/.

[46] Goldberg LR. The structure of phenotypic personality traits. American Psychologist. 1993;48(1):26-34.

[47] Owen JE, Mahatmya D, Carter R. Dominance, Influence, Steadiness, and Conscientiousness (DISC) Assessment Tool. In: Zeigler-Hill V, Shackelford TK, editors. Encyclopedia of Personality and Individual Differences. Cham: Springer International Publishing; 2017. p. 1-4.

[48] Rath T. StrengthsFinder 2.0. Washington, DC: Gallup Press; 2007.

[49] Bradberry T, Greaves J. Emotional Intelligence 2.0. San Diego, CA: TalentSmart; 2009.

[50] Goleman D. Emotional intelligence: Why it can matter more that IQ. New York, NY: Bantam Dell; 1995.

[51] Goleman D. Working with emotional intelligence. New York, NY: Bantam Books; 1998.

[52] Goleman D, Boyatzis RE, McKee A. Primal leadership: Realizing the power of emotional intelligence. Boston, MA: Harvard Business School Press; 2002.

[53] Grunberg NE, McManigle JE, Barry ES. Using Social Psychology Principles to Develop Emotionally Intelligent Healthcare Leaders. Frontiers in Psychology. 2020;11:1917.

[54] Harris LS, Kuhnert KW. Looking through the lens of leadership: A constructive developmental approach. Leadership & Organization Development Journal. 2008; 29(1):47-67.

[55] Rooke D. Transformational leadership capabilities for medical leaders. BMJ Leader. 2018;2(1):3-6.

[56] Kjellström S, Andersson AC. Applying adult development theories to improvement science. International Journal of Health Care Quality Assurance. 2017;30(7):617-627.

[57] Maddi SR, Khoshaba DM. Resilience at Work: How to Succeed No Matter What Life Throws at You. New York, NY: AMACOM Books; 2005.

[58] American Psychological Association. Building your resilience 2012 [June 20, 2021]. Available from: https://www.apa.org/topics/resilience.

[59] Cannon S, Morrow-Fox M, Metcalf M. The strategist competency model: The future of leadership development. In: M. Sowcik, A.C. Andenoro, M. McNutt, Murphy SE, editors. Leadership 2050, critical challenges, key contexts and emerging trends. Bingley, West Yorkshire: Emerald Group Publishing Limited; 2015. p. 189-205.

Chapter 6

Spirituality Leadership Applications in Small and Medium Enterprises (SMEs)

Ahmad Rafiki, Miftahuddin and Atika Rizki

Abstract

This chapter aims to explore the spirituality leadership applications in small and medium enterprises (SMEs). The essence of leadership is crucial in managing the SMEs to achieve effectiveness and efficiency, although the employees would be in small number. Spirituality is not new concept and would be implemented in the modern organizations including the SMEs. The theory of spiritual leadership is also discussed together with the antecedents of spirituality in organizational behavior and its application in modernity context. Spirituality gives an impact to the performance of the organization and improves employees' motivation. An empirical study is required to see the contributions of spirituality in business operation in general.

Keywords: spirituality, leadership applications, SME

1. Introduction

Small and medium enterprises (SMEs) are considered as the backbone of a country because they are related to every aspect of economic and community life. SMEs are also seen as growth engines for economic and social transformation in a country. Nevertheless, there are real limitations faced by SMEs including insufficient employees, lack of financial resources, lack of experience and educational background, and lack of managerial knowledge.

The contribution made by SMEs reaching the micro and macro levels cannot be separated from the successful management of SMEs by effective leaders [1]. The leadership behavior or style of SME leaders is a key element and has a direct influence on organizational performance, competitive advantage, and the success of SMEs [2]. According to Avolio et al. [3], leadership plays an important role in organizational development and growth. Organizational leaders generally consider all business plans and decisions in an effective and timely manner. Leadership becomes more important when faced with new or changing situations. Various micro, small and medium enterprise (MSME) literatures have shown that weak and insufficient leadership skills are a major factor in the failure of SMEs. Therefore, SMEs need to develop their leadership behavior to bring the company through all situations, both calm and crisis.

Over time, the concept of leadership has been discussed and studied in a variety of different theories, approaches, and styles [4, 5]. However, there are no universally accepted concepts and definitions due to differences in organizational forms and contexts [6]. It is also not easy to define the concept given the size of the subject and the general conventions about field analysis.

IntechOpen

Earlier Bass [7] states that the definition of leadership is closely related to the efforts of various possibilities. While Hirtz et al. [8] stated that leadership is a process by which managers for the purpose of directing their subordinates in order to work toward the company. The concept of leadership is also with stimulants and motivations that motivate people to achieve together [9]. This is in line with the statement of Hersey et al. [10] that the essence of leadership involves purpose through people.

Meanwhile, there is one concept called spiritual leadership that is rarely implemented, but it is crucial to be applied by the small and medium enterprises, which usually have a limited number of employees. How this concept could be applied? This would be questioned, and thus, this study aims to explore the application of spirituality leadership in small business. Moreover, this chapter will discuss the essence of leadership, the spiritual leadership theory, antecedents of spirituality in organizational behavior, spiritualism in modernity content, and conclusion.

2. Literature review

2.1 The essence of leadership

Leadership can be seen as a group process, personality attribute, art of encouraging gratification, exercise of influence, certain types of actions or behaviors, forms of persuasion, power relations, and instruments for achieving goals [7, 11]. According to Kotter [12], without leadership, the possibility of mistakes will increase and decrease the chances of success. Leadership enables collaboration, reduces conflict, contributes to creativity, and plays a role in integrating people even if not physically. Alas et al. [13] also look at leadership in terms of individual traits, leader behavior, interaction patterns, role relationships, follower perceptions, influence on followers, influence on task goals, and influence on organizational culture. This view focuses on the relationship between leaders and followers, but not on what conditions must exist for an effective leader to emerge or develop [14].

Kouzes and Posner [15] emphasize leadership issues on leadership methods, how to build and articulate a vision and values, develop strategic awareness and approach to team building. Specifically, the five leadership practices highlighted by Kouzes and Posner [15] are as follows:

1. Model the way—lead by example;

2. Inspire a shared vision—paint a clear picture for everyone to see and understand in achieving the organization's future visions and dreams; belief and ambition; and the importance of dialog;

3. Challenge the process—change from the status quo and innovation (finding and enhancing product and service innovation opportunities; creating the right climate; anticipating risks and uncertainties);

4. Enable others to act—the team effort required to achieve the vision by building trust and strong relationships and encouraging collaboration of all stakeholders;

5. Encourage the heart—the importance of acknowledging contributions, appreciation; a culture of celebrating values and victories; and its relation to performance.

Leadership practice is often associated with the applied leadership style. However, the rapid changes in the environment, communication technology, and the development of community paradigms require the application of a leadership style that is in accordance with these changes. One option in solving these problems is a transformational leadership approach. Transformational leadership is comprehensive and integrated leadership ability for individuals, groups, and organizations to produce transformations marked by changes at every stage of activity. Transformational leadership is developed to deal with change by transforming individual paradigms and values within the organization to achieve organizational goals and vision.

Transformational leadership was first proposed by Downton [16], which was later developed by a sociologist in the field of politics, Burns [17]. Burns [17] connects the role of leadership with followers. As a leader, the task of a leader is to encourage the enthusiasm of his followers to achieve common goals. Transformational leadership has characteristics that emphasize intrinsic motivation and the development of followers [18]. The aspects of transformational leadership are characterized as follows:

1. Transformational leadership arises when members in the organization (leaders and followers) want high motivation and morality. This condition can arise when the organization is facing competition or a lot of customer dissatisfaction.

2. Transformational leadership seeks to motivate and inspire those around them by explaining the urgency of work and challenges. How to motivate this can be done with various approaches such as the needs theory approach, namely the fulfillment of the main needs of followers such as physical, security, social, esteem, and self-actualization needs. In addition, the creation of justice in the permanent system contributes in advancing the organization. Meanwhile, in terms of generating inspiration, it can be done through evaluation of the failures and successes that have been achieved in order to encourage the learning process through discussions, literacy studies, comparative studies, and so on.

3. Transformational leadership is able to reduce the dependence of followers on their leaders. This can be seen through the delegation of authority, developing the ability and confidence of followers, as well as encouraging flexibility in the implementation of teamwork, providing direct access to information, eliminating unnecessary control functions, and creating and empowering a strong work culture.

4. Transformational leadership develops visionary thinking.

5. Transformational leadership develops a collaborative way of working rather than a hierarchical way of working through individual learning and organizational learning. The collaborative way of working results in greater performance than the performance that results from individual systems.

6. Transformational leadership encourages the empowerment of followers so that they are appropriate in dealing with developments in situations and environments that affect the organization.

In addition to transformational leadership, there are other leadership styles that can also be applied in organizations including MSMEs, namely transactional leadership. Transactional leadership is known as a leadership style that motivates and encourages obedience by followers or subordinates through rewards and punishments. With this system the leader can keep subordinates motivated at least in the short term. This leadership style often occurs when someone takes the initiative in making contact with others to exchange things of value [19]. Bass [7] also revealed that transactional leadership is characterized by the provision of assessment through rewards, recognition, salary increases, and career advancement for members who perform well and vice versa, namely the provision of punishment for poor performers. Therefore, transactional leadership is often considered effective in achieving organizational goals [20].

Literally, transactional means "a transaction or exchange." Transactional leadership is concerned with exchanges or transactions between leaders for the desired result by fulfilling the desires of the leader and the expectations of followers, which involves a promise or commitment and trust. Transactional leaders also accommodate the interests of their subordinates by providing incentives, honors, and promises to subordinates who have successfully fulfilled the commitments of leaders or organizations. Transactional leadership is able to encourage followers to perform in accordance with the wishes of the leader in the hope of obtaining rewards and rewards. Transactional leadership also facilitates subordinates to recognize obligations for work and goals to be achieved [21].

Sedarmayanti [22] classifies transactional leadership into:

1. Contingent reward, namely the leader will influence the behavior of subordinates by providing details of the work to be done to subordinates, with incentives as motivation to subordinates to achieve the results of the implementation of tasks;

2. Management by exception, namely the leader will influence the behavior of subordinates by using correction or punishment efforts as a consequence of decreasing performance from predetermined standards. In addition, the leader also influences the behavior of subordinates by actively monitoring the work done by subordinates and by corrective efforts to ensure that work is carried out and completed according to standards.

2.2 Spiritual leadership theory

The spiritual dimension in leadership studies produces a concept referred to as spiritual leadership. For the first time, the phrase "spiritual leadership" was used in an article titled "Spiritual Leadership: Meeting Whole-Self Needs at Work." Several studies have stated the importance of spiritual values in organizations. Spiritual values in leadership are able to motivate and inspire employees in building the vision and culture of the organization and create employee commitment to the organization, which in turn also has an impact on increasing job satisfaction and employee performance. Spiritual leadership theory represents a paradigm shift in the study, research, and practice of leadership that can expand transformational and charismatic theory through ethical and value-based perspectives. According to Fry [23], spiritual leadership includes the following tasks:

a. Developing a purpose that inspires members of the organization to feel called, find significance, and make a difference in their lives.

b. Developing an altruistic love-based social/organizational culture in which leaders and followers truly care about, care for, and respect one another, resulting in a sense of belonging, being understood, and being appreciated.

There are several concepts about this spiritual leadership style [23], including:

a. A causal model of spiritual leadership in which an internal motivation model incorporates vision, belief, compassion for fellow human beings, application of spiritual theory at work, and spiritual endurance, as well as organizational results such as dedication and productivity.

b. Spiritual leadership as a collection of beliefs, attitudes, and behaviors that is inherently necessary to inspire one another in order for them to experience spiritual endurance via calling and membership.

c. Integrating Horton's continuity of God as the supreme force with Smith's perspective that all faiths embrace the vision and fundamental virtues such as humility, compassion, and honesty, the theory of spiritual leadership is able to explain how leaders and followers can be satisfied in their need for spiritual endurance.

Spiritual leadership style in building organizational culture can be done in four steps as follows:

a. The true intention is to build excellent inner qualities in leading, so that the organizational community will have full attention and *istiqomah* in serving their respective duties.

b. Developing a quality culture by building core beliefs and core values to the community that life and work are essentially worshiping God, so they must be done as well as possible.

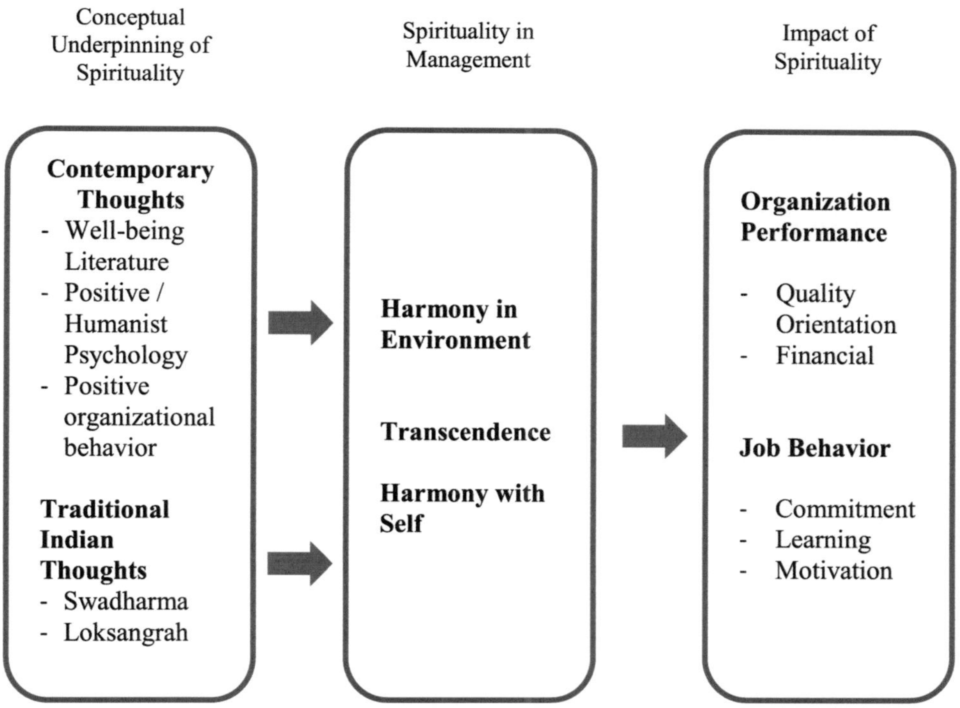

Figure 1.
Spirituality representative schemes in management literature. Source: Pandey et al. [26].

c. Develop brotherhood among community members, so that synergistic cooperation between individuals and groups within the organization can be created to empower maximum potential.

d. Develop ethical behavior at work through the cultivation of gratitude and patience in carrying out the mandate.

Ubaydillah in Muajiz [24] defines spiritual intelligence with intelligence that elevates the function of the soul as an internal device that has the ability and concern to see the meaning behind the reality as it is. Spiritual intelligence is closer to the enlightenment of the soul. Heaton et al. [25] suggested a distinction between two constructs in spirituality, both pure and applied. Pure spirituality refers to an inner experience of pure self-awareness that is quiet and boundless, general praise of perceptions, thoughts, and feelings. An example of pure spirituality in Eastern culture is the technique of meditation. The term “applied spirituality” refers to the source of practical wisdom application and the result of which automatically arises from genuine spirituality’s experience (**Figure 1**; and **Table 1**).

The Spirituality Research by Pawar [27] draws from various literatures that can reflect various attentions on spirituality in the workplace, namely:

1. Spirituality in the workplace is a critical topic that has significant and prospective implications for the well-being of people, organizations, and society [28].

2. Scientific research has the potential to make major contributions to the field of organizational science [29].

3. De Klerk [30] observes about level of attention on spirituality in the workplace and clarifying the notion of the importance of motivation, which no longer necessary. He also places more emphasis on discussing toward spirituality more deeply. Pawar [27] also identified various recent studies on spirituality in the workplace that have different concerns, namely:

    - Focusing on the definition and operationalization of spirituality in the workplace [31–34].

    - Provide a profile of the area of spirituality research in the workplace, and provide an outline guide to the direction and methodology of studies on spirituality [35–38].

    - Describe the manifestation of spirituality at work in organizations [39].

	Subjective approach	**Objective approach**
Pure spirituality	Direct personal experience of silent awakening	Psychological relationship of personal experience on reality
Spirituality Applications	Personal reflection on the consequences articulation which considered conditions of the higher states of consciousness	Quantitative and qualitative research on physiological, psychological, organizational, and social variables before and after transcendental reality
Spiritual Development	Reflection on and articulation of one’s development process	Quantitative and qualitative research on psychological and social development

Table 1.
Methods of research on spirituality in organizations. Source: Heaton et al. [25].

- Describe various organizational views that may facilitate spirituality in the workplace [40].
- Identify different organizational characteristics, such as culture [41], leadership [23], and organizational practices [42], which may aid in the application of spirituality in the workplace.
- Concentrating on the workplace effects of spirituality such as work attitudes [43], organizational productivity [44], and unit performance [45].

It is not easy to find empirical research on spirituality. Most of the writings on spirituality still revolve around the concept and methodology of spirituality. Two empirical studies that discuss spirituality are identified. The first is the study of Kolodinsky et al. [46], and second is Muajiz's research [24]. These two studies represent research abroad and research within the country. While Kolodinsky et al. [46] conducted an empirical test of the effects of spirituality in the workplace.

Muajiz's research [24] examines the effect of auditor training, emotional intelligence, and spirituality on auditor performance at the Directorate General of Taxes. The results showed that training, emotional and spiritual intelligence had a significant positive effect on the performance of auditors either partially or simultaneously. Spiritual intelligence has the greatest influence compared with the other two independent variables. However, the three variables above only have an effect of 23% on auditor performance while 77% are influenced by other factors not examined.

Muajiz's research [24] divides spiritual intelligence into three dimensions:

1. Dimensions of spiritual ± religious relations, with indicators/questions:

    a. Love of God

    b. Better life motivation

    c. Self-understanding as a spiritual being

    d. Be bold in the truth

    e. The feeling of always being watched by God

    f. Patience

2. Social±religious relations, with indicators/questions:

    a. Contribution to the welfare of others

    b. Family ties between people

    c. Love for living things

3. Ethics ± social, with indicators/questions:

    a. Adherence to ethics and morals

b. Amanah (keep promises)

c. Can be trusted

d. Tolerant of difference

e. Anti-violence

f. Match between words and actions

2.3 Antecedents of spirituality in organizational behavior

Pawar [27] states that there are four concepts as the forerunners of the concept of spirituality in organizations that have a concern for transcendent self-interest as discussed in spirituality in the workplace. The four concepts that have preceded spirituality are transformational leadership, organizational citizenship conduct, organizational support, and procedural fairness, all play a role in the workplace. These four concepts have emerged a decade earlier than spirituality in the workplace. Workplace spirituality emerged in the 1990s, while the four concepts described above emerged in the 1980s. This demonstrates that these four ideas are pioneers of workplace spirituality, as well as providing different explanations for the research of spirituality in the workplace, and also assisting the discussion of spirituality at work in the broader study of organizational behavior. However, the four preceding concepts are not the cause of the emergence of spirituality in the workplace. Transformational leadership is the leader's capacity to inspire and encourage subordinates to accomplish more than expected and for higher internal benefits. This kind of leadership encourages followers to strive for transcendental objectives rather than self-interest and toward self-actualization rather than just pursuing stability. Below are the elements of the concept of transformative leadership [47]. The five factors are:

a. Charisma, where the leader is able to gradually instill values, respect, take pride in yourself, and express a vision.

b. Individual attention, which prioritizes employee requirements and offers beneficial initiatives for subordinates' personal development.

c. Intellectual stimulation, in which the leader assists his subordinates in reassessing the issue rationally (encouraging subordinates to be creative).

d. Conditional reward, in which the leader instructs subordinates on how to get the reward they want.

e. Management by exception, where it is possible to allow work to be done without intervening unless the task is not completed on time and at a reasonable cost.

The term "organizational citizenship behavior" (OCB) was coined in 1983 through a study conducted by Bateman and Organ and also by a Smith study in the same year. This is based on what Organ said that measuring employee performance may not cover the overall performance that he actually does [27]. In other words, it does more than what it is supposed to do. This is done because it is driven more by an internal motivation called self-transcendence, rather than personal gains. Five aspects of OCB exist: altruism, conscientiousness, civic virtue, sportsmanship, and politeness. These dimensions represent the many ways in which workers pursue profit is not just to collect values and direct rewards for themselves. This shows that the concept of spirituality in the workplace seems to share the concept of employee transcendence in the OCB concept.

According to Eisenberger et al. [48], the notion of perceived organizational support reflects that organizations are concerned with employee values, well-being, and contributions. If employees perceive organizational support for them, then they will also provide benefits for the organization. This is called the norm of reciprocity, one party will repay the kindness of the party who has given him kindness as well. To a certain extent, this is also related to self-transcendence as well as spirituality in the workplace. This is proven by empirical results, where perceived organizational support has a significant effect on lower absenteeism and employee innovation behavior. This perceived organizational support consists of operational items referring to such things as hearing employee concerns, providing assistance when employees experience problems, and will not be replaced by other employees because there are other people who can replace them with cheaper salaries. From these indicators it appears that the organization is trying to give a sense of being part of the organizational community. Being part of an organizational community is one aspect of spirituality in the workplace and reflects self-transcendence [27]. The concept of procedural justice (perceived fairness) and the procedures used to make this procedural justice are self-interest models and group-value models [27].

According to the self-interest model, the presence of fair processes guarantees that people's personal interests and desired outcomes are safeguarded. While the group-value model argues that individuals will follow the interests of their groups in order to accept the group toward themselves so as to have a psychological impact on their identification as part of the group. This can be seen as meeting the needs of the employee community with a sense of being part of the community. Therefore, procedural fairness may be seen as a means of ensuring a sense of belonging to the community. So that procedural justice can facilitate the self-interest of employees' transcendence. Therefore, the concept of procedural justice in the study of organizational behavior is connected to workplace spirituality [27].

2.4 Spiritualism in modernity context

Spiritualism is not synonymous with religion, but has views and doctrines similar to or close to religion. It is said that spiritualism is a philosophy, doctrine, or (sort of) religion that emphasizes the spiritual aspects of everything. So the basis of spiritualism is the view that spirit is the essence of life and that the spirit is (eternal) and not destroyed by the death of the body or by body. Spiritualism is a religion for people who do not embrace it as religion formally, but at the same time emphasized that belief (spirituality) is based on belief religion.

Now when modern humans want spirituality and meanings of deeper life, they separate it from the things that are underlying spirituality, namely religious rules. Freeing spirituality of religion and science is an act of which both will lead to emptiness and inequality. Because spirituality without the ultimate goal of the Creator has only become a psychological spirituality that will arrive at a state of emptiness, calm, peaceful but no relative and practical things, which benefit others.

According to Comte [49], in the modern society, the religion becomes abandoned. But in reality this opinion is not entirely true. The modern society actually makes people are looking for spiritual values for themselves. Spirituality in fact is not only always related to religion and God, but spirituality also functions as a psychological solutions, obsession, or temporary spiritual need for some of them. Their curiosity about what spirituality is, they only use as a solution to a problem that they cannot deal with only with a ratio but requires their knowledge of their spirituality.

The high passion for the world of spirituality cannot be separated from the construction of modernity. Modernity offers a life of luxury and ease of living for humans, but this kind of life makes people seem to have lost direction and purpose of spirituality in their lives. Modernity makes them finally looking for a spirituality within themselves. This is due to a lack of knowledge about spirituality. They do not seem to find satisfaction in themselves because of their lack of spirituality even though they have a good life with an abundance of luxury and seem to have an easy life.

Spirituality does not only refer to the meaning of religion and God, but spirituality also refers to several aspects, such as referring to nature. Human awareness to restore a natural beauty, which is increasingly being eroded due to the rapid development of modern times. Human awareness of spirituality with nature will make the nature become beautiful again as in previous times. The awakening of spirituality is very much needed in this modern era in order to be able to rebuild what has been damaged and what has been lost due to the development of modern times.

3. Conclusion

The spirituality gives another view in the process of decision-making. Spiritual leadership's goal is to instill the beliefs, attitudes, and behaviors necessary to inspire oneself (intrinsic motivation) and others in order to attain a feeling of spiritual survival as well as to create vision and harmony of values through individuals, empowered teams, organizational levels and assist development in terms of psychological welfare and organizational commitment. While a spiritual leadership style refers to a person who occupies a leadership position must be able to increase the effectiveness of his leadership with high ability to use a situational style, which means a different style in different situations and conditions.

The SMEs will receive benefits on the leaders' role in their organization. Leaders could have 2–3 followers as it exists in the small business, but leaders could manage more than three followers. However, leading few people is easier than many people. In other words, the leaders in small business must be able to influence others to achieve the business goals easily and faster. The essence of leadership in SMEs is shown obviously, and it is would be an important factor to control the SMEs to obtain stability or continuity in their business operations. Leaders are not managers, thus their contributions are helpful to have better performance.

This study expectedly will add literature on leadership context as well as the spiritual leadership. Practically, the application of the spirituality leadership is real and adaptable. It is not always to be associated with the religion teachings but beyond that, it is applicable in various types of organizations particularly the small business. However, a real case in an organization and empirical study is needed to be conducted to see all elements of spiritual leadership play their respective roles.

Author details

Ahmad Rafiki*, Miftahuddin and Atika Rizki
Universitas Medan Area, Medan, Indonesia

*Address all correspondence to: hahmadrafiki@gmail.com

References

[1] Madanchian M, Hussein N, Noordin F, Taherdoost H. The relationship between ethical leadership, leadership effectiveness and organizational performance: A review of literature in SMEs context. European Business & Management. 2016;**2**(2):17-21

[2] Popa BM. The relationship between leadership effectiveness and organizational performance. Journal of Defense Resources Management (JoDRM). 2012;**3**(1):123-127

[3] Avolio BJ, Sosik JJ, Jung DI, Berson Y. Leadership models, methods, and applications. In: Borman WC, Ilgen DR, Klimoski RJ, editors. Handbook of Psychology: Industrial and Organizational Psychology. Vol. 12. Hoboken, NJ: John Wiley & Sons Inc.; 2003. pp. 277-307. DOI: 10.1002/0471264385.wei1212

[4] Ammeter AP, Douglas C, Gardner WL, Hochwarter WA, Ferris GR. Toward a political theory of leadership. The Leadership Quarterly. 2002;**13**(6):751-796

[5] Tirmizi SA. The 6-L framework: A model for leadership research and development. Leadership and Organization Development Journal. 2002;**23**(5):269-279. DOI: 10.1108/01437730210435983

[6] Schaffer B. Leadership and motivation. Supervision. 2008;**69**(2):6

[7] Bass BM. Current developments in transformational leadership: Research and applications. The Psychologist-Manager Journal. 1999;**3**(1):5

[8] Hirtz PD, Murray SL, Riordan CA. The effects of leadership on quality. Engineering Management Journal. 2007;**19**(1):22-27

[9] Senge P. The Fifth Discipline: The Art & Practice of the Learning Organization. New York: Doubleday; 1990

[10] Hersey P, Blanchard KH, Johnson DE. Management of Organizational Behavior: Leading Human Resources. 8th ed. Upper Saddle River, NJ: Prentice Hall; 2001

[11] Zacharatos A, Barling J, Kelloway EK. Development and effects of transformational leadership in adolescents. The Leadership Quarterly. 2000;**11**(2):211-226

[12] Kotter JP. What leaders really do. Harvard Business Review. 1990;**68**: 103-111

[13] Alas R, Tafel K, Tuulik K. Leadership style during transition in society: Case of Estonia. Problems and Perspectives in Management. 2007;**5**(1):50-60

[14] Vardiman PD, Houghton JD, Jinkerson DL. Environmental leadership development: Toward a contextual model of leader selection and effectiveness. Leadership & Organization Development Journal. 2006;**27**(2):93-105. DOI: 10.1108/01437730610646606

[15] Kouzes JM, Posner BZ. The Five Practices of Exemplary Leadership. San Francisco, Milwaukee, WI, USA: Porchlight; 2003

[16] Downton JV. Rebel Leadership: Commitment and charisma in the Revolutionary Process. Free Press; 1973

[17] Burns JM. Leadership. New York: Harper & Row; 1978

[18] Bernard M, Riggio RE. Transformational Leadership. New York: Psychology Press; 2006

[19] Rafiki A. Islamic Leadership: Comparisons and Qualities. Digital

Leadership—A New Leadership Style for the 21st Century. UK: IntechOpen; 2020. pp. 1-16

[20] Afolabi MM, Olasupo FA. The female gender in traditional leadership In Nigeria: A socio-cultural perspective. In: Engendering Leadership through Research and Practice Conference Proceedings. Vol. 21. Perth; 2008, 2008. p. 8

[21] Lo MC, Ramayah T, Min HW. Leadership styles and organizational commitment: A test on Malaysia manufacturing industry. African Journal of Marketing Management. 2009;**1**(6):133-139

[22] Sedarmayanti. Sumber Daya Manusia dan Produktivitas Kerja. Bandung: Mandar Maju; 2009

[23] Fry LW. Toward a theory of spiritual leadership. The Leadership Quarterly. 2003;**14**(6):693-727

[24] Muajiz. Pengaruh Pelatihan, Kecerdasan Emosional dan Kecerdasan Spiritual Auditor Terhadap Kinerja Auditor Pada Direktorat Jenderal Pajak. Jogjakarta: Tesis Magister Akuntansi Universitas Gadjah Mada; 2009

[25] Heaton DP, Schmidt-Wilk J, Travis F. Constructs, methods, and measures for researching spirituality in organizations. Journal of Organizational Change Management. 2004;**17**(1):62-82. DOI: 10.1108/09534810410511305

[26] Pandey A, Gupta RK, Arora AP. Spiritual climate of business organizations and its impact on customers' experience. Journal of Business Ethics. 2009;**88**(2):313-332

[27] Pawar BS. Individual spirituality, workplace spirituality and work attitudes: An empirical test of direct and interaction effects. Leadership & Organization Development Journal. 2009;**30**(8):759-777. DOI: 10.1108/01437730911003911

[28] Sheep ML. Nurturing the whole person: The ethics of workplace spirituality in a society of organizations. Journal of Business Ethics. 2006;**66**(4): 357-375

[29] Giacalone RA, Jurkiewicz CL. Right from wrong: The influence of spirituality on perceptions of unethical business activities. Journal of Business Ethics. 2003;**46**(1):85-97

[30] De Klerk JJ. Spirituality, meaning in life and work wellness: A research agenda. International Journal of Organizational Analysis. 2005;**13**:64-88

[31] Ashmos DP, Duchon D. Spirituality at work: A conceptualization and measure. Journal of Management Inquiry. 2000;**9**(2):134-145

[32] Kinjerski VM, Skrypnek BJ. Defining spirit at work: Finding common ground. Journal of Organizational Change Management. 2004;**17**(1):26-42

[33] Moore TW, Casper WJ. An examination of proxy measures of workplace spirituality: A profile model of multidimensional constructs. Journal of Leadership & Organizational Studies. 2006;**12**(4):109-118

[34] Sheep ML. Nailing down gossamer: A valid measure of the person-organization fit of workplace spirituality. In: Academy of Management Proceedings. Vol. 1. Briarcliff Manor, NY 10510: Academy of Management; 2004. pp. B1-B6

[35] Krahnke K, Giacalone RA, Jurkiewicz CL. Point-counterpoint: Measuring workplace spirituality. Journal of Organizational Change Management. 2003;**16**(4):396-405

[36] Lund Dean KL, Fornaciari CJ, McGee JJ. Research in spirituality, religion, and work: Walking the line between relevance and legitimacy. Journal of Organizational Change Management. 2003;**16**(4):378-395

[37] Tischler L, Biberman J, Altman Y. A model for researching about spirituality in organizations. Business Renaissance Quarterly. 2007;**2**(2):23-37

[38] Giacalone RA, Jurkiewicz CL. In: Giacalone RA, Jurkiewicz CL, editors. Handbook of Workplace Spirituality and Organizational Performance. New York: M.E. Sharp; 2003a. pp. 3-28

[39] Milliman J, Ferguson J, Trickett D, Condemi B. Spirit and community at Southwest Airlines: An investigation of a spiritual values-based model. Journal of Organizational Change Management. 1999;**12**(3):221-233

[40] Ashforth BE, Pratt MG. Institutionalized spirituality: An oxymoron? In: Giacalone RA, Jurkiewicz CL, editors. Handbook of Workplace Spirituality and Organizational Performance. Armonk, New York: M.E. Sharpe; 2003. pp. 93-107

[41] Jurkiewicz CL, Giacalone RA. A values framework for measuring the impact of workplace spirituality on organizational performance. Journal of Business Ethics. 2004;**49**(2):129-142

[42] Pfeffer J. Business and the Spirit: Management practices that sustain values. In: Giacalone RA, Jurkiewicz CL, editors. The Handbook of Workplace Spirituality and Organizational Performance. New York: ME, Sharpe, Armonk; 2003. pp. 29-45

[43] Milliman J, Czaplewski AJ, Ferguson J. Workplace spirituality and employee work attitudes: An exploratory empirical assessment. Journal of Organizational Change Management. 2003;**16**:426-447

[44] Fry LW, Vitucci S, Cedillo M. Spiritual leadership and army transformation: Theory, measurement, and establishing a baseline. The Leadership Quarterly. 2005;**16**(5): 835-862

[45] Duchon DP, Plowman DA. Nurturing Spirit at work: Impact on work unit performance. The Leadership Quarterly. 2005;**16**:807-833

[46] Kolodinsky RW, Giacalone RA, Jurkiewicz CL. Workplace values and outcomes: Exploring personal, organizational, and interactive workplace spirituality. Journal of Business Ethics. 2008;**81**:465-480

[47] Gibson JL, Ivancevich JM, Donnely JH. Konopaske Organizations: Behavior. Structure, Processes. New York: McGraw Hill; 2009

[48] Eisenberger R, Huntington R, Hutchison S, Sowa D. Perceived organizational support. Journal of Applied Psychology. 1986;**71**(3):500-507

[49] Comte A. The Catechism of Positive Religion: Ricahrd Congreve (Trans.). London: John Capman; 1857

Section 3

Leadership in Environment and Workplace Contexts

Chapter 7

Defining Post-Pandemic Work and Organizations: The Need for Team Belongingness and Trust

Joseph Crawford

Abstract

The COVID-19 pandemic has brought forth substantial unrest in the ways in which people work and organize. This had led to disconnection, rapid adaptation, work from home, emergence of a new digital industry, and an opportunity to create anew. This chapter provides a position for the future state of work and organizing, drawing on the belongingness hypothesis, to characterize a revised method of human connection that acknowledges unique differences in online connections. It also explores the role that flexibility and working from home have on organizational outcomes, through changing presenteeism, changes in how people develop trust, and how social resources are deployed. Advancing an understanding of this position creates a possible post-pandemic model of work that acknowledges the current climate and the learnings from before that pandemic. Through genuine acknowledgment of the current and past ways of working, it is possible to build a pathway to heighten employee's sense of belonging and trust. This will support the return to, and evolution of, a form of normality post-pandemic.

Keywords: COVID-19, working from home, sense of belonging, flourishing, belongingness, connectivity

1. Introduction

The word "unprecedented" has perhaps been expressed across 2020–2021 more than any of our past years to describe the novel coronavirus (COVID-19) pandemic, regardless of the discipline or context within which it is represented. The documented and theorized effects of the pandemic continue to emerge as we collectively seek to understand the uncertainty presented to contemporary conceptualizations of organization, work, work-life balance, and human flourishing. And rightly so, prior to 2020, scholars were exploring related concepts; yet these were exacerbated in their application.

For many, this was manifested in visual and physical forms first. The empty streets of lockdown as a society worked from home, the global toilet paper exodus [1] face masks "fiascos" [2], World Health Organization compliant alcohol-based hand sanitizer at every café, and check-in apps and clipboards on each entrance. Each of these pandemic artifacts offers a symptomatic view of how the world operates and operated across 2020–2022. While many of these will become part of comedy skits and long-term legend for future generations, these will likely be archived to history books rather than become business-as-usual in ordinary life. Importantly, and notwithstanding, the pandemic has not operated inside a vacuum; technological innovation, climate change, and inequity are also shaping the future of work.

The contemporary workplace upheaval during early 2020 has had a significant effect on attitudes, appetite, and perception of work and organizations. If contextualized within the last 100 years of work and organization, the post-pandemic nexus offers a new and important turn of our understanding of work and its product(s). The late nineteenth century industrialist philosophy of work suggested that for work to be completed, it is done by industry with minimal governmental intervention (e.g., Laissez-Faire capitalism). The industrialist emphasizes the strength of the individual and their resilience (rugged individualism) and deployment of a survival of the fittest mentality (social Darwinism). Added, division of labor, specialization, positional power [3], the rise of charismatic authority [4, 5], and the growth of scientific inquiry [6] emerged as a modernist pursuit for effective and efficient organizational structures. In response, the postmodernist problematized the dehumanized organization to theorize connected workforces rather than alienated or estranged, with an acknowledgment that informal daily lives and lived experiences were also important. This transition was an important signpost in understanding how humans interact and organize for the purposes of *work*.

Skipping forward to pre-pandemic 2019 where much of the work and the organizational landscape was situated in competing sides of the modernist bureaucratic organization and *still* emergent postmodern post-bureaucratic organization. These tensions gave rise to large scale enterprises embedding activities of meaning, often formulaically, into their bureaucratic organizations: employee assistance programs constrained by fixed numbers of free appointments, workload models to support balance that typically fails to recognize implicit roles, free gym memberships with low uptake, renaming our human resources departments to *People and Wellbeing*, and a mental health and behavior policies with arduous hurdles to reporting and responding. While the workplace of today is far from only these catastrophized examples, they highlight the ongoing challenge of balancing the aim to support workplace-directed human flourishing in a rather complex world.

The pandemic created a catalytic event that has infected every corner of business and organizational practices. It has offered a radical change to the nature of work, with much of the rapid responses focusing on back-of-the-napkin redefined continuity over carefully considered strategy for work productivity. The result has been a multi-year international pilot study on new ways of work, learning, and living characterized by flexibility, agility, continuity, and wellbeing (at times) [7]. Yet, do these work principles remain when the world resumes? Has the pilot created a successful environment for future work? Is the post-pandemic landscape the intervention activity required for scholars to create new ways of working, much like Luthans [8] argued for in the need for positive organizational behavior in the early 2000s.

In the same domain, Avolio and colleagues [9] began a discussion on the e-leader, and later updated its definition to highlight that e-leadership is:

> *"A social influence process embedded in both proximal and distal contexts mediated by AIT that can produce a change in attitudes, feelings, thinking, behavior, and performance" [10].*

Indeed, e-leadership has evolved since 2014, and has likely been accelerated and exacerbated in its use during and beyond the pandemic context. The context was seen as a particularly important conceptual addition between 2001 and 2014 [10], and this chapter seeks to prioritize this conceptual exploration.

In this chapter, I advance a position on the future state of work and organizing beyond the COVID-19 pandemic and do so through a theoretical lens of belongingness [11]. The pandemic literature has yet to progress towards clear theoretical positions on post-pandemic work. I will argue that through the sustained human need to belong, we can better understand how working from home, forms of work-based connectivity and technology, and emotional labor and wellbeing can inform the desired future work context. The positioned end-state is informed from a perspective of positive organizational scholarship, and the human pursuit of flourishing at work.

To advance this position, I begin with a theoretical framework that describes belongingness and the belongingness hypothesis. Following, I describe and justify the critical review approach taken, and continue to discuss connectivity, working from home, and future work redesign. The aim of these sections is to connect an understanding of what leaders can do to better understand and support their followers and staff as work begins to resume. Developing a leader's sense of context is a critical component that underpins diverse conceptualizations of leadership effectiveness [12, 13].

2. Theoretical framework

The belongingness hypothesis argues that humans have a "need to form and maintain strong, stable interpersonal relationships" [11]. Indeed, this hypothesis follows two criteria: a few frequent affectively positive interactions; and the interaction being sustained in a temporally stable mutual affective concern for wellbeing. Belonging, from one perspective, should be analyzed from three lenses: social and economic locations, identifications and emotional attachments, and ethical and political values [14]. In an individual's need to belong, and to become a person who "belongs," they seek intrapersonal and interpersonal attachments to membership, identity, origin, beliefs, and social or economic position. Interestingly, Yuval-Davis laments that the politics of belonging can pose socially constructed boundaries within which a normative person can feel they belong [14].

To provide an example, a person performatively articulates their sense of belonging, "I'm a coffee person" and the social and economic context may moderate their comfort in feeling they can belong to this group. This comment may garner respect among colleagues in the work lunchroom, as the majority likely share of their membership to this group. But such discussions may turn political if followed with "I love kopi luwak," the most expensive and ethically questionable coffee bean. Kopi luwak is the practice of a civit (a catlike creature) partially digesting coffee beans to remove the acidity. This may begin a conversation of competing attachments to ethical values or personal constitution. By this, individual's ability to feel they belong to particular groups may be promoted by socially constructed ideas of being and alienated away from socially unappealing ideals. While established standards for how belonging might occur within existing workplace settings exist (e.g., the post-meeting water cooler conversations), the hybrid digital and face-to-face work environment is driven by pandemic-based lockdowns could reinvent some of these practices.

To extend, existing identities can create a sense of belongingness uncertainty. In one study, students were led to believe they would have few friends in their intellectual domain. White students were unaffected, black students saw a reduced sense of belonging. In a follow-up on mitigating doubts, a shared intervention raised the academic success of black students, but not white [15]. Belongingness uncertainty, as I discuss throughout, is likely to be an unconscious factor that will challenge the extent to which employees may attach themselves and their "worker" identity to their physical workplaces, their home office, or somewhere else. As organizations return to work, there will be a need to consider how employees make sense of their redefined attachment to their colleagues, and to their workplaces.

A focus on understanding and cultivating the human sense of belonging has occurred in education [7, 16], politics [14], and psychology [15]. In this research, I focus on applying aggregate team-level belongingness as a key theoretical foundation for understanding the future design of work. If the belongingness hypothesis [11] holds true, then an individual's feel a sense of belonging to their interpersonal workplace relationships and their sense of individual workplace identity will form a core foundation for how they engage or reengage with work and their organization.

3. Method

This research adopts a critical review method to advance an understanding of the future state of work and organizing beyond the COVID-19 pandemic and do so through a theoretical lens of belongingness. I modeled this work on one of the most significant critical reviews in the field [17]. The focus of this chapter is on creating a clear understanding of how leaders can understand the contextual conditions affecting staff and followers' sense of belonging. While systematic and metanalytic reviews are typically more rigorous, they require an established domain of literature. This chapter focuses on literature and practice that while may have some roots in existing scholarly works, is situated in a context that is largely unknown. Sense of belonging has had a limited discussion in the pandemic literature [7], yet within a future post-pandemic state of work, it requires a critical lens. This critical lens that I apply is focused on examining how existing literature can be synthesized to create a better understanding of the future of work. This remains one of the greatest challenges for post-pandemic leaders.

4. Discussion

4.1 Connectivity

Mutually effective human relationships are a key foundation for a sense of belonging. Prior to the pandemic, work was a common place to meet future friends. However, these relationships tended to have mixed effects on individual wellbeing and workplace performance. While work friendships created higher productivity through trust, creativity, and satisfaction [18], there is also a dark side [19, 20]. These informal social structures, while difficult to adequately capture, likely generate an indirect attachment to workplaces. The morning group coffee, expression of individual-level organizational citizenship behavior on late-night overtime, and establishment of communal norms support individuals to be connected to their peers and their work.

In the early modernist workplace, friendships were likely formed through mutual self-disclosure [21] and perceived similarity [22]. This likely took place in overtime work meetings, the "knock-off drinks," and the indirect or direct benefits attached to physical and proximal workplace connections (e.g., preferential application of existing rules [21]). Contemporary technologies affect this. In one study, social proof (e.g., mutual group membership or group identification) was a central decision rule for when individuals "accept" an online friend request from a person they do not know on Facebook [23]. Yet, there is scant evidence for how digital ways of working affect individual connections in workplaces. Initial pandemic evidence highlights the shift to working from home created higher rates of loneliness, depression, and suicidal ideation [24]. If working from home is poised as a staple in the return, the effect on those employees beginning their career, or with low social supports, may see the greatest risk.

If the return to work includes heightened face-to-face time, it could include elements of social hypochondria, suspicion, and distrust. The return to work arrived with emotional vulnerability for those who are returning, it may also create forms of in/out-group dynamics with those who were employed pre-pandemic and those new employees. New employees will have only engaged with their peers in limited face-to-face capacity; in parts of the world with large-scale lockdowns, perhaps not at all. Arslan found, however, that perceived belongingness to an organization tended to curve individual effects on loneliness [25]. Effective belongingness approaches therefore may engender a more supportive return climate.

In a review of e-leadership [10], a focus on individual, dyadic, and group level leadership was considered. Importantly, a perspective of affective, cognitive, and behavioral attitudes was applied to understanding how e-leadership exists across multiple groups. Connections as the dyadic level are enabled through leaders supporting haptic and emotional recognition and response drivers [26].

The informal organization is an environment by which individuals organize by self-defined means, often within the confines of formal organizational boundaries. This can take shape in the form of social group outings, the selective Secret Santa the boss did not organize, or weekend getaways. As discussed, workplace friendships can create such informality, but also be a place where work is discussed and decided in the absence of full consultation. These environments will likely be more complex when human connectivity is based on primarily digital interactions. In one study, the Sunflower Movement tended to use social media for its promotional activities rather than networking [27], with an assumption that such networking likely took place in offline environments. The proposition proposed by Metaverse rebranding (Facebook parent company) also suggests growing supply-driven movements within the online social landscapes. In a primarily online workplace, therefore, individuals are likely to make their friendships outside of work or sustain workplace relationships with peers they can meet in person.

Likewise, in hybrid workplaces, it will likely be those best equipped for work (e.g., social, or economic resources) that will be able to make more informal connections through physical proximity. Observational mobile phone data was found to predict 95% of friendship dyads based on their extra-role behaviors (e.g., proximity outside of work hours [28]). These relationships may have formed during work hours; however, they appear to be sustained through out-of-hours social activity. This speaks to suggest that despite potential pursuits of organizations to establish positive social relationships among workers, their role may largely be in generating a spark rather than fanning the flame. An understanding such as this creates optimism among some cynical data on the future of work embedded in the online. It offers assurance that with the right forms of organizational connection, that strong interpersonal bonds may remain possible within work teams.

For leaders to facilitate a connection in purely online and hybrid work environments, effort needs to go to examining the ways organizations facilitate work meet-and-greets. Lambert et al. [29] highlight that across multiple contexts, individuals who were primed with a sense of belonging, social support, or social value had heightened levels of perceived meaningfulness. Organizations therefore may not see the same value they once saw in the casual morning teas in the office and need to be more creative in their approaches to generating social goodwill between their employees.

4.2 Working from home

Working from home is not a new concept, but perhaps its current and prospective application during and beyond the pandemic offers novelty. While working from home was often seen, stylized, and reserved for graphic designers and their MacBook in cafes, cultural norms surrounding working from home are beginning to evolve. The literature is also proliferating in recent years on the topic. Google Scholar reports 20,500 results for "working from home" between 2020 and November 2021. Contrast this to 2000–2019 (16,900 results), and pre-2000 (2520 results). While some evidence argues that previous resistance provides a precedent that the working from home reality will not occur as a "new normal" [30], others argue its benefits [31].

Organizational change literature often discusses iterative changes [32], where changes often evolve over time. For working from home individuals, the likely resistance to return to a regimented and rigid environment, any iterative return to hybrid or fully onsite work may lead to resistance. Indeed, while some individual differences characterized the likelihood of voluntary flexible work designs [33], employees who have engaged in working from home have higher rates of positivity towards the flexible work arrangements [34]. This may speak to adoption models whereby broad acceptance may not always emerge until innovators and early adopters have sustained engagement with the "new" way of working. The design of flexible working from home environments however require careful consideration, as I will go on to discuss.

To provide an example from the working from home scholarship, I present unique differences in our understanding in pre-and during-pandemic environments. Working from home experiment at the NASDAQ-listed travel agency Ctrip (n = 249, [31]), identified a 13% increase in performance, with 9% from working more minutes per shift (e.g., less sick leave and fewer breaks), and 4% to call efficiency (e.g., quieter environment shortening call durations). Yet, despite higher employee satisfaction and retention, performance-based promotion rates declined by 50%. Compare this case study to 2020, a working paper surveying 30,000 U.S. workers argue a move from 5to 20% of work time being conducted from home, with an implied 5% gain in productivity in a post-pandemic environment [35].

To explore some of the potential pitfalls of the limited understanding of working from home, the use of existing primarily digital tools may be used as a parallel. In more established online transitions, the Tinder Revolution can be drawn on to understand how we move key components of our lives online. Emergent evidence on online dating indicates 18–25% of Tinder users were in committed relationships, and that these individuals tended to have more casual sexual behavior [36]. Likewise, compulsive use of the app tended to create worse outcomes for individual wellbeing [37]. The progression online during the pandemic likely had similar effects to employee wellbeing: a key focus of effective leaders. Yet, the context still only represents inertia with rapid change. New ways of working, that leverage online connectivity, may require adaption of existing resource deployment to support a technologically connected and physically disconnected workplace. Importantly, the diminished trustworthiness of some in the online dating environment may point to a greater need for training that supports positive character, virtue, and ethical leadership [38, 39]. Leaders build environments that enable commitment, yet if online environments have reduced psychological attachment to existing commitments for employees (or followers), the existing leader and organizational commitment relationships [40] may not as easily apply to the digital context.

This is salient with arguments that while it may be easier to lie online, issue moral intensity may change the outcome [41]. For virtue-based organizational scholarship [42], a focus on doing something for its inherent good may also be a factor, as opposed to consequentialist perspectives that focus on the potential outcome of the lie. The prospective dark side of working from home will be the reduced moral threshold that individuals – without effectively cultivated moral identities – require to make an unethical decision. In practice, a dyad member may find it much easier to "ghost" an individual when their pair is only visible through digital means than if they were next-door neighbors, had adjacent work offices, or shared a favorite morning coffee routine. While the focus of this chapter was not on leaders, dark side leadership [43] will still have the capacity to take place in online environments.

Returning to how working from home may change the way individuals work, Brown et al. identify that technology used for communication, can satisfy the need to belong, but it tends to follow suite with a higher interest in physical interaction [44]. This means that telework models have the propensity to be successful in cultivating human flourishing, but by different means. An individual pivot may be required, and the visibility of home environments (e.g., Zoom backgrounds) may capture unique vulnerabilities. Likewise, the use of artificial video backgrounds or accessing video conferencing without cameras on can create perceived challenges to inclusion or honesty. Meaningful affective relationships tend to form through mutual disclosure, and where digital barriers are established, these environments may be less conducive to productive and high-quality relationship formation. This may especially be true of early-career or low financial resource professionals without adequate space for a dedicated office at home. For e-leaders, there will be changes needed to enable a focus on understanding how leader and follower authenticity changes with self-disclosure [10, 45].

Interestingly, and notwithstanding, is a question of absenteeism and presenteeism. In a study of 25,465 European workers, there was heightened sickness-based presenteeism [46]. This was highest in individuals who teleworked daily and several times a week, contrasted to those less often and never teleworking. For this, employees who were sick attended work more frequently when this was able to be home-based work. The reduced barriers (infection risk, travel, work attire) may have supplemented this, yet it can lead to self-exploitation. Critically, individuals who have trust-based working time tended to self-report higher presenteeism than those with fixed schedules [47]. The potential normalization also creates risks within the working from home environment. On one side, employee monitoring can be deployed to assure productivity, yet much of the theoretical evidence is inconclusive as to the benefits and costs [48, 49]. Yet, where there are home environments involved that employees do not wish to show their Zoom background for, it is quite likely that a decision to implement monitoring in home offices would cause controversy. These vulnerabilities may create pause for followers as they seek to engage effectively with their managers and leaders. Instead, there perhaps is a required need to support effective and flexible workplaces, there may be a need to support high-quality character building as a safeguard against employee deceit; such an approach has greater potential for long-term success than rigid policies. Leaders are, at least in part, measured on their capacity to enable organizational outcomes and absenteeism and presenteeism can create an impediment to such achievement. Leaders have a direct effect on absenteeism, particularly ethical leaders [39]. However, the online environment will make responsiveness to absenteeism and presenteeism less visible (e.g., an empty office versus staff in a blank Zoom meeting room).

4.3 Redesign of work

The third pillar characterizing new forms of work is redesign. In this, there is a need to examine workflow from a new model. This may seem intuitively salient, yet it is not how much of the pandemic response looked like. In the immediate response, there was sustained evidence of an adapt-to-survive mentality. For some organizations, this was taking a seemingly always face-to-face service and delivering these digitally. These ranged from telehealth consultations using Zoom [49], university curriculums being digitalized [50], to boutique restaurants delivering high-end takeaway [51]. These models have created a form of continuity during uncertainty, yet they also likely contain practices that are yet to be effectively assessed for quality. Indeed, while online education may be possible to enable quality outcomes, online education that is simply recorded versions of face-to-face content is likely lower in quality.

Currently, many sector leaders are innovating new business products and services to support their financial viability; yet, when the pandemic ends, what of those things will remain in their existing form? Indeed, it may be their temporal relevance that supports their profitability or their embeddedness in current work. Whereas Zoom, Microsoft Teams, and similar offer high quality and increasingly popular products, what form do these take in an organization that chooses to have only face-to-face meetings? Or how do organizations move to adapt to hybrid meetings where such products and their rooms are not equipped for adaptive user experiences. This limited example offers important insight – whereas some pandemic-produced products and services may sustain, others may be immediately irrelevant, or require rapid innovation.

In the redesign of work too, is a need to reflect on the changing leader-follower and peer-to-peer power dynamics and organizational cultures that existed during the lockdown periods. While full videoconference meetings have varied perspectives of equity [52], there are invariably challenges that will emerge in an environment where some participants attend by videoconference and others attend in person. This will likely be exacerbated by situations where there is a limited number of participants online, and the majority in person. Such satellite meeting situations can create an environment that preferences those in the room (i.e., ignoring the screen), the person on Zoom (i.e., overemphasized interactions from online participants), but rarely balance participation. In leader-member exchange, the emergence of in- and out-groups is common when leaders prioritize their time with those, they have stronger affective relationships with [53]. When mutually affective relationships are considered, leaders may have better employment relationships with those they can see informally more easily (e.g., in-person) [54]. Leader-follower dynamics that exist in temporally consistent but spatially inconsistent locations will be challenging. Organizational politics is likely to add to that complexity [55]. The potential to create an inequitable scenario does require an address.

Many of the assumptions so far have focused on a return-state environment; that is, one where employees employed before the pandemic are returning in some way. This is unlikely to be true, however, with many employees never having met their colleagues in a face-to-face environment yet. In socialization resources theory, identification of resources required for new employees to be successful in their adjustment and socialization is critical for their role longevity [56]. In a return environment, existing employees will return to a different environment than they left in; and this may require adjustment support. However, those individuals who may be entering the physical workplace for the first time will have an unpredictable set of needs and wants to be associated with their acclimatization with geographically specific work conditions. According to Feldman's model of organizational socialization, there are three stages: anticipatory socialization, accommodation, and role definition [57]. Some employees may have been initiated to their tasks and adapt to them (stage one), completed initiations and been accepted in (stage two), and have an established work-life balance (stage three). Yet, when they move from distance to face-to-face, some of these elements will require re-socialization. Where an employee may have once started work "late" and finished "early," they may now need to factor in a train ride causing a stage three reset.

Indeed, the redesign of work may also be an opportunity for a critical review of the existing and residual workplace structures that existed during the modernist pursuit for order. Some of these elements (e.g., fixed timesheets, specialization-based job design, and neat corporate hierarchies) could be assessed for their relative value to the contemporary workforce. If the worker now operates more flexibly, perhaps roles should follow outcomes rather than hours completed. Likewise, if informal organizations provide enormous influence in the formal structure, then should the role they play also be more effectively acknowledged and moderated. Are there ways that positive emotions can be embedded into organizational life [58] to create conditions for human flourishing? Are the organizational constraints actually hindering productivity as much as enabling it? This too, when built on a foundation of belonging also seeks to ask how this might be possible through high quality mutually affective relationships at work.

5. Conclusions

5.1 Theoretical contributions

This chapter focused on the application of the belongingness hypothesis to the future post-pandemic landscape. Leadership theory will be challenged by being conceptually adaptive within the new context, examining what concepts from the broader domain of leadership still holds true when conventional physical proximity changes. Indeed, leader distance has been studied [59, 60] and offers conceptual ambiguity when physical distance is both near and far. Early twenty-first century studies articulate that leader-follower physical distance affects performance [60, 61], this research extended to pose new questions surrounding hybrid environments where a leader has mixed proximal distance from their followers.

Additionally, in presenting the belongingness hypothesis in the post-pandemic organization, there is an opportunity for scholars to begin to better understand how leader-follower dyads are formed and maintained when the environmental conditions are not "traditional." That is, when leaders and followers are: i) sometimes face-to-face and sometimes online (e.g., hybrid); ii) always online (e.g., distance work); and iii) rarely face-to-face (e.g., attending annual events only). The chapter poses questions about the future climate of leadership and invites scholars to continue to examine how leader effectiveness may be enabled in increasingly.

5.2 Practical contributions

There are numerous practical contributions offered in this chapter. Leaders must suspend some of their pre-existing assumptions established in the pre-pandemic environment. While the primary brunt of the pandemic will only last a few years, the rapid digitalization and workforce change observed over this time has likely affected ongoing attitudes towards work. Followers will have different perceptions about the value of attending a physical workplace, and productivity and work teams will be affected as a result. This chapter articulates that effective leaders will need to seek out new environmental conditions to enable their teams to be effective. One way is to enable high-performing teams is through building ongoing and sustained relationships that are built on mutual affective concern for each other's wellbeing. From a practical perspective, this could include establishing replacements for the previous on-campus activities.

5.3 Conclusion

This chapter offered a position on the future state of work and organizing beyond the COVID-19 pandemic. I did this by applying the lens of the belongingness hypothesis. That is, what value is created and what challenges emerge in the current state of work when viewed from a perspective of interpersonal belonging? Within this chapter, connectivity was described as a key challenge. Physical proximity to others supports sustained relationships, and individual assumptions about the relative value of the work contexts in forming meaningful relationships may also offer complexity. Likewise, the influence that digital technologies had on perspectives of working from home was also discussed. The hybrid and flexibility models of work can create inequities within enterprises through inconsistent applications of rules, technologies, and different baselines of moral character. Finally, this chapter discussed how the redesign of work affected future productivity and work-life balance. As the return-state begins, there will be a diverse range of individuals at staggering levels of socialization, and managers may find it difficult to adequately monitor those socialization journeys. This chapter offers a position of hope though, as the potential for humans to build a more enriching and fulfilling workplace may be enabled through support flexibility, but not without appropriate boundaries for working.

Conflict of interest

The authors declare no conflict of interest.

Author details

Joseph Crawford
University of Tasmania, Launceston, Australia

*Address all correspondence to: joseph.crawford@utas.edu.au

References

[1] Paul SK, Chowdhury P. Strategies for managing the impacts of disruptions during COVID-19: An example of toilet paper. Global Journal of Flexible Systems Management. 2020;**21**(3): 283-293

[2] Kefalaki M, Rudolph J, Tan S, Diamantidaki F. Face masks in education: The cases of Greece and Singapore. Thesis. 2021;**10**(1):3-42

[3] Durkheim E. The division of labor in society. Published Dissertation. Translated by G. Simpson. United States of America: Free Press of Glenco, Illinois; 1960

[4] Conger JA. Max Weber's conceptualization of charismatic authority: Its influence on organizational research. The Leadership Quarterly. 1993;**4**(3-4):277-288

[5] Weber M. From Max Weber: Essays in Sociology. Abingdon, Oxon: Routledge; 2013

[6] Taylor FW. Scientific Management: Reply from Mr. FW Taylor. The Sociological Review. 1914;**7**(3):266-269

[7] Tice D, Baumeister R, Crawford J, Allen KA, Percy A. Student belongingness in higher education: Lessons for professors from the COVID-19 pandemic. Journal of University Teaching and Learning Practice. 2021;**18**(4):2

[8] Luthans F. The need for and meaning of positive organizational behavior. Journal of Organizational Behavior. 2002;**23**(6):695-706

[9] Avolio BJ, Kahai S, Dodge GE. E-leadership: Implications for theory, research, and practice. The Leadership Quarterly. 2000;**11**(4):615-668

[10] Avolio BJ, Sosik JJ, Kahai SS, Baker B. E-leadership: Re-examining transformations in leadership source and transmission. The Leadership Quarterly. 2014;**25**(1):105-131

[11] Baumeister RF, Leary MR. The need to belong: desire for interpersonal attachments as a fundamental human motivation. Psychological Bulletin. 1995;**117**(3):497

[12] Antonakis J, Avolio BJ, Sivasubramaniam N. Context and leadership: An examination of the nine-factor full-range leadership theory using the multifactor leadership questionnaire. The Leadership Quarterly. 2003;**14**(3):261-295

[13] Hannah ST, Uhl-Bien M, Avolio BJ, Cavarretta FL. A framework for examining leadership in extreme contexts. The Leadership Quarterly. 2009;**20**(6):897-919

[14] Yuval-Davis N. Belonging and the politics of belonging. Patterns of prejudice. 2006;**40**(3):197-214

[15] Walton GM, Cohen GL. A question of belonging: Race, social fit, and achievement. Journal of Personality and Social Psychology. 2007;**92**(1):82

[16] Allen K, Kern ML, Vella-Brodrick D, Hattie J, Waters L. What schools need to know about fostering school belonging: A meta-analysis. Educational Psychology Review. 2018;**30**(1):1-34

[17] Podsakoff PM, MacKenzie SB, Lee JY, Podsakoff NP. Common method biases in behavioral research: A critical review of the literature and recommended remedies. Journal of Applied Psychology. 2003;**88**(5):879

[18] Sias PM, Gallagher EB, Kopaneva I, Pedersen H. Maintaining workplace friendships: Perceived politeness and predictors of maintenance tactic choice. Communication Research. 2012;**39**(2): 239-268

[19] Methot JR, Lepine JA, Podsakoff NP, Christian JS. Are workplace friendships a mixed blessing? Exploring tradeoffs of multiplex relationships and their associations with job performance. Personnel Psychology. 2016;**69**(2): 311-355

[20] Pillemer J, Rothbard NP. Friends without benefits: Understanding the dark sides of workplace friendship. Academy of Management Review. 2018;**43**(4):635-660

[21] Derfler-Rozin R, Sherf EN, Chen G. To be or not to be consistent? The role of friendship and group-targeted perspective in managers' allocation decisions. Journal of Organizational Behavior. 2021;**42**(6):814-833

[22] Byrne D. Interpersonal attraction and attitude similarity. The Journal of Abnormal and Social Psychology. 1961;**62**(3):713

[23] Belentschikow V, Pfeffel K, Müller NH. Making friends on Facebook: Common group membership as a central decision rule. Computers in Human Behavior. 2022;**126**:107040

[24] Killgore WD, Cloonan SA, Taylor EC, Miller MA, Dailey NS. Three months of loneliness during the COVID-19 lockdown. Psychiatry Research. 2020;**293**:113392

[25] Arslan G. Loneliness, college belongingness, subjective vitality, and psychological adjustment during coronavirus pandemic: Development of the college belongingness questionnaire. Journal of Positive School Psychology. 2021;**5**(1):17-31

[26] MacLean KE. Haptic interaction design for everyday interfaces. Reviews of Human Factors and Ergonomics. 2008;**4**(1):149-194

[27] Tsatsou P. Social media and informal organisation of citizen activism: Lessons from the use of Facebook in the sunflower movement. Social Media+ Society. 2018;**4**(1): 2056305117751384

[28] Eagle N, Pentland AS, Lazer D. Inferring friendship network structure by using mobile phone data. Proceedings of the National Academy of Sciences. 2009;**106**(36):15274-15278

[29] Lambert NM, Stillman TF, Hicks JA, Kamble S, Baumeister RF, Fincham FD. To belong is to matter: Sense of belonging enhances meaning in life. Personality and Social Psychology Bulletin. 2013;**39**(11):1418-1427

[30] Williamson S, Colley L, Hanna-Osborne S. Will working from home become the 'new normal' in the public sector? Australian Journal of Public Administration. 2020;**79**(4): 601-607

[31] Bloom N, Liang J, Roberts J, Ying ZJ. Does working from home work? Evidence from a Chinese experiment. The Quarterly Journal of Economics. 2015;**130**(1):165-218

[32] Rosenbaum D, More E, Steane P. Planned organisational change management: Forward to the past? An exploratory literature review. Journal of Organizational Change Management. 2018;**31**(2):286-303

[33] Lambert AD, Marler JH, Gueutal HG. Individual differences: Factors affecting employee utilization of flexible work arrangements. Journal of Vocational Behavior. 2008;**73**(1):107-117

[34] Giannikis SK, Mihail DM. Flexible work arrangements in Greece: A study of employee perceptions. The International Journal of Human Resource Management. 2011;**22**(02): 417-432

[35] Barerro J, Bloom N, Davis S. Why working from home will stick. Working

Paper 28731. National Bureau of Economic Research Working Paper Series. 2021. Available from: https://www.nber.org/system/files/working_papers/w28731/w28731.pdf

[36] Timmermans E, De Caluwe E, Alexopoulos C. Why are you cheating on tinder? Exploring users' motives and (dark) personality traits. Computers in Human Behavior. 2018;**89**:129-139

[37] Her YC, Timmermans E. Tinder blue, mental flu? Exploring the associations between tinder use and well-being. Information, Communication and Society. 2021;**24**(9):1303-1319

[38] Newstead T, Dawkins S, Macklin R, Martin A. The virtues project: An approach to developing good leaders. Journal of Business Ethics. 2020;**167**(4): 605-622

[39] Hassan S, Wright BE, Yukl G. Does ethical leadership matter in government? Effects on organizational commitment, absenteeism, and willingness to report ethical problems. Public Administration Review. 2014;**74**(3):333-343

[40] Eisenberger R, Karagonlar G, Stinglhamber F, Neves P, Becker TE, Gonzalez-Morales MG, et al. Leader–member exchange and affective organizational commitment: The contribution of supervisor's organizational embodiment. Journal of Applied psychology. 2010;**95**(6):1085

[41] Logsdon JM, Patterson KD. Deception in business networks: Is it easier to lie online? Journal of Business Ethics. 2009;**90**(4):537-549

[42] Newstead T. Being explicit about virtues: Analysing TED talks and integrating scholarship to advance virtues-based leadership development. Journal of Business Ethics. 2021:1-19

[43] Liu D, Liao H, Loi R. The dark side of leadership: A three-level investigation of the cascading effect of abusive supervision on employee creativity. Academy of management journal. 2012;**55**(5):1187-1212

[44] Brown M, Young SG, Sacco DF. Competing motives in a pandemic: Interplays between fundamental social motives and technology use in predicting (non) compliance with social distancing guidelines. Computers in Human Behavior. 2021;**106892**

[45] Klotz AC, Buckley MR. A historical perspective of counterproductive work behavior targeting the organization. Journal of Management History. 2013;**4**

[46] Steidelmüller C, Meyer SC, Müller G. Home-based telework and presenteeism across Europe. Journal of Occupational and Environmental Medicine. 2020;**62**(12):998

[47] Ball K. Workplace surveillance: An overview. Labor History. 2010;**51**(1): 87-106

[48] Martin K, Freeman RE. Some problems with employee monitoring. Journal of Business Ethics. 2003;**43**(4): 353-361

[49] Monaghesh E, Hajizadeh A. The role of telehealth during COVID-19 outbreak: A systematic review based on current evidence. BMC Public Health. 2020;**20**(1):1-9

[50] Crawford J, Butler-Henderson K, Rudolph J, Malkawi B, Glowatz M, Burton R, et al. COVID-19: 20 countries' higher education intra-period digital pedagogy responses. Journal of Applied Learning and Teaching. 2020;**3**(1):1-20

[51] Kostromitina M, Keller D, Cavusoglu M, Beloin K. "His lack of a mask ruined everything." Restaurant customer satisfaction during the COVID-19 outbreak: An analysis of Yelp review texts and star-ratings. International Journal of Hospitality Management. 2021;**98**:103048

[52] Tienken CH. The not so subtle inequity of remote learning. Kappa Delta Pi Record. 2020;**56**(4):151-153

[53] Cropanzano R, Dasborough MT, Weiss HM. Affective events and the development of leader-member exchange. Academy of Management Review. 2017;**42**(2):233-258

[54] Audenaert M, Vanderstraeten A, Buyens D. When affective well-being is empowered: The joint role of leader-member exchange and the employment relationship. The International Journal of Human Resource Management. 2017;**28**(15):2208-2227

[55] Kimura T. The moderating effects of political skill and leader–member exchange on the relationship between organizational politics and affective commitment. Journal of Business Ethics. 2013;**116**(3):587-599

[56] Saks AM, Gruman JA. Getting newcomers on board: A review of socialization practices and introduction to socialization resources theory. In: The Oxford Handbook of Organizational Socialization. 2012. pp. 27-55

[57] Feldman DC. The multiple socialization of organization members. Academy of Management Review. 1981;**6**(2):309-318

[58] Fredrickson BL, Losada MF. Positive affect and the complex dynamics of human flourishing. American Psychologist. 2005;**60**(7):678

[59] Antonakis J, Atwater L. Leader distance: A review and a proposed theory. The Leadership Quarterly. 2002;**13**(6):673-704

[60] Howell JM, Neufeld DJ, Avolio BJ. Examining the relationship of leadership and physical distance with business unit performance. The Leadership Quarterly. 2005;**16**(2):273-285

[61] Meirovich G, Goswami A. Psychosocial and Tangible Distance Between a Leader and a Follower: The Impact on Dyadic Relations. Journal of Leadership Studies. 2021;**14**(4):6-20

Chapter 8

Do Organizations Need Emotionally Intelligent Leadership at the Workplace?

Anurag Mishra

Abstract

Organization is a group of people who are joining together to perform specific tasks. Every organization has a different set of policies and practices which an individual needs to follow. An organization includes teams and team members who have to perform specific tasks on a daily basis. People have to perform their work by proper communication, trust and integrity. Due to lack of these three attributes, conflicts arise among the team members which cause the conditions of anxiety, depression, anger and mood variation, improper response to top management, counter productivity and errors in tasks performance. To overcome such a situation, there is a need for an appropriate style of leadership which can help teams to perform well. The performance of a team depends upon the nature of leadership styles. The kind of leadership style adopted by leaders is sometimes not appropriate completely. To apply appropriate leadership in a particular situation, there is a need to be emotionally intelligent at the workplace. I would like to build a proper relationship between how the traits of Emotional Intelligence will influence positively on the leadership efficiency in organizations. Key findings of the study have focused on the impact of emotional intelligence on organizational growth. The given model has recommended that people with high emotional intelligence can build effective communication, trust and integrity in a team. The attempt has also been made to build a relationship between emotional intelligence and the nature of leadership styles to be adopted in organizations. The finding suggested that transformational style of leadership should be encouraged in an organization. The study of the mentioned topic will help in understanding individual and collective behavior and its effect on the quality of work.

Keywords: Leadership, Emotional Intelligence, Trust, Integrity, Communication

1. Introduction

In the current scenario, due to rapidly changing technology, organizations need to work on those areas which can provide them an edge over others at the workplace. Within an organization, team members have people with different sets of perceptions and personalities. The complexity of tasks and newer technologies have made organizations adapt to new ways of building and maintaining relationships to accomplish organizational goals. Along with the task at hand, there are feelings and emotions of employees that play a major role in building relationships.

How to manage those relationships? What are the best practices to be used in organizations to build those relationships between seniors and subordinates? How to build those relationships for a longer time? These are the major challenges.

To overcome such challenges, there is a need for an adequate style of leadership practices. The proper leadership style can mobilize the team and influence the team members. Leadership can help to build confidence, provide direction to employees, increase motivation and improve efficiency of the employees. A good leadership style can provide job satisfaction, hope and optimism. A good leader can bring out the best abilities of the team members for achieving shared goals. A good leadership style can come by enhancing the level of emotional intelligence. Emotional intelligence is the ability of understanding the feelings and emotions of ourselves and at the same time of the people around us. The capability of understanding emotions and control of emotions can make leaders successful in the organizations. Being able to handle emotions makes it less stressful when we deal with others. A team's emotional intelligence is related to inter-team conflict management and effectiveness of the team. In the cross-sectional study of five south Korean companies: Banking, Investment, Health care, Information technology, and Pharmaceutical industries, results stated that there is a significant relationship between Emotional intelligence and task conflict management [1].

Team leader's emotional intelligence has a positive effect on team's emotional intelligence. The capability of dealing with emotional ups and downs is a powerful asset for building and maintaining relationships. Emotional intelligence is a significant predictor of positive leadership outcomes. This in turn can help in the building good client relationships and business growth for an organization. Emotional intelligence is associated with leadership which can bring effective business outcomes [2].

Emotional intelligence can bring positive business, improve team work, customer service and manage diversity [3]. It is also helpful in recruitment, selection, training and development process at managerial level [4].

Positive emotions such as happiness, joy, hope and enthusiasm have a positive impact on the growth of an organization whereas negative emotions such as anger, disgust, jealousy and frustration brings negativity in an organization. Leaders need to handle their emotions based on the situation. Being emotionally intelligent can help in management of interpersonal relationships within the organizations. Leaders can be more competent in their day to day activities by being aware of the emotional states of people around them. As per previous studies, leaders having low levels of emotional intelligence have difficulty in building good relationships with peers, subordinates and superiors. However, leaders with strong minds can understand others as well and develop better working abilities. The positive leaders emotions bring positive outcomes whereas negative leaders emotions bring negative outcomes [5, 6].

The contemporary study, have attempted to measure the relationship between EI and organizational performance. The results stated that self-awareness, self-management and awareness of others have significant impact on organizational performance [7]. However the study have recommended the future research on role of leadership styles in organization performance. Emotional intelligence is a helpful tool for conflict management, organizational commitment, team effectiveness and task performance. The study also emphasizes cross cultural transportability of EI which needs to be explored [8].

In another study it has been emphasis that employees performance is dependent upon the emotional intelligence, organization culture and adapted leadership style. However which leadership style to be adopted is the question? [9]. Emotional intelligence works as a mediating variable between leadership and organizational commitment. Emotional intelligence leaders can motivate workers to achieve organizations goals [10]. The study among academic leaders have measured the relationship between emotional intelligence and transformational style of leadership. Findings states that direct association between emotional intelligence and transformational leadership [11].

The above studies made an attempt to build a relationship between emotional intelligence and leadership within organizations. Many of the previous theories and studies have looked into the role of emotional intelligence and its positive impact on certain leadership styles in an organization. Researchers have tested and developed models of emotional intelligence for effectiveness of leadership in an organization.

However, there has not been much attention given to find out the association between emotional intelligence and leadership through the variables of trust, integrity and communication. The current study is an attempt to fulfill this gap by adopting these three major components to create an understanding whether the organizations need an emotionally intelligent leadership at the workplace?

Leadership and emotional intelligence are interrelated to each other. The current chapter is going to provide the relationship between emotional intelligence and leadership styles. Also how much do the organizations require to adapt the practices of emotional intelligence to be successful? It is going to address the importance of emotional intelligence within organizations. It will also focus on the styles of leadership which organizations should adopt. By presenting the theories on emotional intelligence and leadership styles, the primary focus has been given to a proposed model that defines the relationship between the two with an emphasis on three major variables of trust, integrity and effective communication. The underlying issues in an organization have been addressed along with suitable suggestions and practical implications.

2. Emotional intelligence

The current changing trends and globalization have raised the level of competitiveness among the organizations. The success of any organization depends upon the maturity level and job performance of employees. The level of maturity is based upon the level of emotional intelligence.

2.1 Mayer and Salovey model

Mayer and Salovey defined Emotional Intelligence (El) as "the ability to monitor one's own and others' feelings and emotions, to discriminate among them and to use this information to guide one's thinking and actions"([12], p. 189). Emotional intelligence is the understanding and management of emotions in appropriate manner to respond consciously and make others comfortable at work.

According to Salovey and Mayer "emotional intelligence as the subset of social intelligence that involves the ability to monitor one's own and others' feelings and emotions, to discriminate among them and to use this information to guide one's thinking and actions" ([13], pg. 5). As per above definitions we can conclude that our own feelings guide intrapersonal skills that include how to conduct oneself, Self-motivation, Inner self control and interpersonal skills which include interaction with other people in a society or in an organization. Emotional Intelligence involves the ability to monitor others moods, emotions and temperaments along with recognition of one's own emotions for solving work related problems. Emotional intelligence can provide a better understanding in the working environment.

Further, in the year 1997, Mayer and Salovey proposed the ability based model of emotional intelligence which has been called the cognitive based model of emotional intelligence. This model has been divided into four branches known as the Four branch model" [14].

The model contains four parts:

1. **Perception, Appraisal and Expression of emotions:** It includes identification of emotions and feelings of our own and people around us.

2. **Assimilation of emotions in thoughts:** Assimilation of emotions encourages us to think in productive ways.

3. **Understanding and Utilizations of emotional knowledge:** This component includes understanding of complex emotions and how they are linked to maintaining relationships with others.

4. **Managing of emotions:** It focuses on emotional, intellectual and personal growth by monitoring feelings and emotions.

Furthermore, Mayer et al. model was purely based on cognitive ability of an individual. It provided knowledge about our inner feelings and thoughts and the capability of understanding relationships based on shift of emotions. Leaders who have higher ability to regulate their emotions are appraised and they can also express their feelings in a positive manner with others [15]. However, the model did not suggest other aspects of emotional intelligence which can help organizations to manage their productivity, improve trust, remove conflicts and motivate employees to perform in a better manner.

2.2 Daniel Goleman model

In 1998, Daniel Goleman in his book *Working with emotional intelligence* came up with the new model of emotional intelligence which is called the 'Model of Affective Regulation'. Goleman has suggested emotional intelligence is the combination of *Personal Competencies and Social Competencies.* Personal competencies are those which help in managing yourself and social competencies are those who can help in managing our relationships. Goleman (1998) defined El as "the capacity for recognizing our own feelings and those of others, for motivating ourselves and for managing emotions well in ourselves and in our relationships" ([16], p. 317).

Goleman has divided emotional intelligence in two major competencies:

1. **Personal competencies:** These competencies help us to understand how to manage our emotions. It includes self-awareness, self-regulation and motivation. These competencies help in understanding our own emotions and develop self-confidence and trustworthiness. Similarly, it motivates us to take initiatives and provides readiness to respond to opportunities.

2. **Emotional competencies:** These competencies determine how we handle relationships. Empathy makes us understand others perspectives in an organization and creates political awareness. Social skills generate leadership styles and develop team handling capabilities.

Goleman has recommended that, to be an emotionally intelligent leader, there is a need for personal and social competencies in an organization. Further, he added the concept of "Emotional competencies" which includes empathy and flexibility. From his book working with emotional intelligence -"One common mistake made by organizations is trying to install emotional competencies like a service orientation or leadership, using the same techniques that effectively teach how to create a business plan which is not enough. Changing a habit based on emotional intelligence demands an entirely new kind of learning strategy. Cultivating emotional competence requires an understanding of the fundamentals of behavior change" ([16], p. 245).

2.3 Reuven Bar-on model

Reuven Bar-On has suggested the model of "Emotional and Social Intelligence". According to him "emotional-social intelligence is a cross-section of interrelated emotional and social competencies, skills and facilitators that determine how effectively we understand and express ourselves, understand others and relate with them, and cope with daily demands" ([17], p. 14). Bar-on's model includes five categories of emotional intelligence respectively: intrapersonal (emotional self-awareness, assertiveness, self-esteem, self-actualization and independence), interpersonal (empathy, interpersonal relationships and social responsibility), adaptability (problem solving, reality testing, flexibility), stress management (stress tolerance, impulse control) and general mood (happiness and optimism) [17, 18].

The above three models have suggested that emotional intelligence provides a competitive advantage to organizations that can help in maintaining good relationships within teams and with business clients. This will in turn facilitate an upward trajectory of growth. Today's business requires smart people who are not only smart at their work but also with their relationships.

3. Organizational leadership

3.1 Concepts of leadership

Organizational leadership is the strategic way of working for achievement of particular goals by influencing people to work in a productive manner. According to Conger ([19], p. 18) " Leaders are individuals who establish direction for a working group of individuals who gain commitment from these group of members to this direction and who then motivate these members to achieve the direction's outcomes" [19]. Similarly Stogdill stated that Leadership may be considered as the process (act) of influencing the activities of an organized group in its efforts towards goal setting and goal achievement [20].

Burns defined transformational leadership as occurring "when one or more persons engage with others in such a way that leaders and followers raise one another to higher levels of motivation and morality" Transformational leadership style inculcates morale and values among the employees ([21], p. 20).

Yukl defined transformational leadership as "the process of influencing major changes in the attitudes and assumptions of organization members and building commitment for the organization's mission or objectives" ([22], p. 204).

Based on the above studies, Bass has segregated the transformational and transactional styles of leadership. Transactional style of leadership provides clear goals and tasks. It also focuses on accomplishment of goals that provide rewards and punishments based on outcomes whereas transformational style of leadership encourages and boosts confidence among the team members. Bass and Avolio, has described the Four "Is "of transformational leadership styles. First is Idealized Influence (II) which displays a sense of power and confidence among followers and makes others proud by being associated with leaders. Second is Inspirational Motivation (IM) where leaders believe in optimistic talk about the future and shows confidence for achieving organizational goals. Third is Intellectual Stimulation (IS) where leaders help others to look into issues from different angles and give suggestions creatively for solving problems. Finally, Individual Consideration (IC) where leaders spend time with other team members, care about followers' needs and help them to develop their strengths [23, 24].

A good leadership style can provide mutual respect, better conflict management, transparency in work and clarity in decision making. Similarly, it also provides an ability to identify meaningfulness in work. However, for achieving such capabilities, there is a necessity to be an emotionally intelligent person.

In the current scenario, organizations are involved in the process of automations and improvement in quality of work done to achieve high demanded targets that may cause heavy workload. The good quality of work requires mental stability at the workplace. Mental stability can only come with self-confidence, flexibility in performing different tasks, self-awareness, building peer bonds and organizational awareness. As per (Goleman, pg. 220) "Research on decision making in management teams shows that having people who possess three qualities of high cognitive capabilities, diverse perspectives, and expertise leads to higher-quality decision making" [16].

The performance of a team depends upon the development and building of a competent leader. Moods and emotions of leaders impact on the performance of teams. However, an adequate style of leadership can help to build strong bonding with a team. Emotional intelligence is a measurful tool for understanding leadership effectiveness in an organization. Emotional intelligence can improve leaders ability to understand and manage the political environment [25].

In the study of Kerr et al., it has been stated that employee perceptions of supervisor's effectiveness are strongly related to the EI of the supervisor. The overall result states that an individual's EI is a key determinant of effective leadership [26]. Proper communication and confronting underperforming team members can only be gained by effective understanding of emotions at the workplace. The study of Ashkanasy and Dasborough have highlighted the importance of emotional intelligence and emotional awareness in an organization. Researchers have described how emotional intelligence has been incorporated into an undergraduate leadership course. The team performance is being predicted by emotional intelligence. Similarly, teaching about emotions and emotional intelligence in leadership courses can affect team performance [27]. Our emotional intelligence helps us to enhance our practical skills at the workplace. It also provides the ability to manage customer and client relationships. Emotional competencies such as trustworthiness and empathy can make an individual more successful in a team. Team performance and motivation of team members can only be built in a highly empathetic environment. If leaders are lacking emotional intelligence skills, they will be inept in leading teams or catalyzing change. The study of Humphrey and hawver have stated that during the conditions of uncertainty, leaders' emotional response i.e. leaders' optimistic emotional displays increase the positive moods and feelings of team members, whereas leaders' negative mood displays results in of frustration among team members [28].

3.2 Emotional intelligence and nature of leadership

Leadership determines how members in an organization interact with each other and the level of harmony among all. Collaboration and cooperation influence all to achieve a shared goal. Similarly, the capability of leaders builds strong professional bonds and creates synergy among team members.

The study of Colbert et al. stated that transformational style of leadership by top managers provides a dyadic relationship and harmony within a team for achievement of goals [29]. The awareness of leaders for adopting style of leaderships depending upon time and situation. Further, flexibility and emotional intelligence are the tools to bring organizational excellence which is need to be covered [30].

Transformational style of leadership is an approach which inspires followers towards their work. It also provides a suitable path for performing work and motivations for achievement of it. Transformational leadership style is significantly correlated with emotional intelligence. Hur et al. studied the role of transformational leadership and team outcome. They focused on the role of emotional intelligence and its effectiveness in organizational leadership and at group level among 859 employees, working in 55 teams in a South Korean public-sector organization. Results concluded a positive relationship between transformational leadership and emotional intelligence [31]. Koman and Koman have stated that team leader influences the team performance. Also, emotional intelligence is the mediator between the role of team leader, emotional competencies and team effectiveness. The study also suggested that organizations can develop emotionally competent groups to develop or hire emotionally competent managers [32]. One study of Milhem et al. states that employee engagement is influenced by transformational leadership style. Leader's emotional intelligence is working as a bridge between transformational leadership and employee engagement. For organizational development and employee engagement, leaders need to learn to develop high self-esteem and the art of influencing people at the workplace [33].

Transformational leadership style is more preferable as compared to transactional and laissez-faire. Emotionally intelligent leaders show concern towards their team members.

Gardner and Stough have examined the components of emotional intelligence and various leadership styles among the top managers. The Multifactor Leadership questionnaire (MLQ) and Swinburne University Emotional Intelligence Test (SUEIT) was conducted among 110 senior level managers. Findings of study concluded that transformational leadership was highly correlated to emotional intelligence as compared to transactional and laissez-faire styles of leadership. The technique of emotional management is helpful in understanding the positive and negative emotions of employees and themselves [34]. Similarly Palmer et al. determined the effect of emotional intelligence on effective leadership styles among 43 Participants of the Swinburne university center for innovation and enterprise programs (CIE). The results concluded that inspirational motivation and individual consideration components of transformational leadership were significantly correlated with both the ability to monitor and manage emotions in oneself and others [35].

4. Emotional intelligence, trust, integrity and effective communication in leadership

The above study has provided the nature of emotional intelligence which can work effectively within the organizations. The study has also proven that a mostly transformational style of leadership is more effective than other kinds of leadership styles. However, the question is whether there is an awareness related to application of transformational leadership styles at the workplace? Are there any training programs about the concepts and practical implications of emotional intelligence and its relatedness with leadership styles at the workplace? Previous researchers have emphasized on the requirement of application of emotional intelligence on leadership and it can be taught (**Figure 1**) [36, 37].

There is a significant impact of trust, integrity and effective communication in an organization. Here, I would like to propose a new model for effective leadership in an organization. This model is based on how emotional intelligence positively influences the three organizational factors of trust, integrity and effective communication. These three factors can be inculcated through practical knowledge of Emotional Intelligence which will in turn create effective and ethical leadership in organizations.

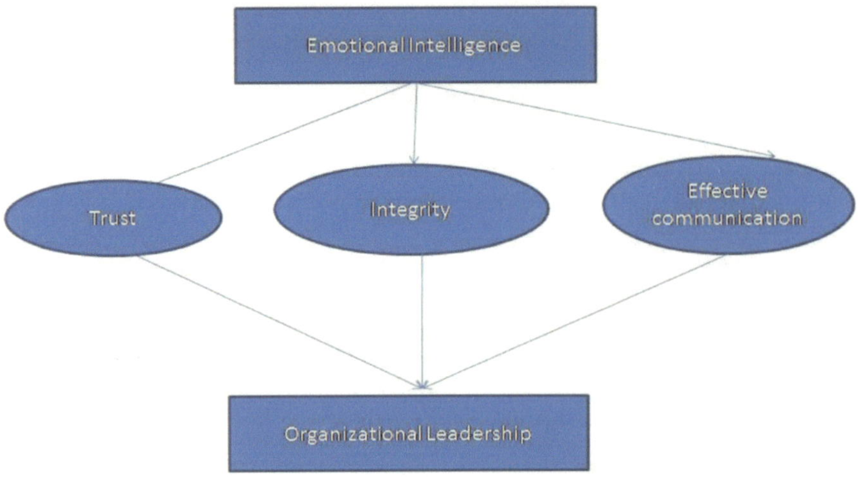

Figure 1.
Proposed model of emotional intelligence, moderating variables and organizational leadership.

4.1 Emotional intelligence and trust in leadership

Trust in an organization can bring a collaborative working environment. Trust reduces the inferiority complex among the group members. Emotionally intelligent leaders treat all the employees in the same manner without any kind of discriminations which can improve the performance of the organization. High level of trust can build mutual respect, motivate workers to perform well and bring in a happy mood at the workplace. If team members are trustworthy and collaborative, there will be transformational or charismatic style of leadership [38].

A study among 178 employees of six manufacturing plants, reveals that transformational leadership and leaders' emotional intelligence have a positive impact on team commitment. Similarly, effective leadership behavior is based on trust which creates team dynamics [39].

Transformational style of leadership and employee championing behavior is being influenced by trust in leadership. In an study among 175 project team members in information technology and software industry, results states that knowledge sharing and leaders trust is influence by ethical leadership. Also, project success is depend upon leaders trust and knowledge sharing [40, 41].

Trust can help to be open to the feelings with others which can reduce the feelings of anxiety, stress and burnout. Leaders need to understand the emotions in themselves and their followers for avoiding the situations like burnout and incivility at the workplace. Study of Knight et al. have revealed the significant association between emotional intelligence and trust among supervisor and staff members respectively [42].

Employees trust plays a mediating mechanism between transformational leadership and organizational performance. At individual and team level, emotional intelligence has positive impact on trust and performance. Trust works as a mediator to build relationship between emotional intelligence and performance [43, 44].

Trust in a team, which can be increased by emotional intelligence is associated with team performance and it can reduce team conflicts. Organizational learning can be achieved by emotional intelligence and trust [45, 46]. Similarly, There is a positive impact of emotional intelligence on job satisfaction and trust which is a major cause of a project's success [47]. Followers trust is influenced by leaders emotional sincerity. Emotional sincerity significantly influences leaders trust, integrity and quality of relationship. There is a positive relationship between integrity, trust on leaders and ethical leadership. The development of leadership is based on integrity, consensus, high-value working environment. Trust and integrity can build a quality of work engagement [48–50].

4.2 Emotional intelligence and integrity in leadership

High integrity builds an innovative and transparent working environment, provides morale support, builds customer loyalty, transparency and adequate corporate culture. Organization's success is defined by the integrity of working people. Integrity refines honesty and moral values in the leaders. When people work with others in an organization, it is necessary to act openly in their tasks and behavior. Integrity makes leaders committed towards their tasks and accountable for their job performance. Work performance is significantly impact by competency, integrity and emotional intelligence [51]. The moral and ethical values of organization depend upon integrity and accountability. Leaders who admit their mistakes, are more honest to their team members. Organizations' partners, vendors and customers prefer a more open and honest style of communication. According to Daniel Goleman "Integrity- acting openly, honestly and consistently- sets apart outstanding performers in jobs of every kind." pg.no 90.

Today organizations require people who are not only capable enough to perform their tasks but also to stand for others in critical conditions, taking responsibility for making mistakes and performing work in an organized manner. The integrity of people in an organization can open up new idea generation and consistent performance of workers. Integrity, courage and empathy are three main essentials of leadership [52]. Emotionally intelligent leaders carry out all the three traits in their behavior. Leaders need to make decisions on a day to day basis. Courageous leaders have the capability to put themselves in uncomfortable zones and take risks for beneficial decision making. There is a strong and significant relationship managerial integrity and employees turnover. Authenticity, constructiveness and reliability of managers helps to overcome employee turnover [53].

Ethical behavior of leaders is influenced by leaders emotional intelligence and perceived integrity. Perception of employees about a leader's integrity is based on the actions of the leader and the moral vision implanted in an organization. Ethical decision making is based on interpretation of others' aspects in the same manner. Highly emotional employees are more adept in taking decisions based on others aspects [54, 55]. Employees performance is significantly impacted by integrity and organization commitment. Moral cultivation for employees can help in achievement of optimal organizational goals [56].

4.3 Emotional intelligence and effective communication in leadership

Effective communication is the part of team performance and organizational success. Leaders who have a high level of communication skills can work smartly with their team members. Effective communication is necessary for resolving conflicts, confusion, and improper responses to top management. Effective style of communication can build empathy, open minded conversations, mutual respect and provide feedback between worker and supervisor. Similarly, people with good communication skills can deal with difficult situations, listen to others carefully and share information in a better manner. Leadership communication helps to creates team building and empowers organizations performance, growth and profitability [57].

Leaders who are able to build emotional bonding with their teams can build long lasting relationships with them. Effective communication and task-relation oriented leadership can provide job satisfaction, motivation and organizational commitment [58]. Among the study 43 medical staff functional (MSF) have found that organizational commitment is influenced by organizational communication and transformational leadership [59].

Leaders' ability to be good with their interpersonal skills are a major source of communication in an organization. Interpersonal skills focus on thoughts, feelings and actions of others. Interpersonal skills can emanate a positive attitude and feelings towards each other. To gain the support from team members, leaders need to be competent with their interpersonal and intrapersonal skills. Team building provides positive communication, continuous growth, trust and leadership potential of team members [60].

Employees' satisfaction with their supervisor is impacted by the supervisor's competency in communication [61]. Emotionally intelligent leaders can build trust with others via interpersonal skills. Emotional intelligence skills play a significant role in development of communication and relational skills [62].

Leaders with a high level of emotional intelligence are able to provide adequate solutions to problems and can easily be adaptable to situations. The traits of negotiations and inspiring others in a group, build a strong relationship within a team. In a study Yue et al. have examined how transformational leadership, transparent communication, and organizational trust impact on employees' openness to change among the 439 employees in the United states. The results suggested that all three factors have positive impact on employees openness to change [63].

Employees creativity and feedback for supervisors is influenced by organizations internal communication. Symmetrical internal communication is positively impacted by leadership communication at senior levels [64].

Similarly, previous studies have emphasized the focus of leader's communication. Good communication of leaders enables and foster; create understanding and build trust which encourages followers to follow a leader. Obstacles and problems of the group can be overcome by certain types of communication competencies; group goals can be achieved by leaders via communication. Leader as a listener, educator and communicator provides positive organizational culture [65–68].

Clearly, group goals can only be achieved by proper style of communication. It is a process of exchange of ideas between two people. Proper communication competencies can help to overcome existing problems and remove ego tussle within a team. The effectiveness and success of a project is based on emotional intelligence and communication among the project managers and team members. Self-awareness and social - awareness competencies can make effective internal communication [69].

Emotional intelligence can help to enhance communication skills. A lack of emotional intelligence can generate the communication problem, which can lead to problems in corporate culture [70].

Emotional intelligence plays a major role in effective communication. A study among 145 employees in educational administrations in Iran has proven that there is a strong association between organization culture, communication effectiveness and emotional intelligence [71].

Leaders' effective communication style makes them more successful in an organization. Self-awareness about our emotions helps us to understand our strengths and weaknesses. Similarly, it also impacts our behavior in positive and negative manner. Emotional intelligence is significantly impacting on leaders' communication [72–74]. Leaders who are self-aware can examine and change their behavior based on situations. Similarly, adaptability brings flexibility in the job. People who are not flexible in their job, have many difficulties in learning new things and communicating their thoughts with others. Emotionally intelligent leaders have the ability to think independently and take accurate decisions in order to reach organizational goals. Similarly, they develop healthy communication and consolidate them with positive feelings at work.

5. Conclusion

I am suggesting that organizations who wish to get growth need to constantly check their leaders' performance and attitude at the workplace. In the above study, I have only focused on Bass's suggested leadership style. Previous studies showed that a transformational style of leadership is more effective for organizations growth. But there are other kinds of styles of leadership which include pace-settings, transactional, Democratic, autocratic, servant style and coach style of leadership. Further studies can focus on these areas. Leadership styles vary from situation to situation. But the major challenge is whether the organizations are aware about the kind of leadership styles that need to be adopted?

Secondly, I have focused on how emotionally intelligent leaders can help in relationship building and business growth for an organization. In addition to that, how they can effectively motivate employees to work and create value for the organization. Since, there is ongoing research in the field of emotional intelligence, it can be developed by practicing. Lack of proper training about self-awareness, political awareness, stress management, client relationship building and conflict management are the major challenges in front of organizations.

Finally, in my proposed model I have focused on three major areas i.e. trust, integrity and effective communication. They are enhanced by adopting the regular practices of emotional intelligence. This will help to create effective leadership. Emotional intelligence creates a positive environment at the workplace which releases positive emotions and thoughts. Effective communication of leaders generates self-motivation in a team. Interpersonal and intrapersonal skills of a leader helps them to be proactive at work. Trust and integrity are the major catalysts in an organization which can be helpful in avoiding conflicts and burnout situations among the team. Emotionally intelligent team building activities are necessary practices which need to be followed by organizations.

5.1 Practical and theoretical contribution

5.1.1 Practical contributions

The above study has stated that leaders' emotional intelligence can affect the productivity and growth of an organization. Involvement in the major practices of emotional intelligence can bring out effective changes in the behavior of people. Leaders who experience emotional awareness build empathetic relationships with their team members.

Another practical finding of the study is to practice and apply emotional intelligence in day to day work. To be emotionally intelligent, there is a need of understanding the complexity of emotions and then responding in an appropriate manner. Since, there is ongoing research in the field of emotional intelligence, it can be developed by practicing. Emotional intelligence program sessions and leadership training should be conducted that can help organizations to perform better at emotional level and at task performance.

5.1.2 Theoretical contribution

Theoretical perspectives of the chapter have included the contributing parts of existing theories. Factors of emotional intelligence. i.e. self and social awareness, relationship building, empathy and motivations have significantly influenced the effectiveness of leadership in organizations. The major findings of above model have suggested the interrelated link between emotional intelligence and effective leadership.

The selected factors i.e. trust, integrity and communication can build confidence in the team. Organizations, employees, client partners and existing shareholders can be benefited by effective style of communication. Similarly, organizational ethics can be established and practiced based on existing theories of emotional intelligence, trust, integrity and communication. This will in turn be helpful in boosting morale of employees, building character and organizational values. Additionally, the application of trust, integrity and communication is a novel attempt to bring more effectiveness in the emotionally intelligent leadership styles.

6. Limitations and future research

Certain limitations of the study have been addressed here for future research work. The major limitation is that I have only suggested three variables to understand the relationship between emotional intelligence and leadership. There are many other variables which can be helpful to understand the effectiveness of emotional intelligence and adapted style of leadership. Understanding about organization politics, decision making strategies of an emotionally intelligent leader and understanding about the learning curve of an employee in an empathetic manner can be a newer set of variables for future research.

Secondly, the above study is based on the suggested model for achievement of organizational effectiveness. Future research can be based on empirical findings.

Author details

Anurag Mishra
Presidency University, Bengaluru, Karnataka, India

*Address all correspondence to: anurag.msr@gmail.com;
anurag.mishra@presidencyuniversity.in

References

[1] Lee C, Wong CS. The effect of team emotional intelligence on team process and effectiveness. Journal of Management & Organization. 2019 Nov;25(6):844-859.

[2] Kerr R, Garvin J, Heaton N, Boyle E. Emotional intelligence and leadership effectiveness. Leadership & Organization Development Journal. 2006 Jun 1.

[3] Bagshaw M. Emotional intelligence–training people to be affective so they can be effective. Industrial and Commercial training. 2000 Apr 1.

[4] Rosete D, Ciarrochi J. Emotional intelligence and its relationship to workplace performance outcomes of leadership effectiveness. Leadership & Organization Development Journal. 2005 Jul 1.

[5] Avolio BJ, Gardner WL. Authentic leadership development: Getting to the root of positive forms of leadership. The leadership quarterly. 2005 Jun 1;16(3):315-338.

[6] Game AM. Negative emotions in supervisory relationships: The role of relational models. Human Relations. 2008 Mar;61(3):355-393.

[7] Krén H, Séllei B. The Role of Emotional Intelligence in Organizational Performance. Periodica Polytechnica Social and Management Sciences. 2021;29(1):1-9

[8] Ashkanasy NM, Daus CS. Emotional intelligence in the workplace. The Wiley Encyclopedia of Personality and Individual Differences: Clinical, Applied, and Cross-Cultural Research. 2020 Sep 18:485-490.

[9] Sharma A, Panicker A. How Ethical Leadership Impacts Employees Performance at the Workplace: A Perspective. International Journal of Business Ethics in Developing Economies. 2020;9(1):18.

[10] Srivastava MS, Kunj V, Sinha S. Emotional Intelligence as a mediating variable in the impact of Leadership on Organizational Commitment.2020

[11] Baba MM, Makhdoomi UM, Siddiqi MA. Emotional intelligence and transformational leadership among academic leaders in institutions of higher learning. Global Business Review. 2021 Aug;22(4):1070-1096.

[12] Salovey P, Mayer JD. Emotional intelligence. Imagination, cognition and personality. 1990 Mar;9(3):185-211.

[13] Salovey P, Mayer JD. Emotional intelligence. Imagination, cognition and personality. 1990 Mar;9(3):185-211.

[14] Mayer JD, Salovey P. What is emotional intelligence. Emotional development and emotional intelligence: Educational implications. 1997;3:31.

[15] Mayer, J, D., Salovey, P„ & Caruso, D. R. (2000). Competing models of emotioral intell- igence. In R, Sternbe g (Ed.). Handbook of human intelligence (pp. 396-420). New York: Cambridge University press.

[16] Goleman D. Working with emotional intelligence.

[17] Bar-On R. The Bar-On model of emotional-social intelligence (ESI) 1. Psicothema. 2006 Dec 31:13-25.

[18] Baron R. The BarOn emotional quotient inventory (BarOn EQ-i). Toronto, ON: Multi-Health Systems Inc. 1997.

[19] Conger, J.A. 'Learning to Lead' San Francisco: Jossey-Bass (1992, p18)

[20] Stogdill RM. Leadership, membership and organization. Psychological bulletin. 1950 Jan;47(1):1.

[21] Burns J. Leadership. New York: Harper & Row. Burris, ER, Detert, J. R., & Chiaburu, DS (2008). Quitting before leaving: the mediating effects of psychological attachment and detachment on voice. Journal of Applied Psychology. 1978;93(4):912-923.

[22] Yukl, G.A. Leadership in Organizations, 2nd ed., Prentice-Hall, Englewood Cliffs, NJ,1989

[23] Bass BM. Leadership and performance beyond expectations. Collier Macmillan; 1985.

[24] Bass BM, Avolio BJ, editors. Improving organizational effectiveness through transformational leadership. sage; 1994.

[25] Hanafi WN, Daud S. Managing sustainable development of government link companies (GLCs) in Malaysia through emotional intelligence and organisational politics. International Journal of Innovation and Sustainable Development. 2021;15(1):126-141.

[26] Kerr R, Garvin J, Heaton N, Boyle E. Emotional intelligence and leadership effectiveness. Leadership & Organization Development Journal. 2006 Jun 1.

[27] Ashkanasy NM, Dasborough MT. Emotional awareness and emotional intelligence in leadership teaching. Journal of education for business. 2003 Sep 1;79(1):18-22.

[28] Humphrey RH, Pollack JM, Hawver T. Leading with emotional labor. Journal of managerial psychology. 2008 Feb 15. pp. 151-168

[29] Colbert AE, Kristof-Brown AL, Bradley BH, Barrick MR. CEO transformational leadership: The role of goal importance congruence in top management teams. Academy of management journal. 2008 Feb;51(1):81-96.

[30] Wyllie TM. Workplace leadership styles: my perspective-Botswana scenario.2020

[31] Hur Y, Van Den Berg PT, Wilderom CP. Transformational leadership as a mediator between emotional intelligence and team outcomes. The Leadership Quarterly. 2011 Aug 1;22(4):591-603.

[32] Koman ES, Wolff SB. Emotional intelligence competencies in the team and team leader: A multi-level examination of the impact of emotional intelligence on team performance. Journal of Management Development. 2008 Jan,27(1):55-57, https://doi.org/10.1108/02621710810840767

[33] Milhem M, Muda H, Khalil A. The effect of perceived transformational leadership style on employee engagement: The mediating effect of Leader's emotional intelligence. Foundations of Management. 2019;11(1):33-42. eISSN 2300-5661, pISSN 2080-7279, DOI: 10.2478/fman-2019-0003

[34] Gardner L, Stough C. Examining the relationship between leadership and emotional intelligence in senior level managers. Leadership & organization development journal. 2002 Mar 1. 23/2:68-78. ISSN 0143-7739, DOI 10.1108/0143773021041919 8.

[35] Palmer B, Walls M, Burgess Z, Stough C. Emotional intelligence and effective leadership. Leadership & Organization development journal. 2001 Feb 1.

[36] Antonakis J, Ashkanasy NM, Dasborough MT. Does leadership need emotional intelligence?. The leadership quarterly. 2009 Apr 1;20(2):247-261.

[37] Sadri G. Emotional intelligence: Can it be taught. Inquiry. 2011;15(3):197-215.

[38] Engelbrecht AS, Heine G, Mahembe B. Integrity, ethical leadership, trust and work engagement. Leadership & Organization Development Journal. 2017 May 2;38(3):368-378. https://doi.org/10.1108/LODJ-11-2015-0237

[39] Schlechter AF, Strauss JJ. Leader emotional intelligence, transformational leadership, trust and team commitment: Testing a model within a team context. SA Journal of Industrial psychology. 2008;34(1):42-53.

[40] Islam MN, Furuoka F, Idris A. Mapping the relationship between transformational leadership, trust in leadership and employee championing behavior during organizational change. Asia Pacific Management Review. 2021 Jun 1;26(2):95-102. https://doi.org/10.1016/j.apmrv.2020.09.002

[41] Bhatti SH, Kiyani SK, Dust SB, Zakariya R. The impact of ethical leadership on project success: the mediating role of trust and knowledge sharing. International Journal of Managing Projects in Business. 2021 Feb 9. https://doi.org/10.1108/IJMPB-05-2020-0159

[42] Knight JR, Bush HM, Mase WA, Riddell MC, Liu M, Holsinger JW. The impact of emotional intelligence on conditions of trust among leaders at the Kentucky Department for Public Health. Frontiers in public health. 2015 Mar 13;3:33. https://doi.org/10.3389/fpubh.2015.00033

[43] Le BP, Tran QT. Leadership practice for building trust of followers: Decisive factors of organizational performance. SEISENSE Journal of Management. 2020 Mar 4;3(2):45-57.

[44] Rezvani A, Khosravi P, Ashkanasy NM. Examining the interdependencies among emotional intelligence, trust, and performance in infrastructure projects: A multilevel study. International Journal of Project Management. 2018 Nov 1;36(8):1034-1046.https://doi.org/10.1016/j.ijproman.2018.08.002

[45] Rezvani A, Barrett R, Khosravi P. Investigating the relationships among team emotional intelligence, trust, conflict and team performance. Team Performance Management: An International Journal. 2019 Mar 11. 25 No. 1/2,:120-137. https://doi.org/10.1108/TPM-03-2018-0019

[46] Bettis-Outland H, Guillory MD. Emotional intelligence and organizational learning at trade shows. Journal of Business & Industrial Marketing. 2018 Feb 5.33(1): 126-133, https://doi.org/10.1108/JBIM-03-2017-0066

[47] Rezvani A, Chang A, Wiewiora A, Ashkanasy NM, Jordan PJ, Zolin R. Manager emotional intelligence and project success: The mediating role of job satisfaction and trust. International Journal of Project Management. 2016 Oct 1;34(7):1112-1122. https://doi.org/10.1016/j.ijproman.2016.05.012

[48] Nisar QA, Basheer MF, Hussain MS, Waqas A. The Role of Leaders' Emotional Sincerity towards Followers' Trust: Leaders' Integrity & Quality Relationship. Journal of Contemporary Issues in Business and Government. 2021 Feb 5;27(1):472-479.https://doi.org/10.1016/j.ijproman.2016.05.012

[49] Engelbrecht AS, Heine G, Mahembe B. The influence of integrity and ethical leadership on trust in the leader. Management Dynamics: Journal of the Southern African Institute for Management Scientists. 2015 Mar 1;24(1):2-10

[50] Duggar JW. The role of integrity in individual and effective corporate

leadership. Journal of Academic and Business Ethics. 2009 Aug 12;3(1):1-7.

[51] Putra AS. The Effect of Competence, Integrity, and Emotional Intelligence on Work Performance. Asian Journal of Law and Governance. 2021 Apr 1;3(1):76-84.

[52] Stefano SF, Wasylyshyn KM. Integrity, courage, empathy (ICE): Three leadership essentials. People and Strategy. 2005 Oct 1;28(4):5.

[53] Akpotu c, ozioko ea. Managerial integrity and employee turnover intention in fast food and restaurant firms in port harcourt. European Journal of Research and Reflection in Management Sciences Vol. 2020;8(1).

[54] Watts DL. The relationship of ethical behavior in the workplace to emotional intelligence and perceived leader integrity. Trevecca Nazarene University; 2013.

[55] Mesmer-Magnus J, Viswesvaran C, Joseph J, Deshpande SP. The role of emotional intelligence in integrity and ethics perceptions. In Emotions, Ethics and Decision-Making 2008 Jul 25. Emerald Group Publishing Limited.

[56] Febrina D, Syamsir S. The Influence of Integrity and Commitment Organizational on Employee Performance. International Journal of Research and Analytical Reviews (IJRAR),. 2020;7(1):799-805.

[57] Colocassides EM. The efficacy of leadership communication under economic challenges. Science and Education. 2021;2(3).

[58] Mikkelson AC, York JA, Arritola J. Communication competence, leadership behaviors, and employee outcomes in supervisor-employee relationships. Business and Professional Communication Quarterly. 2015 Sep;78(3):336-354.

[59] Widyanti R. Do Leadership Style and Organizational Communication Increase to Organizational Commitment? Study Among Hospital Staff. HOLISTICA–Journal of Business and Public Administration. 2020;11(2): 17-24.

[60] Mobolade GO, Akinade ME. Team Building And Teamwork In Organizations: Implications To Managers And Employees In Work Places. International Journal Of Management, Social Sciences, Peace And Conflict Studies. 2021 Mar 11;4(1).

[61] Berman SJ, Hellweg SA. Perceived supervisor communication competence and supervisor satisfaction as a function of quality circle participation. The Journal of Business Communication (1973). 1989 Mar;26(2):103-22.

[62] Petrovici A, Dobrescu T. The role of emotional intelligence in building interpersonal communication skills. Procedia-Social and Behavioral Sciences. 2014 Feb 21;116:1405-1410. doi: 10.1016/j.sbspro.2014.01.406

[63] Yue CA, Men LR, Ferguson MA. Bridging transformational leadership, transparent communication, and employee openness to change: The mediating role of trust. Public relations review. 2019 Sep 1;45(3):101779. https://doi.org/10.1016/j.pubrev.2019.04.012

[64] Lee Y, Kim J. Cultivating employee creativity through strategic internal communication: The role of leadership, symmetry, and feedback seeking behaviors. Public Relations Review. 2021 Mar 1;47(1):101998.

[65] Penley LE, Hawkins B. Studying interpersonal communication in organizations: A leadership application. Academy of Management Journal. 1985 Jun 1;28(2):309-326.

[66] Barrett D. Leadership communication: A communication

approach for senior-level managers. Handbook of Business Strategy Emerald Group Publishing, 2006. Pages 385-390

[67] Barge JK, Hirokawa RY. Toward a communication competency model of group leadership. Small Group Behavior. 1989 May;20(2):167-189.

[68] Allert JR, Chatterjee SR. Corporate communication and trust in leadership. Corporate Communications: An International Journal. 1997.

[69] Belogrudova MZ, Antonova L. Correlation of internal communication with emotional intelligence in project teams in organization "x". In society. Integration. Education. Proceedings of the International Scientific Conference 2021 May 28 (Vol. 6, pp. 540-550).

[70] Jorfi H, Jorfi M. Management: A study of organizational culture and the relationship between emotional intelligence and communication effectiveness (case study in organizations of Iran). Journal of management research. 2012 Jan 1;4(1):1. doi:10.5296/jmr.v4i1.936

[71] Raeissi P, Kalhor R, Azmal M. Correlation between emotional intelligence and communication skills in managers in educational hospitals of Qazvin. Journal of Inflammatory Disease. 2010 Feb 10;13(4):57-62.

[72] Sunindijo RY, Hadikusumo BH, Ogunlana S. Emotional intelligence and leadership styles in construction project management. Journal of management in engineering. 2007 Oct;23(4):166-70. http://dx.doi.org/10.1061/(ASCE) 0742- 597X(2007)23:4

[73] Pryke S, Lunic D, Badi S. The effect of leader emotional intelligence on leader–follower chemistry: A study of construction project managers. Construction Management and Economics. 2015 Aug 3;33(8): 603-624.

[74] Momeny L, Gourgues M. Communication that develops teams: Healthy ministry team dynamics as a function of consistent leader communication of emotional intelligence. Christian Education Journal. 2020 Aug;17(2):283-297.

Chapter 9

Leading in Times of Disruption: Reimagining Leadership and Repositioning Leaders

Tessie H.H. Herbst

Abstract

Peter Vaill's evocative metaphor of "living in permanent whitewater" is very relevant to universities today. Leaders in our institutions (and elsewhere) are navigating unfamiliar territory—and they are doing so without a map. The demands and expectations placed on leaders can be extreme and is testing the abilities of our institutions' leaders to the extreme. Leaders and leadership paradigms has been disrupted and the old model of fear and control do not work. However, the primary leadership challenge is not simply to develop a new leadership competency model—describing a group of behaviours we expect from our leadership. The deeper challenge is to develop a new mindset that anchors, informs, and advances these new behaviours. The ability to question your own deeply entrenched assumptions and well-established worldviews, habits and mindsets will be critical. When unpacking the case for change versus the capacity for change, this chapter surfaced, five kinds of shifts needed to lead in a world characterised by complexity, disruption and uncertainty. I have labelled these shifts as the Awareness shift, the Identity shift, the Mindset shift, the Paradigm shift and lastly the shift from Fear to psychological safety. Are these the only shifts that matter in the current state? I am sure not, we can add many more. But, I believe that these five shifts that demonstrate the complexities of the challenges facing higher education has the potential to reposition and reinvent our leadership for the future.

Keywords: leadership shifts, higher education, complexity, disruption, transformation

1. Introduction

"How do you lead when there is no map? When the territory is unknown? What skillsets and mind shifts are necessary?" [1].

The higher education (HE) sector globally—like other industries—are under enormous pressure to transform itself. However, higher education institutions (HEIs) are struggling to adapt to the fast pace of change and the increasing social, economic, and technological complexity of the challenges facing them. These challenges are becoming increasingly perpetual, pervasive and exponential, compelling HEIs to change and to embrace a new paradigm designed to meet the changing needs of society. The current operating model[1] for HEIs is outdated and is misaligned with the realities of a modern-day society. However, HEIs are acknowledging that they need to radically reinvent themselves or possibly cease to exist [3]. In a recent study by Prof. Bethuel Ngcamu (2017)—one of the leading scholars in the HE field leadership in South Africa—he identifies the following factors hampering the transformation agenda and suggesting inadequate leadership in universities, namely inflexible business processes; lack of reward for performance; inefficient change interventions and centralised decision making [4]. Another study by McGrath found that management styles in universities was either predominantly autocratic or democratic, with employees remarking that academic freedom has diminished significantly. The gap between the current leadership skills and capacity and future leadership requirements is widening—a gap that this chapter aims to address.

Work as we know it is changing rapidly—and subsequently the learning needs of our students. The scope and complexity of the technological revolution of the 4IR—distinguished by the fusion of the physical, biological and digital worlds using diverse new technologies [5]—will profoundly change the way we work, live, and relate to one another. Bryan Penprase [6] in the book *The fourth industrial revolution and higher education* describes the 4IR as "the result of an integration and compounding effects of multiple 'exponential technologies', such as artificial intelligence (AI), biotechnologies and nanomaterials" (p.215). The complexity of the current challenges is forcing universities to reconsider how and what we teach our students and how we lead people. Among the avalanche of impeding changes facing our institutions are the changing demographics of students who are both less prepared for HE and learns in new ways; how to motivate staff to adapt; increased competition; a decline in government funding and public confidence. Furthermore, new technologies offer both the opportunity to increase student access but simultaneously threatens the traditional model of higher education itself. To add to the complexity, is the fact that our current leadership has never had to successfully navigate the impact of an unexpected and disruptive occurrence like the current COVID-19 pandemic, which has triggered an unprecedented need for institutional redesign. To make matters even worse is that while preparing for the future, leaders have to deal with all of these challenges simultaneously. The "tyranny of the urgent"[2] has seldom been felt more acute. The world and work is a different place now. Conditions such as these have been characterised in the leadership and management literature as being VUCA, an acronym for volatile, uncertain, complex, and ambiguous [7].

There are numerous factors that will influence how HEIs respond with no approach that can be applied across the board. Dealing with these conditions requires that leaders change both how they think and behave in order to grow and transform how their institutions respond to the chaos and complexity that abounds. Traditional skills to predict and control outcomes has become redundant and instead resilience, agility and the ability to adapt quickly and recognise patterns has become critical [8]. It requires a shift in our awareness and how leaders perceive and think about their world; moving from an assumption of predictability, stability, continuity, and reliability—to an assumption of volatility, uncertainty, change and ambiguity. Amidst this increasingly complexity, disruption and uncertainty, the

[1] In studying the history of HEIs, Trow (2007) identified three predominant guiding models namely the *elite model*, the *mass model* and more recently the *universal model*. For a more elaborate discussion, see Ref. [2].

[2] Charles Hummel in his book *Tyranny of the Urgent* (1967) contends that a continuous tension exists between the important and the urgent—and that much too often the urgent wins.

question raised by Amit Mrig and Pat Sanaghan [9] concerning the future of higher education is extremely relevant: **"will higher education seize the future or fall victim to it?"**

This chapter aims to address some key issues in developing the leadership capacity needed to enable leaders to navigate the ever-increasing pace of change, disruption, uncertainty and complexity. It proposes five shifts that leaders in HEIs will have to master to enable them to seize the future and create lasting positive impact. It also advocates for a repurposing of leadership development and a philosophy and practice framework that takes an alternative perspective—one in which we view mindset and culture not from the outside in, but from the inside out. I hope that these shifts can guide the future development of leadership development programs in universities.

2. Are leaders as prepared as they think?

To be successful in dealing with these and other challenges, HEIs—like other organisations—need creative, resilient, agile, courageous, and effective leaders throughout their middle management and executive roles. In many ways, the challenges facing our institutional leaders are similar to the challenges encountered by famous explorers like Columbus and Livingston during their expeditions across Africa and the world. Leaders in HE institutions today are navigating unfamiliar territory—and they are doing so without a map. The demands and expectations placed on leaders can be extreme and is testing the abilities of our institutions' leaders to the extreme. As stated by Nasima Badsha in the book *Reflections of South African university leaders* (2017, p. ix) [10]—referring to the unprecedented levels of change in South African higher education:

"Leaders in universities, as well as those responsible for higher education policy in the government and associated statutory bodies, had no neat script to work off, nor 'manuals' or prescripts of 'good' leadership or practice".

Leadership scholars globally agree that universities need leaders who are not only credible scholars but also progressive futurists and inspiring leaders [11–13]. However, leadership remains one of the most sought after yet elusive concepts in the workplace today. The 2020 *State of Leadership Training Market Report* [14] states that over the past decade, one of the most rapidly growing segments in the learning and development (L & D) market has been leadership training. It further states that the leadership training industry—unlike other segments within L & D—has also been growing annually independent of economic trends. However, despite the $3.5 billion spent globally in 2019 alone on leadership development solutions, the literature talks about the failure of an industry. The reason being that leaders soon revert to their old ways of doing things. When we lead in the absence of a map, we often rely mostly on what worked before or what we already know or think we know well. We fall back on our old habits, practices and traditions, losing sight of the originality and resourcefulness needed and the risks we need to take now. We can observe this tendency to rely more on our experience or "smartship" than leadership across all industries, but HEIs are especially prone to it because of the unique weight we assign to intellectualism, knowledge, tenure and qualifications. In their book *How Higher-Ed leaders derail* (2018), Patrick Sanaghan and Jillian Lohndorf talks about the "peril of smartship" as one of the reasons why leaders in HE derail. Therefore, leaders need to take heed and be mindful of the "confirming evidence trap" as described by Hammond et al. (2006), where we tend to look for information that confirms our original—but often outdated—thinking [15].

Amidst all the confusion, if there is one thing we can all agree on—it is that HE—like other industries—is going through a momentous disruption and change. These trends in the world of work are irreversible and the challenges facing our leaders are overwhelming, pushing us (whether we like it or not) to a new normal. These challenges are adaptive challenges—as opposed to technical challenges. Put differently, complicated (technical) problems are not the same as complex (adaptive) problems and require different solutions. Adaptive or complex challenges is defined by Harvard's Heifetz and Linsky [16] as challenges that require risk taking, innovation, and constant learning. To successfully deal with adaptive challenges, the traditional leadership strategies and skill sets of the past are often no longer appropriate or sufficient. Adaptive challenges requires adaptive leaders who can innovate, experiment, engage in continuous learning and adapt to the increasingly complex organisational environments in which they work. Ronald Heifetz [17] states that adaptive leadership is one perspective on the kind of leadership necessary for today's VUCA work environments which he defines as "the practice of mobilizing people to tackle tough challenges and thrive" (p. 14). Furthermore, when facing adaptive challenges, the locus of responsibility for solving the problem is shifting to all employees, and the leader should only help to facilitate this. They regard this role of leadership to be the most difficult. They suggest that leaders should get away from the habit of providing solutions, and devolve this responsibility to find solutions to the "collective intelligence of all employees".

This distinction between "technical" and "adaptive" challenges has important implications for leaders and leadership in higher education. *Technical* or complicated challenges may be very complex and critically important but are situations we have encountered before with known solutions where we can apply our current resources and know-how to deal with them. This does not make technical challenges trivial but only implies that the solution to the problem already exists within the institution's existing repertoire. In contrast, *adaptive challenges*, has no established knowledge and clear solutions as to how leaders and institutions can effectively respond. These challenges require experimentation, creative and innovative thinking and risk taking. It requires from leaders to risk challenging the status quo and naming the elephants in the room—finding a way to push people out of complacency and mobilising the energy needed for transformation. However, in most of our institutions, adaptive leadership is a rare occurrence since adaptive leadership is inherently risky. As such, "the most common cause of failure in leadership is produced by treating adaptive challenges as if they were technical problems" [18]. Most challenges facing our universities is a mixture of technical and adaptive challenges. Therefore, it is important to note that adaptive challenges are not only about change, but also about knowing what needs to continue—the essential elements in the system that should be sustained.

Universities that successfully navigate through these adaptive and technical challenges will emerge more dynamic and stronger, more competitive, and more able to educate students who are future fit for our changing society and workplace. However, the path for change is completely unclear and finding new ways of leading and tackling these "adaptive" [19] challenges will test even the brightest and most capable leaders we have. Nether less, we need to keep on trying to find new ways since the current COVID-19 pandemic has highlighted the life and death impact of leadership, and has also given us the opportunity to reflect on our own ability to deal with the complexity and uncertainty of the current leadership context. As Warren Bennis has said: "It is only when the tide goes in that we can see who has been swimming naked". The current pandemic has placed a spotlight on our existing fault-lines, but at the same time created opportunities for radically new conversations in our universities—one such conversation is how we can reimagine and reinvent leadership. As stated by Amit Mrig and Pat Sanaghan in their recent Future of HE report [20], "Leadership matters; rarely has it mattered more than now".

3. Do we need a new type of leadership?

If we agree that leadership is now more important than ever before, the next logical question would be: **Do we need a new type of leadership for the new VUCA world and the 4IR?** If yes, what is this new leadership we need to help us navigate this uncertainty, disruption and complexity? And—what does complexity-fit leadership look like? As stated by Mrig and Sanaghan,

"The past and current academic leadership model that prizes vision, academic reputation, tenure and track record, communication and charisma is no longer enough to meet our current and future challenges" [21].

The current turbulence and disruption is forcing institutions to reinvent and renew themselves. In doing so institutions need to bring the much-needed clarity regarding their value propositions. It provides HEIs with an once-in-a-lifetime opportunity to ask the most pressing of all questions: **Why do we exist? Who do we choose to be? What do we want to create together?** In his book *Theory-U: Learning from the future as it emerges*, Otto Sharmer [22] states that how we respond to these questions will differ according to the level of consciousness and structure of attention we use to answer them. We can either respond mechanistically from a low level of leadership maturity or we can respond from a more holistic and systemic perspective of social reality creation.

In defining the term "leader", the premise of this chapter aligns with the views of Michael Hamman by defining a leader as:

"Anyone—in any role, at any level of the institution, and within any part of the institution—who are willing to take responsibility for their world and able to influence others in creating that world. In doing so, he/she is steered by a deep inner compass founded upon a profound sense of purpose. In addition, there is a visible willingness to recognise and evolve beyond the limitations of their current ways of seeing the world, of seeing others, and of seeing themselves."

In a VUCA world, we need to shift how we think about and exercise leadership since we are all called upon to lead in some way and at some moment in time. The notion of leadership that happens only at the top cannot possibly address the needs of the 4IR. This is because the VUCA world of work today requires a degree of institutional adaptability that can only be attained when the entire system—not just those at senior and executive levels—is in a state of readiness.

"Leadership is an Everywhere Phenomenon"[3].

4. Why is leadership so tough?

Heifetz and Linsky of Harvard tell us that "to lead is to live dangerously" [24]. Leading academics has been compared to the impossible task of "*herding cats*"—either impossible or pointless [25]. However, we think that most leaders will agree with us that with the current uncertainty and disruption, we have moved beyond herding cats "to riding a tiger". As stated by Priscilla Nelson and Ed Cohen [26]—leadership is like

[3] See Hamman [23].

riding a tiger, not knowing how to get off without being eaten.[4] Therefore, the quote by Margaret Heffernan strikes at the heart of this chapter:

"The organizational adaptability required to meet a relentless succession of challenges is beyond anyone's current expertise. No one in a position of authority—none of us in fact—has been here before."

Therefore, Peter Vaill's (1996)[5] evocative metaphor of "living in permanent whitewater" is very relevant to HEIs today. Without the agility to tolerate discomfort, the courage to see and seize opportunities that others shrink from and do those things that others are not willing to do—effective leadership will be unattainable. The ability to question your own deeply entrenched assumptions and well-established worldviews, habits and mindsets will be critical. In their article *Leadership in a (Permanent) Crisis*, Ronald Heifetz, Alexander Grashow, and Marty Linsky [28], give us a renewed appreciation the value of adaptive leadership. They advocate that leaders should ensure that they surround themselves with diverse people who are willing to challenge ideas (especially the leader's ideas). To address the challenges they are faced with, leaders will need every team-member's help—not their blind loyalty—to follow them on a path to the future using the passion and collective intelligence of the whole team to help them to discover the path. Effective leaders will be the ones that can "confront loyalty to legacy practices" that keep people from taking the institution from 'good to great.' Not completely abandoning legacy practices, but rather not following them blindly [29].

The well-known quote by Ralph Waldo Emerson seems like very relevant advice for leaders now "Do not follow where the path may lead. Go instead where there is no path and leave a trail." To be able to empower innovation and future thinking throughout the institution, leaders will have to lead while not having all the answers. They will have to lead not by telling, not by directing, not even by "going first", or "eating last". They will have to lead by "pointing the way" as explained by Peter Senge [30]. However, in a culture where stability, certainty and predictability are traditionally more valued than innovation and risk-taking, reinventing our institutions will remain a complex challenge. Those who "point the way" or "go where there is no path's" will be met by resistance with people questioning the proposed path likelihood of success. However, this resistance is a trap that lulls leaders into inactivity. That is why the kind of leadership institutions will need going forward will require courage to deal with resistance with new and unproven approaches. Add to that an enthusiasm for continuous learning while leading. To make it even more anxiety providing—you need to do all of this in the full view of everyone. "Most of us are looking for a safe path through—a safe place to be great. There isn't one. There is no safe way to be great, and, there is no great way to be safe. The safe paths have all been taken. The paths left to us require courage. Leadership is inherently risky"[6].

Pollak and Wakid refer to this as "Lewis and Clark problems"[7] where institutions must venture into unfamiliar territory without a clear map [32]. These challenges are not always new, but always require the response to be. Simply applying known solutions—adding new academic programs, offering more tuition discounts, or investing

---

[4] On January 7, 2009, the employees of Satyam Computer Services were shocked to learn about the resignation of the founder and Chairman of their company, Ramalinga Raju. This was after he confessed to a massive accounting scandal. In Raju's words, dealing with his own and others' reactions and trying to survive was "like riding a tiger, not knowing how to get off without being eaten."

[5] See Vaill [27].

[6] See Anderson and Adams [31].

[7] Lewis and Clark problems are ambiguous situations that involve numerous variables with no clear solution or by relying on past knowledge or experience.

in new infrastructure—will no longer be sufficient to set aside public doubt, nor to increase the value and relevance of higher education, nor to ensure our students are future-fit for the 4IR. The immense challenges facing universities have created a watershed moment for HEIs. In their *Future of Higher-Ed Report* Mrig and Sanaghan advocates that leaders in HE recognise that it is senseless to continue to make incremental changes to delay the inevitable reinvention needed. They state very clearly that the tide has turned and that "waiting" is no longer an effective strategy [33].

But, we know that change is hard—in fact, Alan Deutschman contents in his book—*Change or Die*—that even when our lives or institution's survival depend on it, old patterns and behaviours give up their dominance reluctantly [34]. For example, even when their doctors tell cardiac patients they will die if they do not exercise more and change their lifestyle or their diet, only one in seven will change their lifestyle. So, if staring death in the eye is not enough of a threat to invite some change, what will be? For a variety reasons—both neurological and psychological—few leaders actually undertake change. This is exactly the same pattern that plays out with intelligent, motivated managers who attend a leadership development workshop where they are taught new models, techniques and tools to increase their effectiveness as leaders. At the end of the program, everyone makes a commitment for changing their behaviour going forward. However, when they return to the office, they soon fall back into the same old behaviours they had before the program.

So how does all of this start to play into the future of leadership in universities? How do we remap leadership's place in the university within this new landscape of disruption, uncertainty and everything else that comes with the 4IR?

We do not have the research available for universities, but the *MIT 2020 Future of Leadership Global Executive Study and Research Report* [35] provides ample evidence that leaders are holding on to previously effective but now out-dated behaviours that stifle the talents of their employees. The report (based 27 executive interviews and on a survey with 4394 respondents) highlights the mounting mismatch between how many organisations are being led and how they should be led. The majority of respondents were of the opinion that their leaders do not have the right mindsets to lead them forward.

As stated by Mrig and Sanaghan[8] developing leadership capacity is the strategic wedge [36]. However, the primary leadership challenge in the 4IR, is not simply to develop a new leadership competency model—describing a group of behaviours we expect from our leadership. The deeper challenge is to develop a new mindset that anchors, informs, and advances these new behaviours. Behaviour is only a function of mindset. Leadership mindset and style, set the overall tone for institutional culture and overall performance, including how we approach change initiatives. For example, a command and control leadership style does not work for transformational change, yet it is remains the most dominant leadership style most leaders and institutions still rely on. To change our behaviour and our institutional cultures, we first need to change our mindsets about the nature of leadership if we want to produce sustainable behaviour change. To truly lead universities through disruption, **leaders themselves must change. You need to disrupt your leadership**. Furthermore, our ability to change our institutional culture begins with the understanding of how we have helped to create it.

"Personal change must precede or at least accompany management and organization change ... by attempting to change an organization or a management style

[8] See Mrig and Sanaghan [21].

without first changing one's habit patterns is analogous of attempting to improve one's tennis game before developing the muscles that make better stokes possible" [37].

5. A new kind of leadership and a new kind of leader

"The world as we have created it is a product of our thinking. It cannot be changed without changing our thinking". Albert Einstein.

When unpacking the case for change versus the capacity for change, I surfaced, five kinds of shifts needed to lead in a VUCA world characterised by complexity, disruption and uncertainty. Are these the only shifts that matter in the current state? I am sure not, we can add many more. But, I believe that these five shifts that demonstrate the complexities of the challenges facing higher education has the potential to reposition and reinvent our leadership for the future.

I have labelled them as the:

1. Awareness shift
2. Identity shift
3. Mindset shift
4. Paradigm shift
5. The shift from fear to psychological safety

Although each shift will be discussed separately, they are intertwined and interdependent. As I discuss each shift, I would like to invite you to think about how each one of these shifts translate into capabilities. In other words, what are the future proof capabilities for universities in general and your own university that we can extract from this discussion?

5.1 Shift One: The Awareness Shift

In Abraham Kaplan's [38] ground-breaking 1964 book on methodology for behavioural sciences he recites the following classic story:

Late one night, a policeman sees a drunk man on his hands and knees searching for something under a streetlight and asks him what he has lost. He says he lost a coin. The policeman helps him search for the coin for some time and after no luck, asks, "Are you sure you lost the coin here?". The drunkard replies, "No, I lost it in the park over there". The surprised policeman then asked him why then is he searching here, to which the drunkard replies, "This is where the light is."

Various versions of this humorous story referred to as *The streetlight effect*, or the *drunkard's search principle*, has been told for many years across different cultures. The story illustrates a type of observational bias playing out when people only search for something where it is easiest to look, or where we are used to looking, rather than where the answer most likely could be found. This error has limited the progress of science repeatedly.

In their White Paper *Leadership beyond competencies* (2014), Ruderman, Clerkin, and Connolly [39] state that in the field of leadership development, our streetlight has shone on behavioural competencies and skills as the standard for all leadership development. But, leadership encompasses much more than visible behaviours—what happens in the mind or the "inner theatre"[9] of the leader as described by Kets de Vries is just as important for effective leadership [40].

"As a field, we have long considered the mind a "black box"— an unknown and unknowable area—and so, like in the streetlight story, we have looked elsewhere". They suggest that in order to increase their effectiveness and impact, it is time that leaders expand the light to include the mind—calling attention to the dynamics of a leader's internal landscape—and its interplay with their behaviour. Leaders need to shift their awareness from external forces to forces that are less visible such as their physiological, emotional, and mental processes in order to increase the efficacy of their leadership. This is much more than an attitude or even a mindset, but an inner capability (cognitive, psychological and emotional). As such, it must be developed from the inside out—from the level of individual consciousness out and through the level of interpersonal engagement and relationship. And then—and only then—further outward into the institutional territory [41]. Only by developing your inner leadership—your capacity to transcend your own inner uncertainty, insecurities, hesitance, and emotional triggers and to act, instead, from a place of intention, purpose and vision—will you be able to develop in your outer leadership—your ability to readily adopt the skills, practices and thinking needed to catalyse more efficiency and higher performance in the human systems around you.

In the current volatile, unpredictable, complex, and ambiguous world, the term "transformation" has become universal in the organisational change literature. The nature of the current complexity often leaves leaders feeling "in over their heads" recognising all too well that the nature of the complexity, uncertainty and ambiguity—both around them and within them—is beyond their capacity to act with insight, foresight, and grace. This necessitates a broadening of our understanding of the word "transformation"—from a process that applies primarily to the external environment of institutional structures, systems and processes, to include the consciousness from which those very structures, processes, systems and institutions originate—the inner world of the individual leader. This will imply that all us who think of ourselves as transformational leaders, must first catalyse transformation within ourselves before we can hope to catalyse transformation in the people and systems around us.

The well-known psychiatrist Dan Siegel[10] calls this awareness "mindsight"—the ability to observe our internal mental processes unfold, "the capacity to perceive the mind in yourself and others" [42] (Siegel, 2010, p. x). According to Siegel, mindsight is different from the well-known practice of self-reflection in the sense that it is a metacognitive practice that allows us see the internal workings of our

[9] Manfred Kets de Vries [40] describes our "inner theatre" as our unique mixture of motivational needs and fears which determines our character and contributes to the triangle of our mental life—a tightly interlocked triangle consisting of cognition, affect, and behaviour. We all have an "inner theatre" which is filled with our early childhood experiences with people who have influenced, for better or worse, our response patterns as adults. Though we are generally unaware of it, we often relate to others as we once did to early caretakers or significant others. These early relational themes translate into consistent behavioural patterns of relating as adults and contribute to our unique personality style—that develops over time. How we anticipate that others will react to us, and how we in turn react to others is determined by this "basic script" for relating that we developed as coping mechanism in early childhood. As adults, we take these fundamental needs or fears into the context of our workplace relationships. Unfortunately, the life-scripts drawn up in childhood often cause us to behave inappropriately in adult situations—to the detriment of our effectiveness in relationships and in leadership.

[10] Prof. Dan Siegal is a renowned neuroscientist and psychotherapist, Professor of Psychiatry at the UCLA Medical School and co-director of the UCLA Mindful Awareness Research Center, and executive director of the Mindsight Institute. He founded the field of "Interpersonal Neurobiology."

own minds in the present moment. Siegel is of the opinion that this ability to focus internally on our mind (and the minds of others) is a prerequisite for responding with emotional and social intelligence and fundamental to personal growth and transformation. It helps us to become aware of our internal mental and emotional processes or default patterns without it overwhelming us or being blown out of proportion. It is the inner capacity of individuals to sense acutely and to respond gracefully, in the midst of complexity and ambiguity. It enables us to shift out of our autopilot of habitual responses and beyond the reactive emotional patterns we often get trapped in. This awareness allows leaders to "hit the pause button" and to choose a more intentional and appropriate response in the face of emotionally charged or intellectually complex situations. In this way leaders can learn to both observe, as well as shape and shift, how they think, feel, and behave. This increased awareness promotes emotional regulation and mitigates impulsivity and reactivity while simultaneously sharping the leader's understanding of others' emotions and behaviours—skills both necessary and invaluable to leading self and others effectively. In this process we learn to use our self-awareness and inner will to realise our deepest resources and self-leading and self-mastery potential. When we become more self-aware we become more integrated and self-directed individuals taking action based on our values and purpose—becoming more responsive and less reactive.

5.1.1 *Becoming our own best friends*

By internal "tuning in" and paying attention to our mind's intention in a non-judgemental and nonreactive way by self-observation, we become "our own best friends" as described by Siegal. To make this shift from outer to inner awareness, we need to shine light on disciplines not traditionally associated with leadership development, such as neuroscience, contemplative practices, and positive psychology. For example, an increased awareness of our neurological circuitry can help leaders better understand their own and others' behaviours. At its heart, effective leadership development rests on self-awareness and research in the field of neuroscience can helped us improve our understanding of how our internal systems interact to process information and influence behaviour. For example, understanding how the brain processes pleasure and pain can help us to understand how we subconsciously motivate much of how we navigate the world—with huge implications for leaders and institutions.

5.2 Shift Two: The Identity Shift

The second shift is labelled as an Identity shift. This shifts require that leaders disrupt their identities. In their book: *How HE leaders derail* (2018) Patrick Sanaghan and Jillian Lohndorf [43] state that in HE, there is a prevalent myth that the smartest person should be the leader. They talk about the "peril of smartship" and state it as follows:

"We rely more heavily on 'smartship' than leadership. This is a tendency we see in organizations across all industries, but we are especially prone to it in higher education because of the unique weight we assign to hierarchy and tradition".

However, there is a deep humility needed in leaders as a way of facilitating the creativity of employees, especially in an industry changing as rapidly as higher education. The skills that brought us to where we are, does not really fit this complexity. It requires new approaches, new mindsets and new skills. Humility and the willingness to admit mistakes may be two of the most important qualities for a leader in HE. This will require a shift from a performance mindset—that draws on our current knowledge about one's competence—to a learning mindset, fueled by curiosity. A performance mindset is based on our need for favourable judgements—and the avoidance of negative judgements [44].[11] In very simple terms, it means a shift from providing answers to asking questions. What this shift is suggesting is a mindset of experimentation, discovery, partnership, and abundance-thinking. However, it will require that leaders embrace the discomfort of not having the answers and experience the liberation that comes from knowing you do not need to have the answers.

Most of the revolutionary inventions and noteworthy discoveries throughout history are the result of curiosity. Albert Einstein once memorably claimed, "I have no special talents. I am only passionately curious". In *The Businesss Case for Curiosity* [45], a recent issue of the Harvard Business Review, Professor Francesca Gino explains how new research indicates that curiosity is more important than ever to leadership and performance. "When our curiosity is triggered, we think more deeply and rationally about decisions and come up with more creative solutions." Curiosity, humility, and the willingness to admit error go hand-in-hand since you must be humble enough to know you do not have all the answers *and* confident enough to admit it. Traits exhibited by arrogant leaders are exactly the traits we *do not* need if institutions are going to confront the complex challenges facing them. Prof. David Schmittlein, at the MIT Sloan School of Management also advocates the business case for curiosity and states that "great leadership teams in the new economy have a deep and restless curiosity".

Therefore, in a sense, the very elements that make academia strong also make it vulnerable. In higher education, enormous emphasis is placed on smartship or individual intellectual achievement and credentials. "Being right" and having the answers matters—a great deal. Although well meaning, giving people answers as to how to solve problems based on your experience instead of asking powerful questions tends to keep people small and dependent. "You cannot expect people to seriously consider your idea without accepting the possibility that they will challenge it. Accepting that process of engagement as the terrain of leadership liberates you personally."[12]

Making this shift sounds simple, but it is really hard because it requires from leaders to stop trying to prove how smart they are and rather be the person in the room who can facilitate deep thinking and help all the best ideas come out. This shift could be quite challenging for academic leaders. It is also an important part of the shift from being an *academic* to being and *academic leader*. It is a shift that many do not make, or only achieve in part. The thing about these changes is that they are horribly uncomfortable for anyone who has been promoted into management due to their "smartship" or "expertise" and whose identity is built around their individual academic achievements. So, you can imagine—when you shift

---

[11] According to Ames [44] two major goal orientations are at play in any achievement situation: mastery or "task-oriented goal orientation" and performance or "ego-involvement goal orientation". Alternative labels are 'learning goal orientation' and 'performance goal orientation' respectively. The main distinction between these two types of goal orientations is whether learning is valued as a means to reach some external goals or primarily as an end in itself. More specifically, people with mastery-oriented goals focus upon the task, and prefer situations where they can expand their skills and knowledge and mostly assess their success by using "self-referenced standards" such as "Have I learned? Have I improved?" On the other hand, people with a "performance or ego" goal orientation focus upon the self, and prefer situations where they can demonstrate their competence and abilities and compare it with those of others. These students usually assess their success using interpersonal norms, such as "Did I do better than others? Do others think that I am smart?"

[12] See Heifetz [46].

from providing answers to asking questions, your performance mindset—based on your need to get favourable judgements and avoid negative judgements—will be challenged. The question in your mind will be: Will I still be perceived as competent?

In the VUCA world, leaders who set a tone with a mindset of experimentation, curiosity and humility will signal to their teams that they are not preoccupied with creating an image of the leader-as-hero but are committed to developing a remarkable community of leaders at every level in their institutions. Thereby, they will drive home the narrative that co-creating the future through a collective leadership capability is the strongest route to institutional performance in times of disruption.

5.3 Shift Three: The Mindset Shift

"Organizations unintentionally encourage people to choose to maintain what they have, to be cautious and dependent"[13].

The essence of this shift I have labelled the mindset shift, is about the transformation of the word power that we have witnessed over the last couple of years. In their notable study of power conducted in 1959, social psychologists John French and Bertram Raven categorised power as coming from five separate and distinct sources [48]. Legitimate power, reward power, coercive power, referent power and expert power—information power was added later in 1965. But, these all have focused on the LEADER's sources of power and has largely ignored the rest of the organisation. In the VUCA world, this one-directional view of power has become outdated because leadership is about EMpowerment—and in that sense the directionality of the word is wrong. Old-style top-down authoritative leadership will not be enough to lead universities into the future. In their book *How HE leaders derail*, Patrick Sanaghan and Jillian Lohndorf [49], state that the pace of change is too fast and the challenges too complex to be figured out by one individual, irrespective of how smart, experienced or qualified you are. They also mention that the risk aversion that is endemic in many institutions of higher education, throttles empowerment—based on an entrepreneurial, learning culture—stifling it before it can really grow. Unfortunately, according to their research, arrogant and micromanaging leaders (two of the most important causes they have identified for derailment of leaders in HE) often thrive and retain their positions because they operate as "guardians of the status quo". This kind of shift in power is accompanied by a significant change of the centrality of leaders in our universities—a kind of phenomenon we can call UNBOSSING the university and forming an entrepreneurial contract with people, where every staff member accepts ownership for the success of the university as if it was their own. The path to empowerment is to shift from traditional patriarchal, autocratic organisational management and toxic political games where managers believe they have to control people and situations to an entrepreneurial cycle. Empowerment is based on the belief that the most trustworthy source of authority comes from within people. The role of leadership is to help people trust their own instincts, to realise that they are responsible for all of their actions—irrespective of the institutional culture or external environment—and that the local of control for their actions is internal. There is a lot a talk in HE about decolonising the curriculum, however, we also need to decolonise leadership. There is nothing more colonial than to lead people in a way that says: 'I know and you don't'.

---

[13] See Block [47], p. 21.

This shift from power to EMpower also links with the shift from patriarchy to partnership that Peter Block refers to in his book *The empowered manager*[14]. The first version of this book—which validated the shift in control from top management to front line people who are closest to the work—was published in 1987 [47]. Although it had its moment in the sun in the early 90s, the topic of empowerment needs to be reintroduced in institutions of higher learning since it is highly relevant for our current context. Most of our institutions still emphasise a top-down, high control orientation. People are still viewed as just another "resource" or a form of "asset" whose "talent" needs to be carefully managed. We still believe that remuneration drives motivation and performance and that the institutional vision should come from the executive management. People are often told the institution values autonomy and initiative but then they are treated like children by management who believes their role is to control people. In the same line, we hear people constantly call for strong leadership and waiting for management to give direction and vision. According to Peter Block, this is an expression of their dependency—finding comfort in being led—implying that until something above me change, do not expect me to operate much differently.

The patriarchal mindset underlies the choice for safety, predictability and control and nurtures a dependent mentality. The cornerstone of the patriarchal mindset is the belief that the foundation to the organisation's success is the leader or leaders at the top—the more heroic they are, the better. In contrast, the partnership or empowerment approach offered as an alternative to patriarchy by Peter Block, is about placing choice, decision making and control close to and in the hands of the people who do the work. It is about balancing the power between the leaders and those around them. This requires a shift in leaders' thinking and a shift in mindset where a sense of partnership and purpose is cultivated among people at all levels in the institution. When people trust that they have more control over their work, they then become co-creators in defining the institution's vision and purpose. In fact, people need to realise that dependency is no longer the safer path and that there is nothing to wait for from above to create a faculty or department of your own choosing. How we choose to behave and respond at any point in time is either a move in an entrepreneurial or a patriarchal direction. As stated by Peter Block, a hierarchical power-oriented culture breeds hierarchical power-oriented people. The institution then becomes a breeding ground for toxic political playoffs and manipulative tactics driven by personal ambition. The choice for self-assertion and risk is the antidote for caution and maintaining what we have inherited. A university with empowered staff who take ownership is a university that is moving forward. Empowerment also creates a much more positive and fulfilling working environment for everyone, managers included. Empowerment is a sound strategy in the face of all the uncertainty and volatility that is swirling our institutions. "If we have found a way of doing our job that does not entail any risk, then the organization probably does not need us"[15]

Good relationships are based on partnership, not patriarchy. Patriarchy creates a parent–child relationship between management and workers. Empowerment has huge implications for followership and creates a more accountable culture. Partnership is built on empowerment, not dependency. The reason we find partnerships so challenging is that parenting—and its fiercer version, patriarchy—is so deeply etched in our muscle memory and armature that we are often are not even

[14] The Book: *The Empowered Manager: Positive Political Skills at Work* (2017) was the prescribed text book for TUT's LEAD programme in 2019. The theme of the LEAD programme in this year was *We are empowered*

[15] See Block [47], p. 191.

aware of it. In the VUCA world, honesty and transparency is critical. However, the dilemma with patriarchy is that we know that children do not speak the truth to their parents. People do not speak truth in front of power. This difficulty it creates in approaching leaders with open and candid feedback can foster a "seduction of the leader"[16] dynamic—first introduced by Rodney Napier. An insidious dynamic that many senior managers fall victim to as they endeavour to lead their institutions where followers (for whatever reason) are hesitant to provide leaders with pertinent information and honest feedback about their ideas or impact. This in turn stalls quick action and decisive decision-making. However, as so eloquently mentioned by Peter Block, in partnership—not telling the truth is betrayal. Therefore, powerful leadership is not about being a good parent. Good and honest feedback is critical for leaders to become aware of their impact on people and their institutions. Leaders need to constantly and directly engage with their constituents and proactively seek candid unfiltered feedback and input. Without access to this information—honest and valid concerns, viewpoints, ideas and suggestions—leaders are at risk of being seduced into believing people are firmly behind them and that they are on the right track [50].

Unfortunately, in our institutions many of the complaints people have are often around micromanagement and is controlling people. This is because one of the most difficult shifts for leaders to make to go from their own power to orchestrating the energy of others. **The idea of the leader as the conductor of an orchestra is a good metaphor here:**

When you listen to a piece of music—you hear the violin, you hear the clarinet—but do you hear the conductor? We know there is a conductor who orchestrates the whole performance but we do not *hear* the conductor. The following story about the famous conductor Herbert van Karajan is a good illustration of this shift. It is told that in his early years of conducting, Karajan was a very directive conductor giving very precise instructions to musicians about how to perform. However, toward the end of his life, he made a major shift and became very restrained in his gestures when he was conducting. During one of the rehearsals, one of his musicians felt very frustrated by this 'lack of direction' and asked him: "Maestro, with all due respect, when should I start playing my tune?" Karjan responded by saying to him: "when you feel it is the time." During the press conference, one of the journalists asked Karajan: "Maestro why don't you give precise instructions to the orchestra?" To which Karajan wisely responded "that would be the worst damage I could do to them because if I would give them precise instructions then musicians will not listen to one another". In letting go of his need for control he allowed his musicians to make decisions, and also sends the message that I am going to trust you that you will make the right decision about when you are going to play your tune.

Collective and systemic intelligence is driving the new paradigm for leadership. From 'heroic' to 'collective and collaborative' or distributed leadership. However, leadership is often a well-developed misconception and its worth mentioning an interesting article which was published in 1985 by Meindl, Ehrlich and Durkerich. The title of the paper was *The romance of leadership* [51]. In this article the authors discussed our fascination with leadership in our collective consciousness and asked a rhetorical question: Do we glorify leadership? Why are we susceptible to falling

[16] "The seduction of the leader is a term that was first introduced by Dr. Rodney Napier. In short, it describes how (for various reasons) managers often do not receive important information and candid feedback about their impact or ideas because their subordinates or peers are hesitant to provide it to them. This reluctance to "speak truth to power" leaves the leader isolated and misinformed. Followers just go along to get along, which puts the leader—and, ultimately, the institution—at risk.

under the "spell" of leadership? Do we romanticise leaders and do we succumb to the charisma virus. Romanticism can shape conceptions not only of leaders, but also of followers, their agency and their (potential for) resistance to empowerment due to our tendency to over-attribute institutional successes and shortcomings to the leader. Seeing leaders as either charismatic heroes or charismatic villains—both viewpoints are illustrations of falling victim to the romance of leadership. According to the first camp, the leader deserves the credit for any positive outcome even when he had little to do with the achievement. The second group singles out every failure and attribute them to the leader—even when he might have played a minor role in the failure. This article puts forward a question which is very relevant for the times we find ourselves is:

Should we replace the romantic view of leadership with a view of leadership as a collective phenomenon that is shared among all members of an organisation and not the property of a single individual?

Current leadership thinking includes such notions as servant leadership, distributed leadership, authentic leadership, collaborative leadership, and humble or quiet leadership by Robert Greenleaf, David Rock, and Edgar Schein, among others. We need leaders who embrace the mindset of humility—who realise the need to tap into the collective power and capability of the whole university. Jim Collins, the author of the best-selling book *Good to Great* (2001) found in his research that most executives leading lucrative companies were introverted, humble, reserved and self-effacing. They demonstrated "indomitable will" but did not direct their drive and ambition toward their personal interest but toward the goals and purpose of the organisation [52].

Another question for us to reflect about is:

How many of our leaders have this mindset or need to make this mindset shift?

5.4 Shift Four: The Paradigm Shift

The 4IR is not only about technology but how the human experience can be incorporated into technology in order to create an inclusive, human-centred future. The founder of Facebook, Mark Zuckerberg, is renowned for saying that Facebook is as much about psychology and sociology as it is about technology [53]. Steve Jobs said, "It is in Apple's DNA that technology alone is not enough—it's technology married with the liberal arts, married with the humanities, that yields us the results that make our heart sing" [54]. We now have scientific evidence—thanks to the groundbreaking research of the late Dr. David Hawkins—that emotions have measurable energy. This energy can either foster or negate actual cell life. As explained in his book *Power vs. Force* [55], Hawkins reveals how an individual's log level—the measurable level of energy in their magnetic field—increases when positive emotions experienced by the person increase.

So a question to reflect about as leadership is: What Energy Are We Sending?

One of Hawkins's most remarkable findings was that when the log level was below 200, the cells actually started to die. This level below 200, is where the emotions of hate, shame, contempt, anxiety, regret, despair, blame, and humiliation reside. From a leadership perspective, what we can take from Hawkins's research is that it is key that leaders are able to regulate and manage their emotional state (one of the abilities of Emotional Intelligence or EQ), not just for their own emotional well-being and physical health but for the overall well-being of their staff. Leaders need to be able to self-regulate and manage their emotions and emotional impact on people in the face of uncertainty. At the same time they need to be able to support others to deal with their own fears, anxiety and discomfort [56]. Unfortunately, for a long time, especially in universities we have focused mostly on the cognitive intelligence of our leaders. When asked how you *feel* about an issue, the answer often is: 'Who cares, we are here to get a job done, to be rational and logical. A university is not a place to talk about feelings.' In fact, one of the strongest forms of contempt is to say to someone: 'Let's not get into the touchy feely issues'. Both personally and collectively, we pay a high price for denying our own and other people's feelings and denying them the opportunity for self-expression. I have not come across a manager who is not looking for new ways to motivate and engage their staff, but denying people their self-expression and expecting them to exercise self-control (which is different from self-regulation. Expecting people to suppress their emotions is putting a damper on their level of motivation and energy. It also keeps managers from really understanding the impact of their actions on the internal motivation and energy of people and expecting them to 'toe the line'. Our current context asks for a rebalancing of the relationship between IQ and EQ. It requires a paradigm shift from viewing leadership as cognitive labour alone to viewing leadership as emotional labour which requires EQ and a high level of emotional maturity. The complexity of the problems we are faced with is pushing us to make this shift. Is it going to be replace IQ? No—of course we will still need smart leaders, but EQ has been consistently undervalued—I often hear managers say 'I don't do emotions' but in the era of artificial intelligence we can expect a higher premium on the emotional capabilities of leaders—without it you will not be able to tap into the energy of empowerment. Napoleon is famous for saying that leaders are merchants of hope. Leaders in universities can create this much-needed hope by speaking to the collective imagination, hopes, dreams and fears of their people and create a sense of purpose and meaning. However, to accomplish this, they need to develop their emotional intelligence, a process that begins with self-awareness. This is not new of course—it is what the Oracle at Dephi has been telling us all along: **Know Thyself**! [57].

Our emotions guide us by assigning value to things and informing us what is worth striving for in future. Our emotions often contain a wisdom the analytic brain cannot reach—they are not the opposite of reason; they are the foundation of reason [58]. Unfortunately, as stated by Prof. Theo Veldsman [59] "Too often leaders are intelligence giants but maturity dwarfs" with wide-ranging and detrimental consequences for both the leader and the institution.

An overemphasis of IQ at the expense of EQ creates the conditions for toxic leaders. In order to be effective leaders, we need to be driven to seek deep connections and relations with others. These leaders firmly believe that deep change happens through deepening trusting relationships. The World Economic Forum (WEF) now considers EQ an essential skill for the 4IR. In fact, anything that makes us human is becoming very precious. Technology will be able to replicate human intelligence but not human emotions. These straining days of the current COVID-19 pandemic have once again highlighted the significance of a leader's emotional intelligence. The uncertainty about the future, constant disruptions and changes to the academic programme, working from home, stress and anxiety, and getting used to new ways of teaching and communication are all testing us in different ways. You will not be able to deal with the uncertainty and the anxiety it creates both in yourself, your team and your students if you cannot deal with your own and others emotions—or as mentioned before—orchestrate the energy provided by emotions. To do this you will need a highly developed EQ, which will include the ability to step back from your self-protective impulsive, emotional reactions triggered by uncertainty and instead operate from a place of presence and inner calmness. The importance of self-awareness cannot be emphasised enough, since awareness gives us choices about our behaviour.

Without exception, innovation is a social process which requires creative abrasion and constructive dissent—processes that rely on low social friction (as a result of trust) but high intellectual friction (as a result of the diversity of viewpoints). Our ability to be innovative will depend on our ability to be able to tap into the strength of the diversity in our teams. But then again—a word of caution—diversity has huge implications for your leadership. While we all realise that diverse teams can accomplish more than any individual member, we also understand that you just cannot throw a bunch of people in a room and hope for the best. To be able to capitalise on the intended outcomes of diversity, institutions need to focus on fostering an inclusive work environment that are *appreciative* of differences. The role of leadership in generating such an inclusive climate is pivotal. Research has provided clear evidence that diverse teams who are not well lead perform worse than homogeneous teams. Therefore, we need to move beyond diversity to build a deeply inclusive culture for which we need leaders with a highly developed EQ [60].

5.4.1 Shift from fear to psychological safety

"You know the adage 'People resist change.' It is not really true. People are not stupid. People love change when they know it is a good thing. No one gives back a winning lottery ticket. What people resist is not change per se, but loss. When change involves real or potential loss, people hold on to what they have and resist the change."[17]

EQ will also enable us to make the critical climate shift in our institutions from fear to psychological safety. The first key principle is that: **The presence of fear in an organisation is the first sign of weak leadership**. Low levels of psychological safety create a culture of silence. A culture of silence is a dangerous culture in the VUCA world. The book *The fearless organization* [62] by Prof. Amy Edmonson[18] from Harvard Business School is one of the books we discussed in our LEAD Leadership Circles in our own university's leadership development programme. She defines psychological safety as the willingness to "show and employ one's whole self without fear of negative consequences to your self-image, status or career." Furthermore, it is "a shared belief that the team is safe for interpersonal risk taking." Psychological safety, therefore, is a social condition in which you feel that you are included, it is safe to learn and to contribute, and safe to challenge the status quo—all without fear of being punished in any way [63]. Leaders who are humble, authentic, and transparent infuse trust and psychological safety. In turn, psychological safety empowers people to perform to the best of their ability. For our universities to flourish in a world where innovation will differentiate institutions as successful or failing—hiring the smartest academics will not be enough. You must be able to create a climate where it is safe for them to take interpersonal risks and share not only their knowledge and ideas, but also their emotions and feelings. Eliminating fear can promote innovation by freeing people's energy for complex problem-solving and innovative thinking—instead of self-protection. Understanding the importance of psychological safety traces back to organisational change research in the early 1960s. In his book *Personal and Organizational Change through Group Methods* [64], MIT Professor Edgar Schein wrote about the need for psychological safety to help people cope with the uncertainty they experience at work. Schein later noted that psychological safety was vital for allowing people to

[17] See Heifetz [61].

[18] Amy Edmondson is a management Professor at Harvard Business School and has done a tremendous amount of work in the area of psychological safety.

overcome defensiveness and "learning anxiety" when things go wrong and focus on achieving shared goals rather than on self-protection. Psychological safety is essential to producing high performance in a VUCA world. If you have an unsafe culture, you are blocking your team's ability to innovate. Sadly, most leaders are not even aware that they are doing it.

A question for reflection: which of these shifts are most needed in your university? Which of these shifts are most needed in your own leadership?

6. Shaping the future—Are we at a fork in the road?

"The changes are so profound that, from the perspective of human history, there has never been a time of greater promise or potential peril".[19]

According to Prof Klaus Schawab - founder and Executive Chairman of the WEF - and author of *The Fourth Industrial Revolution*, there has never been a time of greater promise, or greater peril. In particular, he makes an appeal to all leaders to:

"Together shape a future that works for all by putting people first, empowering them and constantly reminding ourselves that all of these new technologies are first and foremost tools made by people for people."

As I have attempted to lay out in this chapter, our current and future challenges demand that we take a different view about leadership and the kind of leaders our universities need. Intelligence or functional expertise does not equate to knowing how to lead. Leadership is a deeply human and interpersonal process. Becoming a better leader follows the same process as becoming a better person.

In his book—*The rise of the robots*—Martin Ford forecasts a future that will be terrifying in the absence of public debate and intervention. He systematically sketches the possibilities of artificial intelligence and illustrate the societal implications using a wealth of economic data. Therefore, summarising everything being said in this chapter, the final shift needed would be from leadership to *Stewardship*. Stewardship is the umbrella idea that holds the potential to achieve the fundamental change and reform we seek in the way we lead and govern our institutions. In his book *Stewardship: Choosing service over self-interest* [65] Peter Block defines stewardship as holding something in trust for another—as leaders, we are entrusted with the well-being of people—our students, our staff, our communities, the environment and the planet. Stewardship is a willingness to be accountable for the well-being of our institutions, because we hold our universities in trust for future generations. Stewardship is a willingness to act without needing to control those around us. Imagine how strong our universities would be if everyone were deeply committed and accountable for its success.

In conclusion, steward leadership starts with wanting to the best FOR the world or the university, not only the best IN the world. It is the basic call for all of us to become more than we currently are. However, you can only be more if you, through purposeful action, help others and allow them to be *more than you*. But—you cannot be more if you do not know *how to be less* [66]. Our firm belief in the value of leadership is fundamental to most of our theories about organisational change and transformation. However, this universal and almost religious belief in individual leaders as the answer to transformation and change is precisely what slows the process of fundamentally redesigning institutions and reforming our leadership. Quoting the wisdom of Peter Block (1993:15) "Stewardship offers an alternative approach to reform that puts leadership in the background where it belongs" [67].

[19] Klaus Schwab, WEF.

7. Chapter reflection: what are the leadership skills for the future?

Based on the shifts discussed in this chapter, the next question would be to ask how this translate into the future skills requirements for our leaders? A one-size-fits all approach will not work. To ensure relevance for our context we need to begin a robust conversation in our institutions with all our leaders around the following three questions:

7.1 What are the *eroding* skills?

What are the leadership behaviours that were considered effective in the past but are now considered outdated and even detrimental? Why?

For example, the time for top-down autocratic leadership is over, or should be anyway. This is not the leadership that is going to position our universities for the future.

7.2 What are the *enduring* skills?

What leadership attributes and behaviours have passed the test of time? They are those skills that are still important today, and will be important forever. Why?

For example, in the 4IR, aspects like integrity, trust, and emotional and social intelligence have become even more important. Without integrity, trust and compassion the advancements in technology can do lots of damage to our staff, students and society at large.

7.3 What are the *emerging* skills?

What are the behaviours that might have been regarded as unimportant before but are now considered highly relevant, significant and essential for a leader to be considered effective? Why?

7.4 Crafting a future-fit leadership development strategy

The next logical question to ask when designing a leadership development strategy would be: How can we cultivate the emerging behaviours, combine them with the enduring behaviours and proactively shed the eroding behaviours? However, future fit leadership development requires more than proposing a new list of competencies which leaders will need to acquire (also known as horizontal development)—as if it were just a matter of 'fixing' or 'servicing' our leaders—to transformational development gaining *greater capacity*. This implies expanding the mindsets or the mental models leaders engage when they are thinking—including their identity. It results in more sophisticated ways of thinking or what Hamman [68] refers to as "complexity of mind"—by developing leaders' cognitive and emotional maturity (also referred to as vertical development).[20] Nick Petrie from the Centre for Creative Leadership asserts that if we want to have a better understanding as to why some leaders are so effective, we first have to understand that leaders do not only think differently from each other—they also think from different developmental stages. He states that "most leaders already know what they should be doing. What they lack is the personal development to do so."

[20] The process of horizontal and vertical development often occurs at the same time. However, it is helpful to make a distinction between the two since very often practitioners in the field of leadership development have little or no knowledge of vertical development.

Most leaders today find themselves in the arduous position where the complexity they deal with is overwhelming many leaders' capacity to cope and outpacing both their individual and collective development. For our institutions to thrive in the complicated VUCA world, we will need to develop leaders who can combine wisdom in choosing the right strategies (greater capacity) with the relevant experience and competencies to be able to execute them (competency acquisition). The current challenge however for most universities is that the leadership development interventions they embark on, are predominantly or even exclusively designed around a list of leadership behaviours or competencies. Therefore, we need a leadership development philosophy and practice framework that takes an alternative perspective—one in which we view mindset and culture not from the outside in, but from the inside out. It entails more than training a leader in skills or expanding their knowledge but about transforming the ways a leader thinks. This in turn will have an impact on what they do and how they behave. Only then will leaders be able to create and nurture an institutional culture where innovation can flourish. Leadership development practitioners should design interventions that address the identities, beliefs and mindsets that drives behaviour if they want to prepare leaders with the capabilities to lead successfully in a future that will be perpetually undergoing change.

Acknowledgements

The TUT LEAD programme is funded by Department of Higher Education and Training (DHET) University Capacity Development Grant (UCDG).

Author details

Tessie H.H. Herbst
Tshwane University of Technology, Pretoria, South Africa

*Address all correspondence to: herbstt@tut.ac.za

References

[1] Mrig, A., and Sanaghan, P. (2017). Report: The Skills Future Higher-Ed Leaders Need to Succeed. Academic Impressions. Retrieved from: https://www.academicimpressions.com/PDF/future-skillset.pdf

[2] Trow, M. (2007). Reflections on the transition from elite to mass to universal access: Forms and phases of higher education in modern societies since WWII. In: J. F. Forest, P. G. Altbach, eds. International Handbook of Higher Education (pp. 243-280). Dordrecht, Netherlands: Springer.

[3] Watson, W. R., and Watson, S. L. (2014). Redesigning Higher Education: Embracing a New Paradigm. Educational Technology, May–June, pp. 47-51. Retrieved from: https://www.academia.edu/10400742/Redesigning_higher_education_Embracing_a_new_paradigm?email_work_card=abstract-read-more

[4] Ngcamu, B. S. (2017). The effects of leadership traits on transformation: A case study of a South African University. The Journal for Transdisciplinary Research in Southern Africa 13(1). Retrieved from: https://td-sa.net/index.php/td/article/view/403/615

[5] Penprase, B. (2018). The Fourth Industrial Revolution and Higher Education. DOI:10.1007/978-981-13-0194-0_9

[6] Penprase, B. E. (2018). The fourth industrial revolution and higher education. In: N. Gleason (Ed.). Higher Education in the Era of the Fourth Industrial Revolution (pp. 207-229). Palgrave Macmillan.

[7] Horney, N., Pasmore, B., and O'Shea, T. (2010). Leadership agility: A business imperative for a VUCA world. People and Strategy 33(4):32.

[8] McCormack, T. J., Lemoine, P. A., Waller, R. E., and Richardson, M. D. (2020). Global higher education: Examining response to the COVID-19 pandemic using agility and adaptability. Journal of Education and Development 5(1):10-16.

[9] Mrig, A., and Sanaghan, P. (2018). Report: The Future of Higher Education. Denver, CO: Academic Impressions.

[10] Reflections of South African University Leaders 1981 to 2014 (2016). Published by African Minds and the CHE. Retrieved from: http://www.africanminds.co.za/wp-content/uploads/2016/03/CHEC-Reflections-proof-05a.pdf

[11] Ngcamu, B. S. (2016). An exploratory study on the influence of leadership on transformation in a higher education institution: A case of the Durban University of Technology. Published Thesis. University of KwaZulu-Natal.

[12] Sirat, M., Ahmad, A. R., and Azman, N. (2012). University leadership in crisis: The need for effective leadership positioning in Malaysia. Higher Education Policy 25:511-529.

[13] Herbst, T. H. H., and Garg, A. K. (2017). Transformational leadership potential at a University of Technology. The Journal of Applied Business Research 33(4):741-758.

[14] The State of the Leadership Training Market Report (2020). Retrieved from: https://trainingindustry.com/wiki/leadership/the-leadership-training-market/

[15] Hammond, J., Keeney, R. and Raiffa, H. (2006). The Hidden Traps of Decision Making. Harvard Business Review.

[16] Heifetz, R., Grashow, A. and Linksy, M. (2009). The Practice of Adaptive Leadership. Boston, MA: Harvard Business Review Press.

[17] Heifetz, R. A. (1994). Leadership without Easy Answers. Cambridge, MA: Belknap Press of Harvard University Press.

[18] Heifetz, R., Grashow, A. and Linksy, M. (2009). The Practice of Adaptive Leadership. Boston, MA: Harvard Business Review Press.

[19] Heifetz, R., Grashow, A. and Linksy, M. (2009). The Practice of Adaptive Leadership. Boston, MA: Harvard Business Review Press.

[20] Mrig, A., and Sanaghan, P. (2018). Report: The Future of Higher Education. Denver, CO: Academic Impressions.

[21] Mrig, A., and Sanaghan, P. (2017). The Skills Future Higher-Ed Leaders Need to Succeed. Denver: Academic Impressions.

[22] Otto Sharmer (2009). Theory-U: Learning from the Future as it Emerges. San Francisco: Berrett-Koehler Publishers, Inc.

[23] Hamman, M. (2019). Design for a new kind of leadership and a new kind of leader. Retrieved from: https://static1.squarespace.com/static/5cbe1f34e8ba446390bdf54c/t/5cca02e70d92973d8f127eb2/1556742891314/michael Hamman+-+whitepaper+-+A+New+Kind+of+Leadership+and+a+New+Kind+of+Leader.pdf

[24] Heifetz, R., and Linsky, M. (2002). A Survival Guide for Leaders. Harvard Business Review.

[25] Mccormack, J., Propper, C., and Smith, S. (2013). Herding Cats? Management and University Performance. The Economic Journal 124. DOI:10.1111/ecoj.12105

[26] Nelson, P., and Cohen, E. (2010). Riding the Tiger: Leading through Learning in Turbulent Times. American Society for Training and Development Press.

[27] Vaill, P. (1996). Learning as a Way of Being: Strategies for Survival in a World of Permanent White Water. JosseyBass: San Francisco.

[28] Heifetz, R., Alexander, A. G., and Linsky, M. (2009). Leadership in a (Permanent) Crisis. Harvard Business Review.

[29] Heifetz, R., Alexander, A. G., and Linsky, M. (2009). Leadership in a (Permanent) Crisis. Harvard Business Review.

[30] Senge, P. (2006). The Fifth Discipline: The Art and Practice of the Learning Organization. New York: Doubleday/Currency.

[31] Anderson, B., and Adams, B. Reactive to creative leadership. The Leadership Circle. Retrieved from: https://leadershipcircle.com/wp-content/uploads/2019/01/Reactive-to-Creative-Leadership_edit.pdf

[32] Lauren Pollak and Katherine Wakid. Thriving in Ambiguity: Lessons from Exploratory Organizations. Harvard Business Review, 2010.

[33] Mrig, A., and Sanaghan, P. (2018). Report: The Future of Higher Education. Denver, CO: Academic Impressions.

[34] Alan Deutschman (2009). Change or Die: The Three Keys to Change at Work and in Life. New York: HarperCollins Publishers.

[35] Ready, D., Cohen, C., Kiron, D., and Pring, B. (2020). The New Leadership Playbook for the Digital Age. MIT Sloan Management Review.

[36] Mrig, A., and Sanaghan, P. (2018) Report: The Future of Higher Education. Denver, CO: Academic Impressions.

[37] Covey, S. R. (1985). Transformational vs. Transactional Leadership. Executive Excellence. Retrieved from: http://www.simpsonexecutivecoaching.com/pdf/orgchange/transformational-vs-transactional-leadership-stephen-covey.pdf

[38] Kaplan, A. (2017). The Conduct of Inquiry: Methodology for Behavioral Science. New York: Routledge.

[39] Ruderman, M. N., Clerkin, G., and Connolly, C. (2014). Leadership Development Beyond Competencies: Moving to a Holistic Approach. White Paper, Center for Creative Leadership (CCL). Retrieved from: https://cclinnovation.org/wp-content/uploads/2020/02/leadershipdevelopment competencies.pdf

[40] Kets de Vries, M. F. R., Florent-Treacy, E., and Korotov, K. (2011). Psychodynamic Issues in Organizational Leadership, INSEAD Faculty Research and Working Paper. Retrieved from: file:///C:/Users/HerbstT/Downloads/PsychodynamicIssuesinOrganizational Leadership.pdf

[41] Hamman,M.(2019).FromPredict-and-Plan to Sense-and-Respond. Agile Leadership Institute. Retrieved from: https://static1.squarespace.com/static/5cbe1f34e8ba446390bdf54c/t/5cca05244785d3a55c00ef2a/1556743461276/michael Hamman+-+article+%232-+From+Predict-Plan+to+Sense-Respond+Feb+2019.pdf

[42] Siegel, D. J. (2010). Mindsight: The New Science of Personal Transformation. New York, NY: Bantam Books.

[43] Sanaghan, P., and Lohndorf, J. (2018). How Higher Ed Leaders Derail: A Survival Guide for Leaders. Denver: Academic Impressions.

[44] Ames, C. (1992). Classrooms: Goals, structures, and student motivation. Journal of Educational Psychology 84(3):261-271. DOI:10.1037/0022-0663.84.3.261

[45] Gino, F. (2018). The Business Case for Curiosity. Harvard Business Review.

[46] Ronald A. Heifetz. Leadership on the Line: Staying Alive Through the Dangers of Leading.

[47] Block, P. (2017). The Empowered Manager: Positive Political Skills at Work (2nd Ed.). New Jersey: Wiley.

[48] Forsyth, D. R. (2010, 2006). Group Dynamics. Belmont: Wadsworth, Cengage Learning.

[49] Sanaghan, P., and Lohndorf, J. (2018). How Higher Ed Leaders Derail: A Survival Guide for Leaders. Denver: Academic Impressions.

[50] Sanaghan, P., and Eberbach, K. The Seduction of the Leader in Higher Education. Higher ED Impact. Retrieved from: file:///C:/Users/HerbstT/Downloads/The_Seduction_of_the_Leader.pdf

[51] Meindl, J., Ehrlich, S., and Dukerich, J. (1985). The Romance of Leadership. Administrative Science Quarterly 30(1):78-102. DOI:10.2307/2392813

[52] Collins, J. C. (2001). Good to Great: Why Some Companies Make the Leap ... and Others Don't. New York, NY: HarperBusiness.

[53] Olejarz, J. M. (2017). Liberal Arts in the Digital Age. Harvard Business Review. Retrieved from: https://hbr.org/2017/07/liberal-arts-in-the-data-age

[54] Horace, D. (2011). Steve Job's Ultimate Lessons for Companies. Harvard Business Review. Retrieved from: https://hbr.org/2011/08/steve-jobss-ultimate-lesson-fo

[55] Hawkins, D. R. (1985). Power vs Force: The Hidden Determinants of Human Behavior (5.2.1985). Hay House.

[56] Heifetz, R., Grashow, A., and Linksy, M. (2009). The Practice of Adaptive Leadership. Boston, MA: Harvard Business Review Press.

[57] Kets de Vries, M. (2003). Dysfunctional Leadership. INSEAD Working Paper Series. Retrieved from: https://flora.insead.edu/fichiersti_wp/inseadwp2003/2003-58.pdf

[58] David Brooks (2019). The Second Mountain: The Quest for a Moral Life. New York: Random House.

[59] Veldsman, T. (2017). Maturity makes great leaders. Management Matters 17(2). Retrieved from: file:///C:/Users/HerbstT/Downloads/maturity-makes-great-leaders.pdf

[60] Ashikali, A., Groeneveld, S., and Kuipers, B. (2020). The Role of Inclusive Leadership in Supporting an Inclusive Climate in Diverse Public Sector Teams. Review of Public Personnel Administration. Retrieved from: DOI:10.1177/0734371X19899722

[61] Ronald A. Heifetz. The Practice of Adaptive Leadership: Tools and Tactics for Changing Your Organization and the World.

[62] Edmonson, A. (2019). The Fearless Organization—Creating Psychological Safety in the Workplace for Learning, Innovation, and Growth. New Jersey: Wiley.

[63] Clark, T. R. (2020). The 4 Stages of Psychological Safety: Defining the Path to Inclusion and Innovation (2020th ed.). Berrett-Koehler.

[64] Schein, E. H. (1965). Personal and Organizational Change through Group Methods: The Laboratory Approach. John Wiley & Sons.

[65] Block, P. (1993). Stewardship: Choosing Service Over Self-Interest (1st ed.). Berrett-Koehler Publishers.

[66] April, K., Kukard, J., and Peters, K. (2013). Steward Leadership: A Maturational Perspective. Cape Town: UCT Press.

[67] Block, P. (1993). Stewardship: Choosing Service Over Self-Interest (1st ed.). Berrett-Koehler Publishers.

[68] Hamman, M. (2019). The Anatomy of Sensemaking and Logic. Agile Leadership Institute. Retrieved from: https://static1.squarespace.com/static/5cbe1f34e8ba446390bdf54c/t/5cca3ed23054890001f1d3af/1556758228048/michaelHamman+-+whitepaper+%233-+Anatomy+of+Sensemaking+and+Action+Logic+Feb+2019.pdf

Section 4

Resilience and Sustainable Leadership

Chapter 10

The Social Infrastructure of Organizational Resilience, Agency Capacity and Resilience Spirals: Starting Points for Resilient Leadership

Holger Pfaff

Abstract

The aim of this chapter is to analyze the social preconditions and dynamics of organizational resilience and the role of leadership in managing these conditions and dynamics. The chapter begins with an examination of the concept of organizational resilience, presents an individualistic and systemic perspective on this construct, proposes a social infrastructure model of organizational resilience and describes the phenomenon of resilience spirals. The chapter presents a functional performance level model of organizations and describes the possibility of upward spirals where organizations move up the functional performance levels and the possibility of downward spirals where organizations move down the functional performance levels. The importance of leadership in building and maintaining the social infrastructure of resilience and in managing resilience spirals is emphasized.

Keywords: organizational resilience, collective action, collective agency, resilience spirals, social infrastructure, social capital, leadership

1. Introduction

In times of crisis and adverse events, a certain type of leadership is required which is often called resilient leadership [1–8]. The literature on resilient leadership delivers rich knowledge about the characteristics of resilient leadership [2], the leadership styles of resilient leaders [1, 9], their actions and activities during crisis to foster collective and organizational resilience [4, 9] and ways to enhance resilient leadership [8, 10]. In contrast to this, comparably little is known about the role of leadership in building and maintaining the social foundation of organizational resilience. Some scholars have gone in this direction explaining how leaders could cultivate and activate social and cultural resources which foster organizational resilience [11–13]. The aim of this paper is to continue this work by more closely examining the social preconditions for and dynamics of organizational resilience and the role and starting point of leadership in shaping these phenomena. For this purpose, the chapter focuses first on the concept of organizational resilience, second on the social foundation of organizational resilience and third on the phenomenon of resilience spirals. The role of leadership in building and maintaining this social core of resilience and managing resilience spirals and the starting points to do so are emphasized.

2. Organizational resilience: perspectives and preconditions

This chapter presents two perspectives on the nature of organizational resilience and stresses the importance of examining the preconditions of organizational resilience.

2.1 Two perspectives on the nature of organizational resilience: the individualistic and systemic perspectives

The individualistic perspective on organizational resilience regards the individual resilience of the members of an organization as the main basis for organizational resilience [14–16]. Individual resilience could be defined as "the ability to bounce back from adversity, frustration, and misfortune" [17]. From the individualistic perspective, organizational resilience is the result of the aggregation of the individual resilience of all members. The factors that foster the resilience of individuals are a mixture of pessimism and optimism [14, 16], a proactive orientation [14, 18–20], sense-making abilities [14, 21], autonomy and self-determination [22], risk awareness [16], the ability to connect to others' knowledge [23, 24], the ability to use available resources [24], individual readiness to change [25, 26] and tolerance for ambiguity [27, 28].

The systemic perspective conceptualizes organizational resilience as an attribute of the organization. The literature describes at least four different systemic conceptions of resilience. The ecological resilience concept characterizes resilience as a system's ability to absorb external energy without structural change. This means that "the measurement of resilience is the magnitude of disturbance that can be absorbed before the system changes its structure by changing the variables and processes that control behavior" [29]. The second systemic concept describes resilience as the ability to bounce back to the previous equilibrium. This type of resilience "concentrates on stability near an equilibrium steady state, where resistance to disturbance and speed of return to the equilibrium are used to measure the property" [30]. The third conception of resilience defines resilience as the ability to achieve a new equilibrium, thus attaining a renewal state [16, 31]. The most dynamic systemic conception describes resilience as the ability of a system to switch between different equilibria [32–34] without changing the stable core of the system [33]. This core consists of the "keystone structuring processes which enables systems to adapt across a number of scales, sources of renewal and reformation" [33]. One aim of this chapter is to propose the hypothesis that in the case of social systems, the social infrastructure of collective systems is an important part of this core.

2.2 Preconditions of organizational resilience

There are specific and nonspecific preconditions that contribute to organizational resilience. Scholars have identified specific conditions that promote resilience. According to Hollnagel [35], resilient organizations are characterized by four abilities, namely (1) the ability to anticipate, (2) the ability to monitor possibly dangerous developments, (3) the ability to respond quickly and appropriately and (4) the ability to learn from past events and crises [36]. These abilities can be fostered by different measures [37], such as focused Human Resource (HR) strategic management [19, 22, 31], collective risk awareness tools, critical incident reporting systems [38–40], preparedness strategy [16], uncertainty strategies [19] and analysis tools such as the resilience analysis grid [35, 41].

Nonspecific preconditions for organizational resilience are factors that are necessary but not sufficient for resilience. They are useful not only for coping with crises but also for managing routine, everyday demands. Nonspecific preconditions lay the foundation for resilience but are unable to produce resilience on their own. Research into organizational resilience has identified many attributes in organizations that could contribute to resilience in a nonspecific way [37]. Identified nonspecific preconditions for organizational resilience include ritualized ingenuity [14, 42], flexibility [42], elasticity [28], adaptive capacity [16], organizational readiness to change [26, 43], proactiveness [19, 44], robustness [16], redundancy [16], resourcefulness [16], rapidity [16] and the regeneration capacity of an organization [45]. Other nonspecific preconditions are financial resources [46, 47], technical resources [28, 47] and informational resources [28]. With regard to the social foundations of organizational resilience, it is worthwhile to more closely examine the social resources which have been identified as relevant for organizational resilience. These are communication (to exchange information and knowledge relevant in times of crisis) [16], commitment and emotional attachment to the organization [16, 24, 26], common values [21, 48], trust and open communication [26, 28, 48–50] as well as social capital, sense of belonging and relational reserves [16, 26, 28, 46, 51].

3. The social infrastructure of collective agency: the social foundation of resilience management and organizational resilience

One purpose of this paper is show, that the stable core, which Gunderson [33] describes as a property of higher order resilient systems, is—in the case of social systems—equivalent to the social infrastructure of these systems. This social infrastructure guarantees that fast collective decisions and action could be made and that the collective systems experiences collective agency during normal times and during crisis. This social infrastructure consists of at least four infrastructural components: adaptive structures, goal-attaining structures, integrative structures and pattern maintenance structures. According to the infrastructural model of organizational resilience (see **Figure 1**), these structures together heighten the agency capacity of an organization, which is its basis for collective action and collective agency. Collective agency itself is a general precondition for all management activities in an organization as long as these activities are based on collective action. This is also true for resilience management, which if properly done leads to a higher amount of organizational resilience. Additionally, organizational resilience is not only dependent on resilience management alone but also on infrastructure, agency capacity and collective agency in a direct way. The amount of organizational resilience in turn influences the amount and quality of the social infrastructure of collective agency (**Figure 1**).

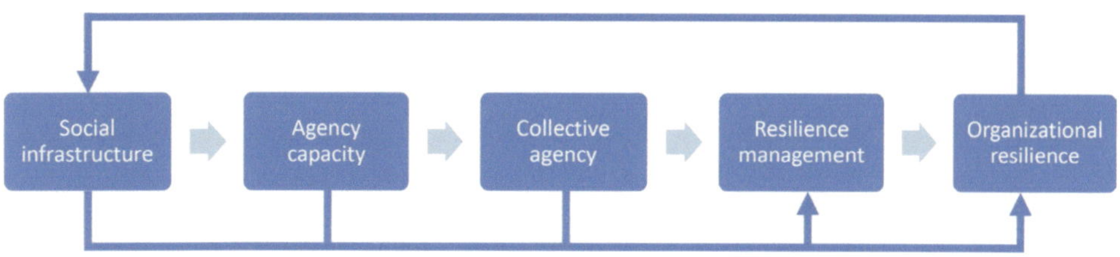

Figure 1.
The social infrastructure model of organizational resilience.

3.1 The social infrastructure of collective action and agency capacity

According to the structural-functional theory, I distinguish functions from structures. The underlying hypothesis is that certain structures may have certain functions [52–54]. The structure is then a solution to a systemic problem. Talcott Parsons' structural-functional theory further states that a social system has to fulfill four functions to act and survive: adaption (A), goal attainment (G), integration (I) and latent pattern maintenance (L; AGIL functions). The hypothesis here is that if all four functions are fulfilled, the collective possesses systemic agency capacity (see **Figure 2**) and by this, the ability to be an autopoietic social system. This autopoietic system is "self-producing or self-constructing" [55]. In this case, all four functions work together, forming the systemic agency capacity (**Figure 2**) and making a collective system able to act and react, to regulate itself according to its own value-based standards and to rebuild and reconstruct itself in times of crisis. Thus, if the metafunction systemic agency capacity exists within an organized collective, the emergence of an autopoietic social system from this collective is highly probable.

I now more closely examine the structures necessary to fulfill these four functions. They form the social infrastructure for collective agency and action. Adaptive structures enable a collective to produce (common) goods and deliver services and thus obtain resources from the environment in exchange, which can be used as general resources to adapt to new situations [53]. Goal-attaining structures enable a collective to make consensual decisions, set goals, control the goal-attaining process, analyze the gains and losses in a reflective way and redirect activities that have not been helpful to achieve a goal [56]. Integrative structures are necessary to prevent disintegration, subgroup conflicts and noncohesiveness and to build social capital. Integrative structures include reciprocity-based and trustful social networks [51, 57, 58]. Latent pattern maintenance structures [59], such as a system of values, knowledge, beliefs and symbols are necessary to guide and evaluate action with regard to the systems´ own value standards. Institutionalization and socialization agents and processes are part of this structure because they have the task of transferring the values, knowledge, beliefs and symbols into the collective system and to the next generation of individual members (see **Table 1**).

3.2 Agency capacity and collective agency

Organizational resilience requires (a) fast and consensual collective decision-making to react to new events in a timely fashion; (b) common collective actions of the leaders and followers to execute resilience management in an impactful way; and (c) a robust organization with a stable core, absorptive capacity and the property of general agency, which enables organizational fitness. The first point should not be taken for

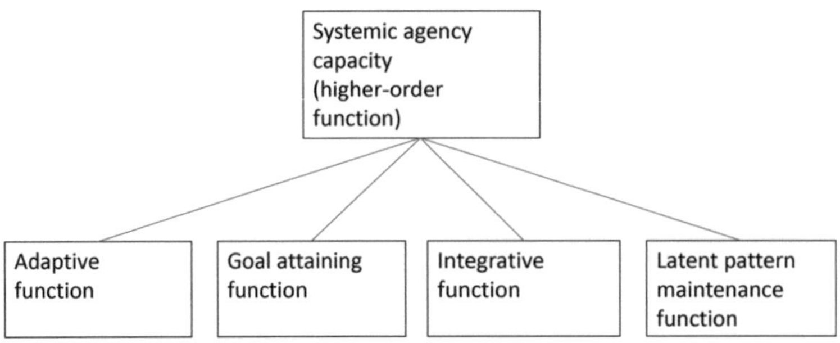

Figure 2.
Systemic agency capacity as a higher-order function of the AGIL functions.

Adaptive structures	Goal attainment structures
Integrative structures	Latent pattern maintenance structures

Table 1.
The social infrastructure of collective agency.

granted within organized collectives, especially within management boards [60] and top management teams [61], where leadership in singular is replaced by leadership in plural. Leadership in plural is the new normal [62]. In sum, resilient organizations need collective agency and the general capacity to execute this agency as the foundation for fast, united and impactful collective action with regard to adverse events.

Collective action could be defined as "joint activities by a wide group of actors on the basis of mutual interests" [63]. Because people often do not have mutual interests, collective inaction is commonly observed [63, 64]. To overcome the default tendency of collective inaction and enter the state of collective action, collectives have to transform themselves into a collective agent [63] and in the long run into an autopoietic social system [65, 66].

A collective agent "is a collective (...) that can (...) be the subject of attitudes and can perform actions as a collective" [67]. An important property of a collective agent is collective agency. According to the social cognitive theory perspective, "people's shared beliefs in their collective power to produce desired results are a key ingredient of collective agency" [68]. This includes not only "shared knowledge and skills of its different members, but also (...) the interactive, coordinative, and synergistic dynamics of their transactions" [68]. According to Bandura, "perceived collective efficacy is not simply the sum of the efficacy beliefs of individual members (...) it is an emergent group level property" [68].

Systemic agency is a special type of collective agency. It is produced if the collective transforms itself into an autopoietic social system [69] by incorporating additional structural features. The social ontology perspective within collective research [67] delivers some hints about these necessary features. According to this approach, the collective agency of an autonomous collective agent consists of at least three components. First, a collective which possesses collective agency should be a "social entity that consists of an unspecified number of individuals who share some properties that allow for their identification as a collective" [67] and which "exhibit a certain degree of persistence regarding their own identity in the case the identity of their constituents is changed" [67]. Examples of this are common values or even a common worldview of the members of the collective. Second, a collective agent which possesses collective agency should be clearly distinguishable from its environment and able to actively shape this environment and evaluate its own behavior with regard to normative standards and values, which are generated by the collective itself [67]. Third, the collective agency should be a significant property of the collective agent as a whole [67]. Out of this perspective, collective agency is a potential: "possessing agency (...) does not imply that the collective actually performs any particular action or holds a specific attitude at any instance", but it implies "that it would be possible for it to do so" [67]. To distinguish this form of collective agency from the term used by Bandura [68], I propose to call the social-ontological-based term "systemic collective agency" or "systemic agency".

The amount of collective and systemic agency depends on functional preconditions. As in the case of humans where personal agency requires that the human body is able to fulfill basic functions like body coordination [70], collective agency requires that the collective system is able to fulfill basic functions necessary for acting and surviving as a social unit. The agency capacity is the most important of

Stages of collective development	Basic function	Social infrastructure	Type of capacity	Type of collective (perspective of action theory)	Type of social systems (perspective of system theory)
Stage 1	—	—	None	Mere collective	Absence of a social system
Stage 2	I	Integrative structures	Action-shaping capacity	Cohesive collective	Social system capable of shaping action
Stage 3	GI	Integrative & goal-attaining structures	Collective agency capacity	Collective agent	Social system capable of acting
Stage 4	AGIL	Integrative, goal-attaining, adaptive & maintenance structures	Systemic agency capacity	Corporate actor	Autopoietic social system

Legend: I = Integration; G = Goal attainment; A = adaptation; L = Latent pattern maintenance.

Table 2.
Stages of collective development, AGIL functions and capacity type.

these basic functions. The amount and quality of the agency capacity of a collective corresponds with the development stage of the collective (**Table 2**).

A mere collective (stage 1 collective) is transformed into a cohesive collective (stage 2 collective) by adding social cohesion to the disorganized mere collective. In this case, the group fulfills the function of integration (I-function). The social group is therefore able to shape the actions and behavior of its members, producing conformity, group think and behavior change [51, 71–73]. This enables cooperation between individuals, including those with divergent interests [57, 74]. In cohesive collectives, social cohesion bundles otherwise chaotic individual energies and transforms these into social energy [56]. This kind of collective system can be called an action-shaping social system or social system capable of shaping action [75], and the type of capacity this collective possesses can be called action-shaping capacity.

If a cohesive collective is also able to set goals and attain them and if the members of this collective develop a sense of purpose [76], the goal attainment function (G-function) is fulfilled. Stage 3 collectives fulfill the G-function plus the I-function. This leads to the "GI factor" [56, 77]. This factor "produces collective energy within a group and gives this energy a direction, producing goal-oriented collective action" [56]. The result is a collective with "a sense of purpose and unity", speaking with one voice [56, 77] and possessing shared beliefs of collective efficacy [68]. This kind of collective system could be called a collective agent or, from the social system perspective, a social system capable of acting [75]. These types of collectives possess "collective agency capacity".

Social systems capable of acting (collective agent) could further transform themselves into an autopoietic system by fulfilling two functions, namely the adaptive function (A-function) and the latent pattern maintenance function (L-function).

The A-function is achieved if the collective produces goods and services for the environment to receive needed resources in exchange in order to accumulate needed resources as well as slack resources like social, human, economic and cultural capital [60, 78, 79]. The A-function is also fulfilled if the collective internally produces slack resources and flexible structures to be able to adapt to new situations in turbulent times [79, 80].

The L-function is fulfilled if the collective has incorporated value systems, knowledge systems, belief systems and symbolic systems (a) which serve as guiding standards and values against which the collective system's behavior is evaluated by itself and (b) which could be transferred to the next generation of members via socialization and internalization [54, 81]. Additionally, the L-function is fulfilled if these cultural elements are institutionalized into the collective system by roles, positions and norms [54, 64, 81]. This leads to an organization-culture fit [82]. By these three means—socialization, internalization and institutionalization of cultural structures—social systems, which are capable of acting, are additionally able to maintain the latent pattern of these systems over time. This and the ability of the social system to evaluate its own behavior by the cultural values which the system has generated itself ensure self-organization and autopoiesis independent of the strategies and personalities of the individuals who are temporarily members of this system.

If a social system fulfills all four AGIL functions, systemic agency capacity is produced (see **Figure 2**). This is a necessary condition for sustainable agency and the emergent birth of an autopoietic social system. From Coleman's action theory perspective, this type of system can be called a corporate actor [57]. From the sociological systems theory perspective, such a collective can be called an autopoietic social system [65, 66, 83–85].

3.3 Resilience management

Resilience management comprises different dimensions [86–88]. As already outlined, resilience management rests on four abilities: the ability to anticipate, the ability to monitor possibly dangerous developments, the ability to respond quickly and appropriately and the ability to learn from past events and crises [35]. The basis for these abilities is the capacity to perform collective action in a self-organized way. Without a minimum amount of this agency capacity, resilience management would be less impactful.

Resilience management could be defined as the process of collective coping with an adverse event and its consequences with the aim to prevent and reappraise adverse events and to buffer their impact or compensate for losses or damages. The concept of resilience management presented here consists of four types of collective resilience management, namely (1) appraisal-focused, (2) problem-focused, (3) impact-focused and (4) spiral-focused resilience management.

With regard to appraisal-focused resilience management, leaders can shape and influence the collective perception and appraisal of a given or expected situation with regard to its threat and loss potential. Leaders are also able to shape and influence the collective appraisal of the coping resources available to handle the situation properly. Additionally, they can support the collective reappraisal of a given situation [89]. In a positive scenario, a perceived threat could with the help of the leader be reappraised collectively as less threatening or as no longer threatening [90]. Charismatic leaders in particular are good at this [90].

Problem-focused resilience management aims to prevent adverse events in the future by altering the dangerous environment in the midterm and long term and/or decreasing the burden of the existing adverse event. Measures that fall into this category of resilience management include altering by political, regulatory or technological means the natural, technical, biological and psychosocial environment with the goal to minimize the probability and severity of adverse events in the future [91]. Other measures within this category include monitoring of possible threats, learning from crises (e.g., [92]), critical incident reporting [38, 39], preparedness strategy [16] and uncertainty management [19].

Impact-focused resilience management aims to manage the consequences of the adverse event. The aim of the measures in this category is not to solve the primary problem but to prevent the occurrence of follow-up problems caused by the primary adverse event and to mitigate the impact of the adverse event and the follow-up problems on the organization and their members. Measures within this category include using financial reserves, staff overhang, organizational slack, storage capacity, social capital and other impact-absorbing structures and resources (e.g., [47, 92, 93]). Other measures are to compensate for losses or impairment and to ameliorate the collective pain caused by the adverse event by organizing, for example, positive events to replace negative emotions with positive emotions. Another form of impact-focused resilience management is to accept the negative structural consequences of the adverse event and to adapt the organization to the new situation by restructuring it and attaining a new, often lower equilibrium. The fourth form of resilience management—the management of resilience spirals—is explained later in detail.

3.4 Organizational resilience

Organizational resilience occurs if an organized collective is able to prevent, appraise, absorb and cope with adverse events and their consequences in such a way that the organized collective can either (a) maintain the previous equilibrium; (b) bounce back to the previous equilibrium; (c) find a new, satisfying equilibrium; or (d) find new equilibria by maintaining a stable core within the system [33, 37, 94]. An optimal form of organizational resilience is obtained when an external adverse event can be managed by the organized collective without loss of collective performance.

The concept of functional performance levels outlined here proposes a hierarchical model of optimal organizational resilience. This model consists of five main levels of equilibria and five levels of a functional performance (see **Table 3**). The levels of equilibria are the (1) nonautonomous, (2) autonomous, (3) routine, (4) innovation and (5) resilience equilibria levels. These levels are separated by five functional thresholds: (a) survival, (b) autonomy, (c) routine, (d) innovation and (e) resilience. If an organized collective system falls below a threshold, it immediately moves to a lower functional performance level.

Level 5	The autonomous organized collective system is able to manage routine work, to be innovative and to cope with disruptions and troubles (resilience level)
T 5	Threshold of coping with disruptive events
Level 4	The organized collective system is able to act and to manage the professional routine work as well as tasks to innovate and change (innovation & exploration level)
T 4	Threshold of coping with the innovation and change tasks
Level 3	The organized collective system is autonomous and able to manage professional routine work (routine & exploitation level)
T 3	Threshold of coping with routine demands
Level 2	The organized collective system is able to act without help from outside (autonomous level)
T 2	Threshold of acting autonomously
Level 1	The organized collective system is able to act but depends on help from outside (nonautonomous level)
T 1	Threshold of surviving
Level 0	The organized collective system is not surviving

Table 3.
The concept of functional performance levels of organizations.

An organized collective system which is located on the functional performance level 5 fulfills all the requirements for good organizational resilience while still accomplishing innovation work as well as routine work in a parallel way. An organized collective system at functional performance level 4 (see **Table 3**) is able to innovate and do routine work but is unable to manage disruptive events without damaging innovation management and routine processes. This functional status is close to the status known in the management literature as ambidexterity. Ambidexterity is defined as an organization's ability to simultaneously exploit the present (by routine work) and explore the future (by innovation management) [95, 96]. Ambidexterity is regarded as a prerequisite for organizational survival [97], and there are empirical results that support this hypothesis [98]. Ambidexterity could be regarded as a prerequisite for resilience [99, 100] because "ambidextrous firms are better than others at responding to disruptive new business models and emerging technologies" [101]. Factors that promote ambidexterity include a collaborative community [102], support [103] and trust [103]. These factors are important parts of the social infrastructure of collective action as previously shown in this article.

If organized collective systems are unable to perform at level 3, they fall below the routine threshold, which means that they act autonomously but cannot manage routine tasks in the necessary quantity, quality, efficiency or timeliness.

If organizations also fall below the autonomy threshold, they reach functional performance level 2. This means that they need external support to act and survive. This external support could stem from the government or investors. An example of this are the bailouts of airlines during the COVID-19 pandemic [104] or bankruptcy. Some scholars argue that bankruptcy leads to a relief of financial burdens, but it does not change the structures and processes that led to bankruptcy. Therefore, without changing structures and processes and achieving a new equilibrium, long-term survival is doubtful in these cases [105].

If organizations also fall below the survival threshold, the organization will no longer survive.

4. Resilience spirals

Organizations differ with regard to the levels of their functional abilities and can be located according to these abilities on the functional performance ladder already shown in **Table 3**. Organizations that are close to bankruptcy are at the bottom of this ladder, and organizations that are flourishing are at the top. The important point is that first, organized collective systems are able to move up or down this functional performance ladder and that second, this move takes on the form of a spiral: an upward spiral in the case of organizational success and a downward spiral in that of organizational failure.

The reciprocal nature of the relationship between organizational success and organizational resources nurtures the organizational spiral. During upward spirals, the availability of resources leads to organizational success, this success leads to additional resource gains and so on. Some of the resources gained through success include financial or human resources (e.g., attracting young talent). This resource gain provides fertile ground for even more success in the future. In short, success breeds success. This effect is also known as the Matthew effect [106], which is the central pillar for upward spirals. Organizations on an upward spiral experience an accumulation of institutional advantages over time. Contrary to this, in downward spirals, a depletion of resources could provoke organizational failure, and this organizational failure reduces the probability of gaining additional resources in the near future. The causal path "resource depletion > failure > resource depletion > failure"

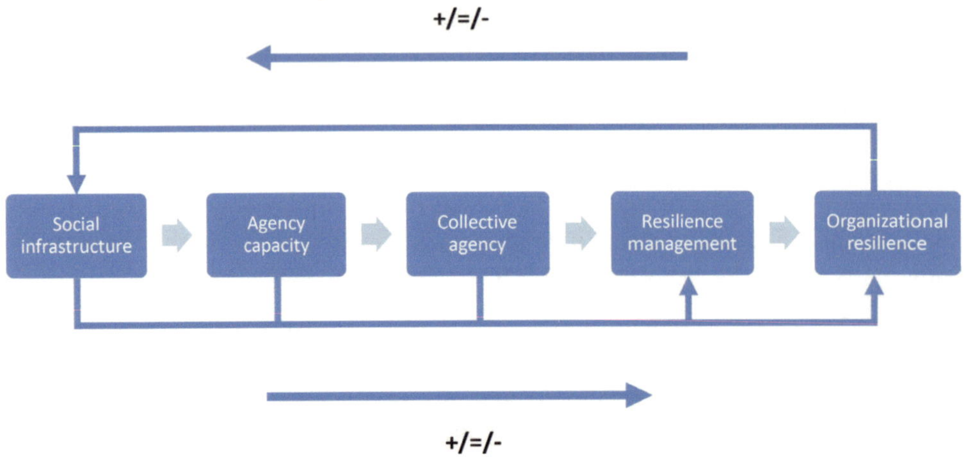

Figure 3.
The resilience spiral: downward spirals (-), upward spirals (+) and steady state (=).

produces a downward spiral. Organizations on a downward spiral experience an accumulation of institutional disadvantages over time [107].

Resilience spirals are a subtype of organizational spirals. The basic causal path is illustrated in **Figure 3**. The social infrastructure promotes organizations' agency capacity. This agency capacity enables collective agency, which is necessary to execute resilience management. Additionally, this collective agency leads to strong organized collective systems, which due to their stable "social infrastructure" core can withstand even strong disruptive events by their mere stability and absorptive structures. If an organization is resilient by its mere presence and stability, it is able to gain resources even during times of trouble. This gain in resources could further foster the infrastructure of the social system, which leads to a causal chain of "infrastructural resources → organizational resilience → gain in infrastructural resources → gain in organizational resilience". This pattern could be called an upward resilience spiral.

In the case of a downward resilience spiral, the causal chain is "weak organizational resilience → loss of infrastructural resources → weaker organizational resilience → additional loss of infrastructural resources". For example, the collective learning process after a disaster could lead to the conclusion that the organization needs to strive for a new equilibrium. A move from the previous equilibrium to the new one could be associated with a gain or loss of resources (see also [108]). If the new equilibrium is on a higher functional level, the move is associated with a resource gain, while if the new equilibrium is on a lower functional level, there is a loss of resources. In this last scenario, the organization is stabilized on a weaker resource level than before. This loss of resources leads to lower collective agency, which could weaken organizational resilience and heightens the possibility of further loss of resources. In this case, there will be a downward resilience spiral. Upward resilience spirals are based in part on the Matthew effect [106]. Downward spirals are characterized by an accumulation of systemic disadvantages. This can be described as a negative Matthew effect.

Upward and downward resilience spirals are processes where old equilibria are abandoned and new equilibria achieved: lower ones in the case of downward spirals and higher ones in the case of upward spirals. In all these cases, the core of the system—the social infrastructure and the resulting agency capacity—should be protected to ensure stability during change and to make change possible. If this protection is no longer possible, the downward spiral has reached a critical phase.

This critical phase occurs when further resource loss leads to a situation where the social infrastructure and the corresponding agency capacity function is impaired in such a way that the functioning of the collective system, meaning its ability to act and to do this in effective way, is endangered.

5. Leadership and organizational resilience: starting points

Resilient leadership exists if leaders care about organizational resilience in at least three ways. One way is to lay the groundwork for long-term organizational resilience by building the social infrastructure for collective action. Another way is more specific, namely to develop resilience management, run it and activate it fully in times of trouble. In addition to these two leadership strategies, there is a third one, namely the strategy of managing organizational spirals in general and resilience spirals in particular. Therefore, we distinguish three starting point for resilient leadership: (1) the social infrastructure of collective action and agency, (2) resilience management and (3) resilience spirals. Because we already discussed resilience management, we now focus on how leaders could foster the social foundation and then on how they are able to manage resilience spirals.

5.1 Leadership: building up, maintaining and modernizing the social infrastructure of collective action and agency

A central leadership task is building and maintaining the social infrastructure for collective action by accumulating and conserving the adaptive, political, integrative and cultural structures. These structures are necessary to fulfill all four basic AGIL functions and their higher-order function systemic agency capacity. Leaders who manage social systems, which possess systemic agency capacity, are more successful in reaching their goals. This is greatly independent from the content of the goals and measures as long as they are compatible with the value system of the organized collective. Organizational resilience is an example of such a goal.

In times of rapid change, leaders have to build up structures which enable adaptation. This fosters the A-function and the capacity to adapt to new situations [109]. The primary way to do this is to promote adaptive leadership [110]. This is the ability of leaders "to become more fit with the environment in which they operate, including but not limited to modifying existing procedures, adjusting to new circumstances, and updating knowledge and skills to meet new situational demands", [110] and it includes the "need to continually learn, change and keep a flexible mindset" [110].

The second task of leaders with regard to social infrastructure is to establish and optimize collective decision-making structures as well as the process of strategic goal-setting, −controlling and -attaining. There is broad knowledge about how to conduct and organize managerial decision-making [111] even in complex environments [112] and how to conduct and measure strategic goal-setting and -attaining [51, 113–115].

The third task of leaders is to strengthen the social integration and cooperation within the collective they lead. Leaders are responsible for building and maintaining solidarity and cohesiveness within the organized collective. This strengthens the social capital and the integrative structures of the collective they lead. Leaders can contribute to this by (1) a "consideration" leadership style which stresses the orientation toward good social relationships [116, 117]; (2) a transformational leadership style which combines having vision with creating a "we-feeling" among the followers [118] in such a way that they are willing to transfer the vision into practice; (3)

cohesive leadership [119], which promotes social cohesion within the followers; or (4) collaborative leadership [120–124], which "recognizes the need for appropriate balance—between power sharing and control, between process and results, between continuity and change, and between interpersonal trust and formalized procedures" [123] and which is most appropriate in professional organizations, knowledge work organizations and partnership networks [123, 125, 126]. Therefore, enhancing the social capital and cooperation within organizations is central for fulfilling the I-function and is one of the top tasks of leaders within organizations [76, 127].

The fourth task of leaders with regard to the infrastructure for collective agency is to build up the cultural structures within the collective they lead [128, 129]. Cultural structures comprise the value system, knowledge system, belief system and symbolic system. Leaders can shape the culture of an organization in many ways [59, 130–135]. They shape the culture of the collective by being a role model with regard to the common values of the collective [134, 136]. Additionally, they should be aware that their decisions send cultural signals to their followers with regard to the values the organized collective prefers [76, 133]. This is the case, for example, with job promotion (e.g., which person with which attitudes and values is the preferred one?) [76]. Additionally, leaders should organize the transfer of values, knowledge, beliefs and worldviews to their followers and the next generation. Organized collectives often try to establish a person-culture fit to reproduce their culture by employing individuals who fit into the organizational culture [82, 137]. However, if leaders want to change the culture of organized collectives, they should change the personnel selection team and the selection criteria in order to not reproduce the old culture by recruiting the same way the same sort of people as always.

The fifth function of leaders with regard to social infrastructure is to organize and manage the maintenance and modernization of these four structural elements: the maintenance and modernization of organizational culture [134, 138–140]; the maintenance, reproduction and modernization of the social structures which produce solidarity and integration [76, 141]; the maintenance and modernization of the adaptive structures like machines and technologies; [142] and the maintenance and modernization of the goal-attaining and decision-making structures [143, 144]. This guarantees the sustainability and adaptability of the collective system and its long-term survival.

5.2 Leadership: managing resilience spirals

Leadership plays a central role in the management of organizational spirals in general and resilience spirals in particular. The main task of resilience-oriented leaders is to manage the collective system they lead in such a way that the reciprocal mechanism (see **Figure 3**) stabilizes the system in a steady state where resource gains equal resource losses. In this scenario, there is a strong probability that organizational resilience can be maintained on a given level (either a low or a high level) [145]. If the level is low, one of the critical tasks of leaders and managers is to move the organization or organizational unit up the functional performance levels. They are able to accomplish this by using the causal pathway (see **Figure 3**) to higher resilience via fostering the social infrastructure of collective action by establishing adaptive structures, by investing in the social capital of the organization (integrative resources), by creating efficient decision-making structures and processes (political resources) and by working on common values, visions and knowledge (cultural resources). The second way is to manage the activities of the members in a goal-oriented and motivating way. The third way is by building up systematic resilience management through the implementation of specific resilience measures, such as resilience engineering, resilience analysis and threat monitoring (e.g., [92, 94, 146]).

Another important point of resilient leadership is to heighten the capacity of the collective system to be ambidextrous. This enables an organization to do routine as well as innovation work in an efficient and robust way with enough room and energy to also cope with adverse events. Another important task of leaders is to build up an early warning system which signals to them that a downward resilience spiral is just beginning and which delivers evidence-based suggestions [147] about how to stop the downward spiral in a fast and efficient way.

6. Limitations and conclusions

The main limitation of this article is its nonempirical foundation. The article presents theoretical thinking about the social foundations and social dynamics of organizational resilience. The hypotheses presented are not supported by empirical evidence. Thus, as long as these concepts and hypotheses have not been empirically tested and proven, it is necessary to be cautious with practical conclusions. However, it has to be stressed that the concept of the social infrastructure rests on the theoretically proven AGIL concept of Talcott Parsons [53] which has been used or discussed by several social theorists like Habermas [138, 141], Luhmann [148], Münch [149, 150] and Gerhardt [52, 151] and which has been tested empirically in part in some studies [56, 152].

With this limitation in mind, it is possible to draw some tentative practical conclusions from the concepts outlined. The first conclusion is that leaders should take care of followers by enhancing the integrating forces among them [76, 127]. The second conclusion is that leaders should be aware of the importance of effective and efficient decision-making structures and processes and goal-attaining structures (e.g., the controlling system) within the organizational unit they lead in order to enhance the unit's agency capacity. Third, leaders should foster the adaptive structures of their unit by building processes and structures to produce goods and services efficiently and by accumulating resources to obtain organizational slack which can be used in times of crisis. The fourth conclusion is that leaders should install knowledge and value management to stabilize and enhance the organization's cultural capital. The fifth practical conclusion is that leaders are better off if they install systematic resilience management which protects the organizational units in times of crisis [153, 154]. The sixth conclusion is that leaders should build up early warning systems to detect the beginning of downward spirals [155].

7. Summary

The aim of this paper was to describe the social foundations and dynamics of organizational resilience and the role of leadership in building and steering these social phenomena. The two main hypotheses were that organizational resilience depends on collective resilience management and the agency capacity of the organization. This capacity was conceptualized as a higher-order function combining the four AGIL functions. These functions are fulfilled if four AGIL-promoting structures are present, namely adaptive, goal-attaining, integrative and latent pattern structures. The reciprocal relationship between the social infrastructure of collective action and organizational resilience could lead to a resilience spiral going either upward or downward. In sum, the task of resilient leadership is to build and maintain the social infrastructure of collective action, foster the agency capacity of their own organization, execute resilience management and prevent downward spirals.

Author details

Holger Pfaff
University of Cologne, Cologne, Germany

*Address all correspondence to: holger.pfaff@uk-koeln.de

References

[1] Dartey-Baah K. Resilient leadership: A transformational-transactional leadership mix. Journal of Global Responsibility. 2015;**6**:99-112. DOI: 10.1108/JGR-07-2014-0026

[2] Drath K. Resilient Leadership. London: Routledge; 2016

[3] Eliot JL. Resilient leadership: The impact of a servant leader on the resilience of their followers. Advances in Developing Human Resources. 2020;**22**:404-418. DOI: 10.1177/1523422320945237

[4] Everly GS, Smith KJ, Lobo R. Resilient leadership and the organizational culture of resilience: Construct validation. International Journal of Emergency Mental Health and Human Resilience. 2013;**15**:123-128

[5] Giustiniano L, Cunha MP, Simpson AV, Rego A, Clegg S. Resilient leadership as paradox work: Notes from COVID-19. Management and Organization Review. 2020;**16**:971-975. DOI: 10.1017/mor.2020.57

[6] Arond-Thomas M. Resilient leadership for challenging times. Physician Executive. 2004;**30**:18-21. Available from: https://www.proquest.com/scholarly-journals/resilient-leadership-challenging-times/docview/199984879/se-2?accountid=10218

[7] Suryaningtyas D, Sudiro A, Eka TA, Dodi IW. Organizational resilience and organizational performance: Examining the mediating roles of resilient leadership and organizational culture. Academy of Strategic Management Journal. 2019;**18**:1-7. Available from: https://search.proquest.com/scholarly-journals/organizational-resilience-performance-examining/docview/2238485074/se-2?accountid=10218

[8] Wicks RJ, Buck TC. Riding the dragon: Enhancing resilient leadership and sensible self-care in the healthcare executive. Frontiers of Health Services Management. 2013;**30**:3-13. Available from: https://journals.lww.com/frontiersonline/Fulltext/2013/10000/Riding_the_Dragon__Enhancing_Resilient_Leadership.2.aspx

[9] Madi Odeh RB, Obeidat BY, Jaradat MO, Masa'deh R, Alshurideh MT. The transformational leadership role in achieving organizational resilience through adaptive cultures: The case of Dubai service sector. International Journal of Productivity and Performance Management. 2021. Ahead-of-print. DOI: 10.1108/IJPPM-02-2021-0093 [ahead of print]

[10] Lombardi S, Pina e Cunha M, Giustiniano L. Improvising resilience: The unfolding of resilient leadership in COVID-19 times. International Journal of Hospitality Management. 2021;**95**:102904. DOI: 10.1016/j.ijhm.2021.102904

[11] Everly GS. Building a resilient organizational culture. Harvard Business Review. 2011;**10**:109-138

[12] Southwick FS, Martini BL, Charney DS, Southwick SM. Leadership and Resilience. In: Marques J, Dhiman S, editors. Leadership Today: Practices for Personal and Professional Performance. Cham: Springer International Publishing; 2017. pp. 315-333

[13] Teo WL, Lee M, Lim W-S. The relational activation of resilience model: How leadership activates resilience in an organizational crisis. Journal of Contingencies and Crisis Management. 2017;**25**:136-147. DOI: 10.1111/1468-5973.12179

[14] Coutu DL. How resilience works. Havard Business Review. 2002;**80**:46-56

[15] Home JF, Orr JE. Assessing behaviors that create resilient organizations. Employment Relations Today. 1997;**24**:29-39. DOI: 10.1002/ert.3910240405

[16] Kantur D, Iseri-Say A. Organizational resilience: A conceptual integrative framework. Journal of Management and Organization. 2012;**18**:762

[17] Ledesma J. Conceptual frameworks and research models on resilience in leadership. SAGE Open. 2014;**4**:1-8. DOI: 10.1177/2158244014545464

[18] Kahana E, Kahana B, Lee JE. Proactive approaches to successful aging: One clear path through the forest. Gerontology. 2014;**60**:466-474. Epub 2014/06/11. DOI: 10.1159/000360222

[19] Conner D. Managing at the Speed of Change: Guidelines for Resilience in Turbulent Times. New York: Villard Books; 1993

[20] Kahana E, Kahana B. Contextualizing Successful Aging: New Directions in an Age-Old Search*. Invitation to the Life Course: Toward New Understandings of Later Life. New York: Routledge; 2018. pp. 225-255

[21] Weick KE. the collapse of sensemaking in organizations: The Mann Gulch disaster. Administrative Science Quarterly. 1993;**38**:628. DOI: 10.2307/2393339

[22] Doe PJ. Creating a resilient organization. Canadian Business Review. 1994;**21**:22

[23] Granovetter M. The strength of weak ties. The American Journal of Sociology. 1973;**78**:1360-1380

[24] Horne JF III. The coming age of organizational resilience. Business Forum. 1997;**22**:24-28

[25] Hower KI, Pförtner T-K, Pfaff H, Lee S-YD, Ansmann L. Child-oriented drug counseling in Germany: Evaluating the implementation of the program "Fitkids" and its association with readiness for change. Human Service Organizations: Management, Leadership & Governance. 2019;**43**:421-442. DOI: 10.1080/23303131.2019.1661929

[26] Hind P, Frost M, Rowley S. The resilience audit and the psychological contract. Journal of Managerial Psychology. 1996;**11**:18-29. DOI: 10.1108/02683949610148838

[27] Mallak L. Putting organizational resilience to work. Industrial Management. 1998;**40**:8-13

[28] Mallak L. Toward a theory of organizational resilience. In: PICMET '99, editor. Portland International Conference on Management of Engineering and Technology. Proceedings Vol-1: Book of Summaries. 1999

[29] National Academy of Engineering, editor. Engineering Within Ecological Constraints. Washington, D.C.: National Academies Press; 1996

[30] Holling CS. Engineering resilience versus ecological resilience. In: Schulze P, editor. Engineering Within Ecological Constraints. Washington, D.C.: National Academies Press; 1996. pp. 31-44

[31] Lengnick-Hall CA, Beck TE, Lengnick-Hall ML. Developing a capacity for organizational resilience through strategic human resource management. Human Resource Management Review. 2011;**21**:243-255. DOI: 10.1016/j.hrmr.2010.07.001

[32] Gunderson LH, Holling CS. Panarchy: Understanding Transformations in Human and Natural Systems. Washington, D.C.: Island Press; 2002

[33] Gunderson LH. Ecological resilience—In theory and application.

Annual Review of Ecology and Systematics. 2000;**31**:425-439. DOI: 10.1146/annurev.ecolsys.31.1.425

[34] Holling CS. Understanding the complexity of economic, ecological, and social systems. Ecosystems. 2001;**4**:390-405. DOI: 10.1007/s10021-001-0101-5

[35] Hollnagel E. How resilient is your organisation? An introduction to the resilience Anal-Ysis Grid (RAG). 2010

[36] Badura B, Ducki A, Schröder H, Meyer M, editors. Fehlzeiten-Report 2021: Betriebliche Prävention stärken – Lehren aus der Pandemie. Berlin, Heidelberg: Springer Berlin Heidelberg; 2021

[37] Braithwaite J, Wears RL, Hollnagel E. Resilient health care: Turning patient safety on its head. International Journal for Quality in Health Care. 2015;**27**:418-420. DOI: 10.1093/intqhc/mzv063

[38] Petschnig W, Haslinger-Baumann E. Critical Incident Reporting System (CIRS): A fundamental component of risk management in health care systems to enhance patient safety. Safety in Health. 2017;**3**:1-16. DOI: 10.1186/s40886-017-0060-y

[39] Sendlhofer G, Schweppe P, Sprincnik U, Gombotz V, Leitgeb K, Tiefenbacher P, et al. Deployment of Critical Incident Reporting System (CIRS) in public Styrian hospitals: A five year perspective. BMC Health Services Research. 2019;**19**:412. Epub 2019/06/24. DOI: 10.1186/s12913-019-4265-0

[40] Mannion R, Braithwaite J. False dawns and new horizons in patient safety research and practice. International Journal of Health Policy and Management. 2017;**6**:685-689. DOI: 10.15171/ijhpm.2017.115

[41] Chuang S, Ou J-C, Hollnagel E, Hou S-K. Measurement of resilience potential—Development of a resilience assessment grid for emergency departments. PLoS One. 2020;**15**: e0239472. Epub 2020/09/21. DOI: 10.1371/journal.pone.0239472

[42] Mallak L. Measuring resilience in health care provider organizations. Health Manpower Management. 1998;**24**:148-152. DOI: 10.1108/09552069810215755

[43] Helfrich CD, Blevins D, Smith JL, Kelly PA, Hogan TP, Hagedorn H, et al. Predicting implementation from organizational readiness for change: A study protocol. Implementation Science. 2011;**6**:76. Epub 2011/07/22. DOI: 10.1186/1748-5908-6-76

[44] Covin JG, Slevin DP. The development and testing of an organizational-level entrepreneurship scale. Frontiers of Entrepreneurship Research. 1986;**1**:628-639

[45] Bhandarker A, Rai S. Toxic leadership: Emotional distress and coping strategy. IJOTB. 2019;**22**:65-78. DOI: 10.1108/IJOTB-03-2018-0027

[46] Gittell JH, Cameron K, Lim S, Rivas V. Relationships, layoffs, and organizational resilience. The Journal of Applied Behavioral Science. 2006;**42**:300-329. DOI: 10.1177/0021886306286466

[47] Tengblad S. A resource-based model of organizational resilience. In: Tengblad S, Oudhuis M, editors. The Resilience Framework. Singapore: Springer; 2018. pp. 39-54. DOI: 10.1007/978-981-10-5314-6_3

[48] Weick KE. Sensemaking in Organizations. Foundations for Organizational Science. Thousand Oaks, Calif: Sage Publ.; 1995

[49] Pfaff H, Hammer A, Ernstmann N, Kowalski C, Ommen O. Safety culture: Definition, models and design. Zeitschrift für Ärztliche Fortbildung

und Qualität im Gesundheitswesen. 2009;**103**:493-497

[50] Weick KE. Prepare your organization to fight fires'. Harvard Business Review. 1996;**74**:143-148

[51] Hammer A, Arah OA, Dersarkissian M, Thompson CA, Mannion R, Wagner C, et al. The relationship between social capital and quality management systems in European hospitals: A quantitative study. PLoS One. 2013;**8**:e85662. Epub 2013/12/31. DOI: 10.1371/journal.pone.0085662

[52] Gerhardt U. The social thought of Talcott Parsons. In: Methodology and American Ethos. London: Taylor and Francis; 2016

[53] Parsons T, Smelser NJ. Economy and Society: A Study in Integrations of Economic and Social Theory. London: Routledge; 1956

[54] Parsons T. The Social System. New York: The Free Press; 1964

[55] Mingers J. Can social systems be autopoietic? Assessing Luhmann's social theory. The Sociological Review. 2002; **50**:278-299. DOI: 10.1111/1467-954X. 00367

[56] Pfaff H, Braithwaite J. A Parsonian approach to patient safety: Transformational leadership and social capital as preconditions for clinical risk management-the GI factor. International Journal of Environmental Research and Public Health. 2020;**17**. Epub 2020/06/04. DOI: 10.3390/ ijerph17113989

[57] Coleman JS. Foundations of Social Theory. 3rd ed. Cambridge, Mass: Belknap Press of Harvard University Press; 2000

[58] Putnam R. Bowling Alone: The Collaps and Revival of American Community. New York: Simon&Schuster; 2000

[59] Mannion R, Davies HTO, Marshall MN. Cultural characteristics of "high" and "low" performing hospitals. Journal of Health Organization and Management. 2006;**19**:431-439. DOI: 10.1108/14777260510629689

[60] Ansmann L, Vennedey V, Hillen HA, Stock S, Kuntz L, Pfaff H, et al. Resource dependency and strategy in healthcare organizations during a time of scarce resources: Evidence from the metropolitan area of cologne. Journal of Health Organization and Management. 2021;**35**:211-227. DOI: 10.1108/ JHOM-12-2020-0478

[61] Hambrick DC. Top Management Teams. Wiley Encyclopedia of Management; 2015. pp. 1-2

[62] Denis J-L, Langley A, Sergi V. Leadership in the plural. The Academy of Management Annals. 2012;**6**:211-283. DOI: 10.1080/ 19416520.2012.667612

[63] Wijen F, Ansari S. Overcoming Inaction through Collective Institutional Entrepreneurship: Insights from Regime Theory. Organization Studies. 2007;**28**:1079-1100. DOI: 10.1177/ 0170840607078115

[64] Abdelnour S, Hasselbladh H, Kallinikos J. Agency and institutions in organization studies. Organization Studies. 2017;**38**:1775-1792. DOI: 10.1177/0170840617708007

[65] Luhmann N. The autopoiesis of social systems. In: Geyer RF, van der Zouwen J, editors. Sociocybernetic Paradoxes. Observation, Control, and Evolution of Self-steering Systems. London, Beverly Hills, Calif: Sage Publications; 1986. pp. 172-192

[66] Hernes T, Bakken T. Implications of self-reference: Niklas Luhmann's autopoiesis and organization theory. Organization Studies. 2003;**24**:1511-1535. DOI: 10.1177/0170840603249007

[67] Hainz T, Bossert S, Strech D. Collective agency and the concept of 'public' in public involvement: A practice-oriented analysis. BMC Medical Ethics. 2016;**17**:1. DOI: 10.1186/s12910-015-0083-z

[68] Bandura A. Exercise of human agency through collective efficacy. Current Directions in Psychological Science. 2000;**9**:75-78. DOI: 10.1111/1467-8721.00064

[69] Luhmann N. Social Systems. Stanford, Calif: Stanford Univ. Press; 1995

[70] Wirtz MA, Voigt-Radloff S. The international classification of functioning, disability and health-orientated occupational therapy assessment: A Rasch analysis of its domains. International Journal of Rehabilitation Research. 2008;**31**:23-32. Available from: http://journals.lww.com/intjrehabilres/Fulltext/2008/03000/The_International_Classification_of_Functioning,.4.aspx

[71] Borek AJ, Abraham C. How do small groups promote behaviour change? An integrative conceptual review of explanatory mechanisms. Applied Psychology: Health and Well-Being. 2018;**10**:30-61. DOI: 10.1111/aphw.12120

[72] Marmarosh CL, Sproul A. Group cohesion: Empirical evidence from group psychotherapy for those studying other areas of group work. In: Parks CD, Tasca GA, editors. The Psychology of Groups: The Intersection of Social Psychology and Psychotherapy Research. Washington: American Psychological Association; 2021. pp. 169-189

[73] Forsyth DR. Recent advances in the study of group cohesion. Group Dynamics: Theory, Research, and Practice. 2021;**25**:213-228. DOI: 10.1037/gdn0000163

[74] Diekmann A. Sozialkapital und das Kooperationsproblem in sozialen Dilemmata. Analyse & Kritik. 1993;**15**: 22-35. DOI: 10.1515/auk-1993-0103

[75] Der SU. mangelnde Akteursbezug systemtheoretischer Erklärungen gesellschaftlicher Differenzierungen - ein Diskussionsvorschlag. Zeitschrift Für Soziologie. 1985;**14**:421-434

[76] Prusak L, Cohen D. How to invest in social capital. Harvard Business Review. 2001;**79**:86-93

[77] Pfaff H, Hammer A, Ballester M, Schubin K, Swora M, Sunol R. Social determinants of the impact of hospital management boards on quality management: A study of 109 European hospitals using a Parsonian approach. BMC Health Services Research. 2021;**21**:70. DOI: 10.1186/s12913-020-06053-0

[78] Mattingly JE, Olsen L. Performance outcomes of investing slack resources in corporate social responsibility. Journal of Leadership & Organizational Studies. 2018;**25**:481-498. DOI: 10.1177/1548051818762336

[79] Daniel F, Lohrke FT, Fornaciari CJ, Turner R. Slack resources and firm performance: A meta-analysis. Journal of Business Research. 2004;**57**:565-574. DOI: 10.1016/S0148-2963(02)00439-3

[80] Cyert RM, Cyert RM, March JG. A behavioral Theory of the Firm. 2nd ed. Malden, MA: Blackwell Publishing; 2006

[81] Parsons T. Societies; Evolutionary and Comparative Perspectives. Englewood Cliffs, New Jersey: Prentice-Hall; 1966

[82] Athanas C, Athanas SP, Friese E-M, Pfisterer N. Cultural Fit Studie. Berlin, Bochum: Meta HR und Employou; 2016

[83] Radosavljevic M. Autopoiesis vs. social autopoiesis: Critical evaluation and implications for understanding firms as

autopoietic social systems. International Journal of General Systems. 2008;**37**:215-230. DOI: 10.1080/03081070701251018

[84] Brans M, Rossbach S. The autopoiesis of administrative systems: niklas luhmann on public administration and public policy. Public Administration. 1997;**75**:417-439. DOI: 10.1111/1467-9299.00068

[85] Seidl D. Luhmann's theory of autopoietic social systems. Munich Business Research. 2004;**2**:1-28

[86] McManus S, Seville E, Brunsden D, Vargo J. Resilience Management: A Framework for Assessing and Improving the Resilience of Organisations. New Zealand: Resilient Organizations; 2007

[87] Häring I, Sansavini G, Bellini E, Martyn N, Kovalenko T, Kitsak M, et al. Towards a generic resilience management, quantification and development process: General definitions, requirements, methods, techniques and measures, and case studies. In: Linkov I, Palma-Oliveira JM, editors. Resilience and Risk. Dordrecht: Springer Netherlands; 2017. pp. 21-80

[88] Bjarte R, David L, Marianthi T, Christer P. From risk management to resilience management in critical infrastructure. Journal of Management in Engineering. 2020;**36**:4020039. DOI: 10.1061/(ASCE)ME.1943-5479.0000795

[89] Miller AJ, Slater MJ, Turner MJ. Coach identity leadership behaviours are positively associated with athlete resource appraisals: The mediating roles of relational and group identification. Psychology of Sport and Exercise. 2020;**51**:101755. DOI: 10.1016/j.psychsport.2020.101755

[90] LePine MA, Zhang Y, Crawford ER, Rich BL. Turning their pain to gain: Charismatic leader influence on follower stress appraisal and job performance. Academy of Management Journal. 2015;**59**:1036-1059. DOI: 10.5465/amj.2013.0778

[91] Pfaff H, Schubin K. Zukünftige Gesundheitsrisiken: Was kommt auf die Gesellschaft zu. In: Badura B, Ducki A, Schröder H, Meyer M, editors. Fehlzeiten-Report 2021: Betriebliche Prävention stärken – Lehren aus der Pandemie. Berlin, Heidelberg: Springer; 2021. pp. 43-63

[92] Wears RL, Hollnagel E, Braithwaite J. Resilient Health Care, The Resilience of Everyday Clinical Work. Vol. 2. Farnham: Ashgate Publishing Limited; 2015

[93] Tengblad S, Oudhuis M. The Resilience Framework. 2018. DOI: 10.1007/978-981-10-5314-6

[94] Hollnagel E, Braithwaite J. Resilient Health Care. London: CRC Press; 2019

[95] O'Reilly CA, Tushman ML. The ambidextrous organization. London: Havard Business Review. 2004;**82**:74-81

[96] O'Reilly CA, Tushman ML. Organizational ambidexterity: Past, present, and future. AMP. 2013;**27**:324-338. DOI: 10.5465/amp.2013.0025

[97] O'Reilly CA, Tushman ML. Ambidexterity as a dynamic capability: Resolving the innovator's dilemma. Research in Organizational Behavior. 2008;**28**:185-206. DOI: 10.1016/j.riob.2008.06.002

[98] Junni P, Sarala RM, Taras V, Tarba SY. Organizational ambidexterity and performance: A meta-analysis. AMP. 2013;**27**:299-312. DOI: 10.5465/amp.2012.0015

[99] Iborra M, Safón V, Dolz C. What explains the resilience of SMEs? Ambidexterity capability and strategic consistency. Long Range Planning.

2020;**53**:101947. DOI: 10.1016/j.lrp.2019.101947

[100] Stokes P, Smith S, Wall T, Moore N, Rowland C, Ward T, et al. Resilience and the (micro-)dynamics of organizational ambidexterity: Implications for strategic HRM. The International Journal of Human Resource Management. 2019; **30**:1287-1322. DOI: 10.1080/09585192.2018.1474939

[101] Tarba S, Jansen J, Mom T, Raisch S, Lawton T. A microfoundational perspective of organizational ambidexterity: Critical review and research directions. Long Range Planning. 2020;**53**(6)

[102] Adler P, Heckscher C. The collaborative, ambidextrous enterprise. Universia Business Review. 2013;**10**:34-51

[103] Gibson CB, Birkinshaw J. The antecedents, consequences, and mediating role of organizational ambidexterity. AMJ. 2004;**47**:209-226. DOI: 10.5465/20159573

[104] Jackson T, Brickley J, Smith C, Hughes C, Tabas J, Zupan M. University of Rochester roundtable on bankruptcy vs. bailouts: The case of General Motors and the U.S. auto industry. Journal of Applied Corporate Finance. 2020;**32**:58-79. DOI: 10.1111/jacf.12389

[105] Lu L, Sheng Y. Successful metamorphosis or not? A case study of the bankruptcy reorganization of northeast special steel. Modern Economy. 2019;**10**:1419-1429

[106] Merton RK. The matthew effect in science: The reward and communication systems of science are considered. Science. 1968;**159**:56-63

[107] Moran KA. Organizational resilience: Sustained institutional effectiveness among smaller, private, non-profit US higher education institutions experiencing organizational decline. Work. 2016;**54**:267-281

[108] Allen CR, Angeler DG, Garmestani AS, Gunderson LH, Holling CS. Panarchy: Theory and application. Ecosystems. 2014;**17**:578-589. DOI: 10.1007/s10021-013-9744-2

[109] Uhl-Bien M, Arena M. Leadership for organizational adaptability: A theoretical synthesis and integrative framework. The Leadership Quarterly. 2018;**29**:89-104. DOI: 10.1016/j.leaqua.2017.12.009

[110] Castillo EA, Trinh MP. Catalyzing capacity: Absorptive, adaptive, and generative leadership. Journal of Organizational Change Management. 2019;**32**:356-376. DOI: 10.1108/JOCM-04-2017-0100

[111] Aharoni Y, Tihanyi L, Connelly BL. Managerial decision-making in international business: A forty-five-year retrospective. Journal of World Business. 2011;**46**:135-142. DOI: 10.1016/j.jwb.2010.05.001

[112] Cramp DG, Carson ER. Systems thinking, complexity and managerial decision-making: An analytical review. Health Services Management Research. 2009;**22**:71-80. DOI: 10.1258/hsmr.2008.008015

[113] Curtright JW, Stolp-Smith SC, Edell ES. Strategic performance management: Development of a performance measurement system at the Mayo Clinic. Journal for Healthcare Quality. 2000;**45**:58-68

[114] Kotter JP. Accelerate. Building Strategic Agility for a Faster-Moving World. Boston: Harvard Business Review Press; 2014

[115] Pfaff H, Zeike S. Controlling im Betrieblichen Gesundheitsmanagement: Das 7-Schritte-Modell. Wiesbaden: Springer Fachmedien Wiesbaden; 2019

[116] Judge TA, Piccolo RF, Ilies R. The forgotten ones? The validity of consideration and initiating structure in leadership research. The Journal of Applied Psychology. 2004;**89**:36-51. DOI: 10.1037/0021-9010.89.1.36

[117] Schriesheim CA, Bird BJ. Contributions of the Ohio state studies to the field of leadership. Journal of Management. 1979;**5**:135-145. DOI: 10.1177/014920637900500204

[118] Hammer A, Ommen O, Röttger J, Pfaff H. The relationship between transformational leadership and social capital in hospitals—A survey of medical directors of all German hospitals. Journal of Public Health Management and Practice. 2012;**18**: 175-180. DOI: 10.1097/PHH. 0b013e31823dea94

[119] Pommerening C. Kurswechsel in der Führung: Mehr Mut und Verantwortung. In: Pommerening C, editor. New Leadership im Finanzsektor: So gestalten Banken aktiv den digitalen und kulturellen Wandel. Wiesbaden: Springer Fachmedien Wiesbaden; 2020. pp. 159-205

[120] Chrislip DD, Larson CE. Collaborative Leadership: How Citizens and Civic Leaders can Make a Difference. San Francisco, Calif.: Jossey-Bass; 1994

[121] Vangen S, Huxham C. Enacting leadership for collaborative advantage: Dilemmas of ideology and pragmatism in the activities of partnership managers. British Journal of Management. 2003;**14**:S61-S76

[122] Huxham C, Vangen S. Leadership in the shaping and implementation of collaboration agendas: How things happen in a (not quite) joined-up world. Academy of Management Journal. 2000;**43**:1159-1175. DOI: 10.5465/1556343

[123] Alexander JA, Comfort ME, Weiner BJ, Bogue R. Leadership in Collaborative Community Health Partnerships. Nonprofit Management Leadership. 2001;**12**:159-175. DOI: 10.1002/nml.12203

[124] Lawrence RL. Understanding collaborative leadership in theory and practice. New Directions for Adult and Continuing Education. 2017;**2017**:89-96. DOI: 10.1002/ace.20262

[125] Adler PS. Market, hierarchy, and trust: The knowledge economy and the future of capitalism. Organization Science. 2001;**12**:215-234

[126] Adler PS, Heckscher C. Towards collaborative community. In: Heckscher C, Adler PS, editors. The Firm as a Collaborative Community. Reconstructing Trust in the Knowledge Economy. Oxford: Oxford University Press; 2006. pp. 11-105

[127] Cohen D, Prusak L. In Good Company. How Social Capital Makes Organizations Work. Boston: Harvard Business School Pr; 2001

[128] Villaluz VC, Hechanova MRM. Ownership and leadership in building an innovation culture. Leadership & Organization Development Journal. 2019;**40**:138-150. DOI: 10.1108/ LODJ-05-2018-0184

[129] Jung DI, Bass BM, Sosik JJ. Bridging leadership and culture: A theoretical consideration of transformational leadership and collectivistic cultures. Journal of Leadership Studies. 1995;**2**:3-18. DOI: 10.1177/107179199500200402

[130] Dixon-Woods M, Baker R, Charles K, Dawson J, Jerzembek G, Martin G, et al. Culture and behaviour in the English National Health Service: Overview of lessons from a large multimethod study. BMJ Quality & Safety. 2014;**23**:106-115. Epub 2013/09/09. DOI: 10.1136/ bmjqs-2013-001947

[131] Peterson KD, Deal TE. How leaders influence the culture of schools. Educational Leadership. 1998;**56**:28-31

[132] Groysberg B, Lee J, Price J, Cheng J. The leader's guide to corporate culture. Harvard Business Review. 2018;**96**:44-52

[133] Kane-Urrabazo C. Management's role in shaping organizational culture. Journal of Nursing Management. 2006;**14**:188-194. DOI: 10.1111/j.1365-2934.2006.00590.x

[134] Schein EH. Organizational Culture and Leadership. San Francisco, Calif.: Wiley; 2010

[135] Mannion R, Davies H. Understanding organisational culture for healthcare quality improvement. BMJ. 2018;**363**:k4907. DOI: 10.1136/bmj.k4907

[136] Bass BM, Avolio BJ. Transformational leadership and organizational culture. Public Administration Quarterly. 1993;**17**:112-121. Available from: http://www.jstor.org/stable/40862298

[137] Der DC. "Betriebsclan": Der japanische Organisationstypus als Herausforderung an die soziologische Modernisierungstheorie. Soziale Welt. 1987;**2**:133-147

[138] Habermas J. The Theory of Communicative Action. 1. Reason and the Rationalization of Society. Cambridge: Polity Press; 2015

[139] Trice HM, Beyer JM. Cultural leadership in organizations. Organization Science. 1991;**2**:149-169. DOI: 10.1287/orsc.2.2.149

[140] Banaszak-Holl J, Castle NG, Lin M, Spreitzer G. An assessment of cultural values and resident-centered culture change in U.S. nursing facilities. Health Care Management Review. 2013;**38**:295-305. DOI: 10.1097/HMR.0b013e3182678fb0

[141] Habermas J. The Theory of Communicative Action. Lifeworld and Systems, a Critique of Functionalist Reason. 1st ed. Vol. 2. New York: John Wiley & Sons; 2015

[142] Jasiulewicz-Kaczmarek M, Gola A. Maintenance 4.0 technologies for sustainable manufacturing—An overview. IFAC-PapersOnLine. 2019;**52**:91-96. DOI: 10.1016/j.ifacol.2019.10.005

[143] Dennis AR, Rennecker JA, Hansen S. Invisible whispering: Restructuring collaborative decision making with instant messaging. Decision Sciences. 2010;**41**:845-886. DOI: 10.1111/j.1540-5915.2010.00290.x

[144] Akinci C, Sadler-Smith E. Collective intuition: Implications for improved decision making and organizational learning. British Journal of Management. 2019;**30**:558-577. DOI: 10.1111/1467-8551.12269

[145] Arbeit PH. Technik und Gesundheit: Ergebnisse einer sozialepidemiologischen Studie. Das Gesundheitswesen. 1995;**57**:532

[146] Sunol R, Wagner C, Arah OA, Kristensen S, Pfaff H, Klazinga N, et al. Implementation of departmental quality strategies is positively associated with clinical practice: Results of a multicenter study in 73 hospitals in 7 European countries. PLoS One. 2015;**10**:e0141157. DOI: 10.1371/journal.pone.0141157

[147] Sunol R, Wagner C, Arah OA, Shaw CD, Kristensen S, Thompson CA, et al. Evidence-based organization and patient safety strategies in European hospitals. International Journal for Quality in Health Care. 2014;**26**:47-55. DOI: 10.1093/intqhc/mzu016

[148] Luhmann N. Warum AGIL?(Pourquoi AGIL?). Kolner Zeitschrift für Soziologie und Sozialpsychologie. 1988;**40**:127-139

[149] Münch R. Theorie des Handelns. Zur Rekonstruktion der Beiträge von Talcott Parsons, Emile Durkheim und Max Weber. Frankfurt am Main: Suhrkamp; 1988

[150] Münch R. Theory of Action. Towards a New Synthesis Going Beyond Parsons. London: Taylor & Francis e-Library; 2010

[151] Gerhardt U. Ideas About Illness. An Intellectual and Political History of Medical Sociology. New York: New York University Press; 1989

[152] Talcott TS. Parsons' AGIL schema-based system identification of administrative problems of north-east vocational education in Thailand. Chinese Business Review. 2013;**12**: 747-761

[153] Duchek S, Raetze S, Scheuch I. The role of diversity in organizational resilience: A theoretical framework. Business Research. 2020;**13**:387-423. DOI: 10.1007/s40685-019-0084-8

[154] Duchek S. Organizational resilience: A capability-based conceptualization. Business Research. 2020;**13**:215-246. DOI: 10.1007/s40685-019-0085-7

[155] Martin GP, McKee L, Dixon-Woods M. Beyond metrics? Utilizing 'soft intelligence' for healthcare quality and safety. Social Science & Medicine. 2015;**142**:19-26. DOI: 10.1016/j.socscimed.2015.07.027

Chapter 11

Green Transformational Leadership and Green Growth

Natalia Aleksandrovna Zhuravleva and Milos Poliak

Abstract

The ongoing global crisis of the world economy requires the search and substantiation of an alternative model for achieving sustainable development, taking into account environmental safety factors. The aim of the study is to substantiate a scientific hypothesis of the impact of transformational leadership on green growth. The methodology is based on the theory of transformational leadership as a new type of effective management activity, the concept of the digital platforms and ecosystems. Based on the concept of sustainable development and the theory of destabilization, which explains the changes in the business models of transport organizations, the authors substantiated the dependence of the effectiveness of these models on the activity of transformational leadership. The main results of the study are confirmation of the proposed scientific hypothesis. It has been proven that the current transactional leadership metrics (Key Performance Indicator and variance management) do not meet the requirements of effective management. A model for quantitative assessment of the conformity of the impact of transformational leadership on the goals of sustainable development and green growth of transport companies has been developed. It is proved that transformational leadership, intersectorality, is becoming a new type of management activity that ensures the growth of long-term profitability from green investments.

Keywords: transformational leadership, sustainable development, green growth, business model

1. Introduction

The global financial crisis has vividly demonstrated the instability of the modern financial and economic system and made it particularly urgent for the world community to find an alternative model for achieving economic growth based on digital technologies, taking into account the factors of social and environmental security.

The current stage of development of economic science requires a rethinking of the basic concepts of all transformations taking place in the world through the prism of scientific and technical changes, both general and specific, associated with changes in human behavior, competition, data, innovations, and values.

Before the theory of transformational leadership appeared in the literature [1–3], most researchers relied on transactional factors of effective leadership behavior. Rewards and recognition were explained as the most important factors in achieving goals in organizations [4]. The evolution of further research has shown significant changes in the understanding of leadership [5].

Nevertheless, the structure of modern commodity markets, the gravity of intersectoral balances of countries and territories are changing significantly. Most of the technologies and management decisions that were in demand until recently are of no interest to anyone today. The areas of knowledge and competencies of personnel are changing. Transformational leadership is emerging as a response to the rapid changes in society, economics, and politics. It offers a toolkit for promoting changes leading to a socially oriented, equitable green society, thereby contributing to the creation of new technologies, innovations, and some kind of a social progress. That is why every industry in our time requires, first of all, competent leadership and only then management.

The emergence of transformational leadership, used as a tool for the development of business and society, has spread to many areas of the world's leading countries, including nongovernmental organizations. Transformational leadership in the modern business world is positioning itself as a new type of management activity that has shifted the management paradigm from excellent task performance to leadership or the right choice of what to do.

The results of numerous studies have shown that green transformational leadership has a significant impact on the internal motivation and creativity that employees need to produce ecologically pure products and services [6, 7]. At the same time, research on the interaction of the areas of leadership and economics is not enough to present the completeness and diversity of the influence of leadership on business efficiency and the development of society. The study [8] that demonstrates the potential benefits of leadership research in achieving economic goals should be noted. In particular, the authors link the evolution of the concept of leadership with the corresponding tasks of economic development. The research [9] analyzing studies that combine economics and leadership argues that the behavior of a leader, his choices and actions determine the results of the organization and indicate new strategic objectives.

Special attention of researchers is focused on understanding the actions of corporate leaders. Predicting the behavior of a future leader emphasizes the importance of understanding the context (conditions, economic situation) in which a leader acts, how valuable capital is created, capital markets' conditions, as well as the general trend of society development [10].

We are careful in our research, because we take into account the reasoned opinion of [11] about the demystification of the impact of transformational leadership on the performance of an organization under conditions of environmental uncertainty.

These studies allowed us to support our statement about the impact of transformational leadership on the sustainable development of society and green growth. At the same time, we see a significant number of unexplored areas, in particular, (1) for many corporations, including with state participation, transactional leadership instruments being still dominant, while it is obvious that they are economically losing their meaning; (2) the effectiveness of green infrastructure development projects and "green financing" has not been proven; (3) the influence of transformational leadership on the sustainable environmental development of industries is practically absent. It was the latter circumstance that determined the choice of the transport industry, as the most significant in the context of the green growth of Russia, as an object of scientific research.

Under the influence of all the above circumstances, significant changes are taking place in the world transport systems. First, the intensification of the construction and launch of high-speed roads is based on fundamentally new green technologies, materials, and energy. Secondly, the inclusion of transport systems in sustainable development projects as an essential part of ensuring the development of new product markets and the growth of social mobility. Thirdly, the designed transport systems in the world strive to conform to the new consumption model.

The transport system is moving into the format of an environmentally friendly (safe), social (highly mobile), and economical ESG system. At the same time, the E-factor takes into account the reduction of CO_2 emissions by the company, the volume of consumption of water resources and land, as well as the introduction of waste processing. The factor of social criteria (S-factor) reflects the level of observance of human rights, ensuring safety in the workplace and protection of customer information, the availability of training programs. The corporate governance paradigm (G-factor) is based on independence and efficiency of management, transparency and quality of financial reporting, as well as disclosure of nonfinancial information of the company.

The purpose of this study is to develop and test a scientific hypothesis that determines the role of transformational leadership in enhancing sustainable development processes, first of all, green growth. The scientific hypothesis is subject to quantitative assessment of this impact on the efficiency of the operating and business models of Russian transport organizations.

The object of the research is the largest transport companies in four transportation segments: rail, urban rail passenger transportation, road, and sea.

The subject of the research is the methodology for the development of transformational leadership in the new economic order, methods and models for assessing its impact on the effectiveness of green projects of transport organizations.

The research is based on the hypothesis of the positive impact of transformational leadership on the sustainable development of the transport and logistics business, first of all, its "green" growth. Two main results of the study that are directly related to the backbone organizations of the Russian transport system are highlighted: (1) the current metrics of transactional growth do not meet the requirements of sustainable development and "green" growth and do not stimulate the personnel of companies to work effectively; (2) the positive impact of transformational leadership on the transformation of transport companies in the direction of green growth has been quantitatively confirmed.

2. Scientific hypothesis

There is some (but limited) support for the impact of transformational leadership on green growth. So, many modern management theories, in terms of style and management methods, are based on the understanding of "leadership" [12]. The most commonly considered types of leaders are authoritarian, democratic, laissez-faire, transactional, and transformational. The systems theory of leadership, exploring many options for the behavior of leaders, is basic in understanding the evolution of this concept [13]. In our study, we rely on the concept of transformational leadership as the most appropriate to the new economic order [14, 15]. At the same time, we understand that the previous model of transactional leadership, when the goals and objectives of the business are predetermined, and the leader uses reward and punishment to motivate the entire staff of the company, becomes ineffective in some cases. We studied the impact of Key Performance Indicator (KPI) on the efficiency of business models of the largest Russian transport and logistics companies and came to the conclusion that there should be other metrics for team and personal efficiency.

In this regard, on the basis of the provisions of the situational leadership theory, namely the study of the dependence of the leadership style on the situation in the team and the leader's clear orientation toward solving the problem, we have established the positive influence of situational leadership (from the development of monofunctional products or services that satisfy a certain need) for the growth of the value of the product or service itself [16–18].

The third step of our research was based on the modern interpretation of the systems theory of leadership [13]. Within the framework of this theory, leadership and the leader are considered from the point of view of group dynamics. The group is viewed as a system, leadership is the organization of relations in the group, the leader is the subject of managing this process. We applied these provisions to the concept of the evolution of digital platforms and ecosystems, which today maximally reflects the level of development of the object of our research—transport and logistics systems [19]. The introduction of digital technologies in the supply chain of goods and services satisfies the demand of society and the economy in the growth of mobility, speed, flexibility, and the ability to compress space. At the same time, the threshold between reality and virtuality loses its clear outline. Today, most services can exist in the format of digital products, and their set forms an entire ecosystem.

Digitization embodies the model of the development of consciousness. Its processes reflect our thinking and the way we interact with the world. Developers of digital systems are repeating the path of development of the human mind—from adaptability to creativity. This, in its essence, is transformational leadership—it is a type of leadership that causes transformation (change) in subordinates, which leads to an understanding of changes in business [20]. Our conclusions are confirmed by the following logic of the development of the theory of transformational leadership.

It is a known fact that the term "transformational leadership" was first introduced by James V. Downton (1973). However, this concept was developed by James MacGregor Burns in his book "Leadership" published in 1978 [1, 21]. He expanded this concept, moving away from a simple interpretation of transformational leadership as a set of certain personal qualities to a process in which a leader and a follower, interacting in a certain way, raise each other to a higher level of motivation and personal, moral development. In our study, this is an important understanding of how leadership can contribute to the implementation of the goals of sustainable development, green growth. It substantiates the position that the activities of transport and logistics organizations within the framework of the ESG (Environmental, Social, Governance) concept and compliance with the principles of responsible investment (PRI—Principles for Responsible Investment) contribute to the growth of transport infrastructure development projects and the improvement of business models of transport organizations [22].

The tasks of transformational leadership in ensuring green growth are extremely important, since they raise awareness of the company's personnel about the importance and value of the intended results and how to achieve them and, in turn, motivate them to go beyond their immediate selfish interests for the sake of the mission and vision of the organization, its involvement in sustainable development of society. Charismatic and inspiring qualities are observed at all levels of organization management [23].

Transformational leadership implements an individual approach to building teamwork, which is extremely important in the context of the COVID-19 pandemic, when business has switched to the work of "hybrid teams", i.e., partly on-line, partly off-line [24, 25]. We consider individualization of work with personnel as a method of timely transfer of information to subordinates. It provides ongoing observation and feedback and, more importantly, links the individual's current needs with the organization's mission and enhances those needs when appropriate.

The most important component of transformational leadership is intellectual stimulation [26, 27]. An intellectually stimulating leader awakens in subordinates an awareness of problems, awareness of their own thoughts, as well as recognition of their beliefs and values. It is through the intellectual stimulation of subordinates that new methods of fulfilling the organization's mission are explored. Following this statement, we have developed a methodology for assessing the impact of transformational leadership on the transformation of transport and logistics systems in a green growth economy in the context of global economic destabilization.

Each particular question of business and society how to survive and sustainably realize itself in an unstable world has a generalized abstract or demarcation answer. This answer requires an assessment of the processes of destabilization in the context of asymmetric competition in the business models of organizations that follow the trend of sustainable development [28, 29]. For the reliability of the study, we rely on the provisions of the theory of destabilization, which distinguishes ordinary competition from destabilization, the process of assessing potentially destabilizing threats, as well as the methodology that allows forming methods of countering destabilization, taking into account the sustainable development of organizations based on green technologies.

We relied on two approaches to methodological research: specific scientific and technological. It is these two levels of our research methodology that are of particular interest for describing the impact of transformational leadership on digital technological change, which is essentially a set of theoretical and experimental studies conducted in order to obtain substantiated baseline data for the successful implementation of green business models of transport organizations.

The concept of sustainable development, influencing the consciousness of the manufacturer and the consumer, first of all, significantly changes the views on value for the consumer (Environmental, Social, Governance), offers new methods of creating added value. Moreover, in order to methodologically reliably describe the impact of transformational leadership on the sustainable development of business models of organizations, it is necessary to assess the business through the prism of a new quality of value of a service or product and also why digital technologies, intangible assets (data), and customer networks are so important in this context.

Specific scientific methodology made it possible to generalize the signs of the influence of transformational leadership on the behavior of economic agents, which is used in the development of social, economic, and environmental policies [30]. In fact, the "demand economy" and "supply economy" are being transformed into a new digital entity that changes both the behavior of the consumer and producer and the scientific apparatus that describes these processes. Above all, digital transformation addresses fundamental constraints in each of the areas in which business strategy operates, proposing new methods of connecting with consumers and new methods of creating added value and competition, where the role of a transformational leader is growing.

Analyzing information on the adherence of transport and logistics systems to the requirements of sustainable development, we applied a logical-conceptual approach to identifying the relationship between transformational leadership and sustainable growth of organizations [31].

Mathematical calculations made it possible to assess the fundamental changes in the supply chains of goods and services associated with the growing importance of the category of time or the emergence of the concept of "mobility of supply chains" [32].

The resources-processes-values (RPV) theory explains why established transport companies have such a hard time adopting disruptive green technologies [33, 34].

It is the resources (what is at the disposal of transport companies today, primarily the energy that provides traffic), processes (the existing patterns of the company's work), and values (what the company strives for) in general determine the advantages, disadvantages, as well as "blind zones" of its strategic development. A company can successfully take advantage of disruptive green technologies only when it has the necessary resources (for example, sources and generation of maglev energy), when processes facilitate, rather than impede, the necessary actions, and when corporate values allow making a promising project a priority.

Using the theory of rational behavior, it can be stated that in the current situation, the model of human behavior is shifting toward maximizing utility (including previously unknown values) under conditions of limited resources. This means that the choice of a product or service is solely caused by its value (utility) and becomes a purely "economic choice." Thus, passengers strive to ensure the monetization of their mobility, transport companies—to optimize costs and stay in their market segment, the state pursues various, often contradictory, goals related to ensuring stability, economic efficiency, socioeconomic equality of society members, etc. Obviously, the rationality of behavior will lead to a change in the value of transport services: there are obvious examples of violation of the rationality of behavior during the period of isolation and the uncertainty of getting out of it, which directed attention to the search for an assessment of new psychological factors that change the behavior of consumers of transport services and transport organizations [35, 36].

3. Data

First of all, we examined the basic documents that define the Sustainable Development Goals (SDGs), in particular, the concept of sustainable development adopted by the United Nations (UN) in 2015, the UN Resolution, data from the International Energy Agency. The documents confirming the national adaptation of the SDGs in Russia have been analyzed, on the basis of which a table has been formed showing the relationship between the SDGs and national goals, projects, and state programs for the green development of the transport industry. The data are grouped in **Table 1** [39–41].

The data in **Table 1** show that green infrastructure (transport) projects are being launched in response to numerous environmental challenges. At the same time, they can solve other—social and economic problems.

We analyzed the current and planned expenditures of Russia on the ecology in the context of the state program "Environmental Protection" for 2015–2024, the indicators of national projects: "Comprehensive plan for the modernization and expansion of the main infrastructure," "Safe and high-quality highways," and "Digital economy of the Russian Federation" [42–46]. We confirm the trend of significant growth in the volume of budgetary funds under these programs.

We used data on the global green finance market and found that green bonds account for the largest share in its structure. In substantiating our hypothesis, we relied on data from the World Bank Group on green bonds, since Russian transport companies (in particular, Russian Railways) use this very tool in the development of railway infrastructure projects. Green bonds are issued for new and existing transport projects that comply with the International Capital Market Association (ICMA) Green Bond Principles (GBP).

By examining the forecast data of the Global Infrastructure Hub [47] for the next decade, we have estimated the growth of the world needs for financing infrastructure to support sustainable development by 2030 at about 0.3% of world GDP. PwC data indicate that the amount of capital for responsible investment has grown by one-third every 2 years from 2014 to 2018, and at the beginning of 2021, about half of all managed assets in Europe are attributed to responsible investment assets [48].

According to a 2018 World Bank Group study, Russia's transition to the best available technologies as part of the "greening" and "decarbonization" of the economy will require financing in the amount of about 4–8 trillion rubles, of which 13% for urban and mainline transport.

Sustainable development goals	National goals	Nationa projects	State programs
Resilient infrastructure, inclusive and sustainable industrialization and innovation	• Acceleration of technological development • Ensuring accelerated adoption of digital technologies • Entry of the country into the top-5 largest economies in the world	• "Comprehensive plan for the modernization and expansion of the main infrastructure," "Safe and high-quality highways" and • "International cooperation and export"	• "Development of the transport system" • "Scientific and technological development"
Transition to sustainable consumption and production patterns	• Acceleration of technological development. • Ensuring the accelerated adoption of digital technologies. • Entry of the country into the top-5 largest economies in the world	• "Environmental protection" • "Economic development and innovative economy" • "Development of industry and increasing its competitiveness" • "Reproduction and use of natural resources"	• Ecology
Strengthening the means to achieve sustainable development and revitalizing global partnership mechanisms	Ensuring accelerated digital adoption	• "Digital economy" • "International cooperation and export"	• "Economic development and innovative economy" • "Development of foreign economic activity" • "Scientific and technological development of the Russian Federation"

Table 1.
Parameters of compliance of the development strategy of transport organizations of the Russian Federation with the goals of sustainable growth. Compiled by: [37, 38].

Important for our study is the conclusion of the World Bank analysts that the transition to a green economy in Russia is possible through the development of green public procurement, especially taking into account that the state as a customer is a significant segment of consumption in a country with a market accounting for about a third of GDP. This confirms our hypothesis that in Russia, the transformational leadership of public authorities will be critical to green growth.

For an empirical assessment of the obtained scientific results, we conducted a survey of four Russian transport companies in relation to the detection of signs of transformational leadership and the determination of their weight value in making sustainable development decisions. The sample is determined by the importance of these organizations in the transport services market. The survey involved managers and specialists of the following companies:

- JSC Russian Railways (JSC RZD) —a company that owns the entire public railway infrastructure, railway rolling stock and is the largest operator of passenger and freight traffic.

- Transport concession company—the leader of green projects in the segment of urban rail passenger transportation, corresponding to ICMA;

- State company “Russian Highways” (Avtodor), which has 3771 km of road length in trust;

- Ust-Luga seaport, the largest universal port in the Baltic, the second largest in Russia, and the fifth in Europe.

- The analysis lacks data for air transport companies.

4. Methods

Using the method of grouping data obtained as a result of questioning top-level managers (self-assessment and assessment by colleagues, management, subordinates) of four transport companies in the field of rail freight transport, road transport, land rail transport, and sea transport, we have formed a scale of the main features of transactional and transformational leadership. We used the Multifactor Leadership Questionnaire (MLQ) [49, 50]. At the same time, we have updated the questions, in particular:

- Does the management of the company use an individual approach or leadership by developing people toward the concept of sustainable growth? (To turn followers into leaders of transformations. Generation of fundamentally new ideas and solutions);

- Is the company’s policy on intellectual stimulation evident or leadership by stimulating people’s thinking: ecology, social responsibility, responsible management? (Reaching a consensus with employees on the values of the organization);

- Is there real motivation or leadership by inspiring people to design and implement green growth projects? (An appeal to such values as freedom, environmental safety, and responsibility);

- How charismatic is the leader (top management) of the company? The leader tries to be a role model, sacrifices his own selfish interests: social responsibility, environmental behavior.

Each answer was assigned a value for the weight of the indicator corresponding to the rating scale. The final assessment was used in the correlation analysis of the hypothesis substantiation: a) the dependence of the presence and increase of green growth projects on the obvious signs of transformational leadership in the company; b) dependence of the growth of efficiency of business models of organizations on green transport projects.

We applied the methods of mathematical description of the value of transport services (speed of transportation, development of transport networks, and availability of a set of necessary digital services), formed under the influence of intellectual stimulation of transformational leadership, which made it possible to form a set of indicators of sustainable development and green growth, applicable to all types of transport: the effect of growth in the profitability of green projects (E-factor), caused by green investments, an increase in network density (S-factor), and the speed of movement or compression of space (G-factor).

On their basis, it is possible to generate a complex indicator—*a unit of value* for the impact of transformational leadership on green growth projects.

5. Results

The research results presented below confirm the main provisions of our scientific hypothesis:

- The effectiveness of the use of transactional leadership tools, primarily based on KPI indicators and variance management, has reached its limit. The current metrics do not meet the requirements of sustainable development and green growth.

- Transformational leadership tools influence the efficiency of the operating and business models of transport organizations implementing green growth projects.

Below is a sequence of evidentiary actions in confirming these provisions of the scientific hypothesis.

1. Based on the survey, an analytical scale was developed for the correspondence of indicators of transformational leadership of the leading companies in the main sectors of the Russian transport market (**Table 2**).

As follows from the survey, organizations make the most of transactional leadership indicators (KPIs and deviation management), while everyone notes the low utility of these indicators. Moreover, in the largest transport companies, the costs of periodic calculations and the formation of these indicators in complex hierarchical structures with overlapping business processes exceed the effect of their application.

Analysis of the aggregate weights of the assessment of indicators of transformational leadership in Russian transport companies allows us to conclude about the presence and development of its processes in the following sequence:

First step (from 0 to 10): realizing the organization's need for changes associated with increased competition in the transportation markets, the decrease in the effectiveness of existing business models, and the achievement of the maximum level of labor productivity while maintaining existing technologies in the supply chains.

Second step (from 10 to 15): creating a new vision of sustainable development and, above all, green growth. The vision is not the product of a single leader, but is

Company	Assessment of transactional leadership metrics KPI / deviation management	Assessment of transactional leadership indicators				Aggregate weights of the assessment IS+IC + IM + II
		IS	IC	IM	II	
JSC Russian Railways	5	5	3	4	2	14
Transport Concession Company	4	5	4	5	5	19
"Russian highways" (Avtodor)	5	3	2	2	2	9
Ust-Luga seaport	5	3	2	2	3	10

Legend: IS – Intellectual Stimulation; IC – Individualized Consideration; IM - Inspirational Motivation; II – Idealized Influence.
Weighted assessments: 2 – Not at all; 3 – Sometimes; 4 – Often; 5 - Almost always.

Table 2.
Indicators of transformational leadership of the leading Russian transport companies. Note: 1. Calculated taking into account the weights of the scale of compliance of indicators of transformational leadership in the company, the presence of active green projects (funded by Green Bond), compliance of green bonds with ICMA standards. 2. Calculated according to information on the Internal Rate of Return (IRR) and the value of the Green Bond coupon.

formed as a result of team discussion and decision-making during the development and implementation of the project.

Third step (over 15): institutionalization of changes. It involves changes in the organization of business processes, project teams, operational and financial business models of the organization.

As can be seen from the table, transformational leadership focused on green growth is just beginning to develop in Russian transport organizations. Therefore, it is extremely important to show the dependence of the effectiveness of sustainable development and green growth projects on the understanding and formation of transformational leadership.

Based on the representations of [51], we examined how eco-friendly human resource management interacts with the interrelationships between green transformational leadership, green innovation, and environmental indicators.

2. The assessment of the conformity of the influence of transformational leadership on the transformation of transport companies in the area of green growth and the goals of sustainable development is made (**Table 3**).

The following designations are used in the table:

a. the projects of the company (Transport Concession Company) are aimed at the availability of public transport for the population of the agglomeration, increase the convenience of urban transport users, and contribute to the reduction of CO_2 emissions when using personal transport.

b. projects of the Russian Railways involve the construction of new railway lines, implement programs to reduce the impact on the environment; electrification of track sections to reduce greenhouse gas emissions; construction of treatment facilities to reduce emissions of pollutants.

c. Avtodor plans to use alternative low-carbon modes of transport; how environmentally friendly the road infrastructure under construction is.

Company	Ongoing green growth projects	Planned projects (investments) of sustainable development	Impact of transformational leadership green growth projects (average correlation r)	Impact of green transport projects on the efficiency of business models (IRR of the project)
JSC Russian Railways	(b) (d) (f)		=.77	2.2–7.25%%
Transport Concession Company	(a) (d) (f)		=.83	10–12%%
"Russian highways" (Avtodor)		(c) (d) (f)	=.24	No completed projects
Ust-Luga seaport		(e) (f)	=.15	No completed projects

Table 3.
Assessment of the impact of transformational leadership on the transformation of transport companies toward green growth and sustainable development goals. Compiled by: [37, 52, 53].

d. projects for the implementation of certain digital mobility technologies that increase passenger traffic and supply chains in order to reduce the longest and most air-pollution-related travel.

e. the planned investments in the development of the Ust-Luga seaport are shifting from infrastructure consolidation to a renewable infrastructure, and successful port terminals will be recognized primarily by the high degree of use of green technologies (connected devices, route optimization, energy efficiency, problem detection and troubleshooting).

f. projects that increase the spatial and technical possibilities of creating remote workplaces to accommodate more "hybrid" teams working online to reduce the need for commuting.

The results show that indicators of transformational leadership are highly correlated between green growth projects and the growth of project performance in companies that are strategically targeting and implementing environmental development programs for their businesses. These strategies provide companies that are realigning their business models for sustainable development, the growth of competitiveness, and efficiency [54, 55].

With regard to seaports, it is extremely difficult to assess the economic effect of investments in green technologies in specific numbers, and most often only indirect results can be seen. For example, the Solvo.TOS automated management system for ports and terminals can reduce the operating costs of a cargo terminal by 5–35%. The spread is large enough to predict a return on investment. However, at the same time, the system at least allows increasing the level of service provided to the terminal's clients, which is one of the indicators of its sustainable development. Likewise, it is difficult to assess fragments of Avtodor's projects.

3. Transformational leadership, open to the publicity and social responsibility of business, helps to attract cheaper investments than the financial market offers. The market evolution of finance has formed a set of green finance: bonds,

loans, stock investments, and green insurance [56]. The use of these tools involves the implementation of projects with clear environmental benefits that are assessed, including quantitatively, by issuers, investors, credit institutions, and insurance companies. In other words, they require disclosure of information and absolute openness of the company's management in confirming the necessity for assessing the impact of investments on the environment.

For Russian transport companies, more than ever, there is a problem of attracting investment in projects for the development of urban and mainline transport infrastructure. Moreover, these projects have special features: long payback periods and a low rate of return, generate efficiency mainly with a high density of passenger traffic, and active supply chains. The COVID-19 pandemic has reduced global passenger traffic by 50–60% for various types of transportation, changed the gravity of supply chains and the structure of goods, which led to a decrease in the profits of transport companies. At the same time, the deficit of investments in financial markets has increased with a simultaneous increase in their value. Thus, the estimated supply potential in the investment market of infrastructure projects in the world is $10.2 trillion, while the required investments are estimated at $11.3 trillion—an investment gap of $1.1 trillion.

For Russia, attracting green, cheaper financing is the most important economic and social task of ensuring sustainable development, including transport infrastructure. The global financial market recognizes that the format of sustainable development of railway transport in Russia on the basis of green projects is not only useful in terms of protecting and restoring the environment, but also relatively profitable, since it generates the idea of environmentally friendly transport as financially attractive. It is quite obvious that transformational leadership as the ability of management to transform its worldview to solve social and environmental problems can activate Russian business, government bodies, and political forces to move to a new world of sustainable development.

This is confirmed by the experience of green growth of the Russian Railways company, which has already invested more than 4 billion rubles in green projects. The general director of the company, Oleg Belozerov, annually increases the costs of sustainable development projects, primarily green growth projects, despite the fact that the load on the environment of railway transport is the lowest of all modes of transport.

The leader of the company not only declares the importance of high environmental friendliness of transportation as the main vector of development, but also initiates projects in the field of ecology, clean transport, and social responsibility of the transport business. At the same time, the company fully complies with the principles of "green" financing, placing the third tranche of green bonds.

5.1 Implications for theory

This study has theoretical implications for the leading infrastructure industries in Russia, the effectiveness of which is associated with sustainable development and "green" growth. It expands the possibilities of studying potential internal drivers of transport and logistics organizations and complements the growing body of knowledge in the study of environmental and digital leadership.

5.2 Implications for practice

This study also has a number of practical implications that stem from the increased global interest in sustainable growth and ecological responsibility. It enables transport and logistics organizations to evaluate the effectiveness of their operational and business models in green growth projects.

5.3 Limitations and suggestions for future research

It is important to recognize that this study, despite the results obtained, has a number of limitations. Firstly, it was limited by a relatively small sample size consisting of four basic, mainly state-owned, transport companies that occupy more than 50% of the market for the corresponding modes of transport. Undoubtedly, the work that will expand the sample taking into account the market operators of transportation will be useful. We understand that it is necessary to increase the number of variables in the factor analysis of the impact of transformational leadership indicators on the effectiveness of business models of organizations.

6. Conclusion

The scientific hypothesis presented in this study confirms the direct impact of transformational leadership on the activation of sustainable development processes, first of all, green growth. Our evidence shows the impact of these processes on the growth of the operational and business models of Russian transport companies.

We found that intellectual stimulation, as a critical sign of transformational leadership, is shaping a new digital approach to transport infrastructure development projects, supply chains, and population mobility, which is reflected in the green growth of the national economy.

Our analysis has shown that the inspiring motivation of a transformational leader can spur complex green growth processes in such complex systems as rail transport. The concept of sustainable growth and the environmental goals of Russian Railways under the Long-term Development Program until 2025 confirms this conclusion.

A survey of the management of the largest Russian transport companies showed that the idealized influence and individualization of decision-making inherent in transformational leadership are supported by the choice of people and reflect the views of a society that is willing to pay 15–30% more for products and services produced with ESG in mind, and 80% of millennials choose to work for companies with strong sustainability practices.

We can quantify another transformational leadership trend—ethical choice. More and more top managers of Russian transport companies are beginning to think about what value their company brings to the world, what problems it solves, and whom it helps. This allows them to cope with burnout and gain moral satisfaction from their work.

6.1 Next steps

Expanding on this study, we will be able to calculate indices of the impact of transformational leadership on the efficiency of supply chain mobility. Mathematically, they reflect the weighted average sum of three subindices: the impact of green transport projects on society (mobility), the environment, and the ability of businesses to grow in innovation (efficiency).

Conflict of interest

The authors declare that they have no known competing financial interests or personal relationships that could have appeared to influence the work reported in this paper.

Author details

Natalia Aleksandrovna Zhuravleva[1*] and Milos Poliak[2]

1 Emperor Alexander I St. Petersburg State Transport University, Saint Petersburg, Russia

2 University of Žilina, Žilina, Slovak Republic

*Address all correspondence to: zhuravleva_na@mail.ru

References

[1] Burns JM. Leadership. New York: Harper and Row Publishers Inc. Hardcover; Harpercollins; 1978. ISBN-13: 978-0060105884

[2] Bass BM. Leadership and Performance. N.Y: Free Press; 1985

[3] House RJ. A 1976 Theory of Charismatic Leadership. Working Paper Series 76-06. Ontario: Toronto Univ.; 1977. p. 38

[4] Bass BM, Avolio BJ, Jung DI, Berson Y. Predicting unit performance by assessing transformational and transactional leadership. Journal of Applied Psychology. 2003;**88**(2):207-218. DOI: 10.1037/0021-9010.88.2.207

[5] Global Definitions of Leadership and Theories of Leadership Development: Literature Review. [Internet]. Available from: https://cisl.cam.ac.uk [Accessed: 2022-01-03]

[6] Li W, Bhutto TA, Xuhui W, Maitlo Q, Zafar AU, Ahmed BN. Unlocking employees' green creativity: The effects of green transformational leadership, green intrinsic, and extrinsic motivation. Journal of Cleaner Production. 2020;**255**:120229. DOI: 10.1016/j.jclepro.2020.120229

[7] AlNuaimi BK, Singh SK, Harney B. Unpacking the role of innovation capability: Exploring the impact of leadership style on green procurement via a natural resource-based perspective. Journal of Business Research. 2021;**134**:78-88. DOI: 10.1016/j.jbusres.2021.05.026

[8] Garretsen H, Stoker JI, Weber RA. Economic perspectives on leadership: Concepts, causality, and context in leadership research. The Leadership Quarterly. 2020;**31**(3):101410. DOI: 10.1016/j.leaqua.2020.101410

[9] Hiller NJ, Piccolo RF, Zaccaro SJ. Economic assumptions and economic context: Implications for the study of leadership. The Leadership Quarterly. 2020;**31**(3):101352. DOI: 10.1016/j.leaqua.2019.101352

[10] Fitzsimmons TW, Callan VJ. The diversity gap in leadership: What are we missing in current theorizing? The Leadership Quarterly. 2020;**31**(4): 101347. DOI: 10.1016/j.leaqua.2019.101347

[11] Sheehan M, Garavan TN, Morley MJ. Transformational leadership and work unit innovation: A dyadic two-wave investigation. Journal of Business Research. 2020;**109**:399-412. DOI: 10.1016/j.jbusres.2019.10.072

[12] Northouse PG. Leadership: Theory and Practice. Eighth Edition. Western Michigan University. Thousand Oaks: SAGE Publications; 2018. p. 729. ISBN: 9781506362311

[13] Ahmed T. All about leadership theories [Internet]. 2021. Available from: https://blog.vantagecircle.com/leadership-theories [Accessed: 2021-10-22]

[14] Bass BM, Avolio BJ, Atwater L. The transformational and transactional leadership of men and women. Applied Psychology: An International Review. 1996;**45**:5-34. DOI: 10.1111/j.1464-0597.1996.tb00847.x

[15] Bass BM, Riggio RE. Transformational Leadership. 2nd ed. Mahwah, New Jersey; UK: Lawrence Erlbaum Associates Publishers; 2006. p. 263. ISBN: 0-8058-4761-8

[16] Fiedler FE, Garcia JE. New Approaches to Leadership, Cognitive Resources and Organizational Performance. New York; USA: John Wiley and Sons Inc; 1987. p. 240. ISBN 10: 0471874566

[17] Blanchard KH, Zigarmi P, Zigarmi D. Leadership and the One Minute Manager: Increasing Effectiveness through Situational Leadership. New York (US): William Morrow & Co; 1985. p. 111. ISBN: 0688039693

[18] Blanchard KH, Johnson SMD. The New One Minute Manager. India: HarperCollins; 2016. 85 p. ISBN 10: 8172234996

[19] Indeed Editorial Team. Data Leadership: A Definitive Guide [Internet]. November 25, 2021. Available from: https://www.indeed.com/career-advice/career-development/data-leadership?from=careeradvice-US [Accessed: 2021-12-01]

[20] Liao Z, Zhang M. The influence of responsible leadership on environmental innovation and environmental performance: The moderating role of managerial discretion. Corporate Social Responsibility and Environmental Management. 2020;**27**(1):2016-2027. DOI: 10.1002/csr.1942

[21] Goethals GR, Sorenson GJ, Burns JMG. Encyclopedia of Leadership. Thousand Oaks, Calif: Sage Publications; 2004. p. 1558. ISBN: 9781452265308

[22] A Legal Framework for the Integration of Environmental, Social and Governance Issues into Institutional Investment. Produced for the Asset Management Working Group of the UNEP Finance Initiative. UK: Freshfields Bruckhaus Deringer; 2005. p. 154

[23] Odumeru JA, Ogbonna IG. Transformational vs. transactional leadership theories: Evidence in literature. International Review of Management and Business Research. 2013;**2**:355

[24] Ishkov D. Hybrid theory: how combining the real with the digital changes the format of work. [Internet]. 2021. Available from: https://incrussia.ru/specials/hybridtheory/ [Accessed: 2021-12-02]

[25] Stamford C. Gartner survey finds 1-in-5 workers consider themselves digital technology experts since COVID-19. Reliance on digital collaboration tools and IT self-service requirements changed workers' relationships to technology. [Internet]. April 26, 2021. Available from: https://www.gartner.com/en/newsroom/press-releases/2021-04-26-gartner-survey-finds-1-in-5-workers-consider-themselves-digital-technology-experts-since-covid-19 [Accessed: 2021-12-02]

[26] Dilts RB, DeLozier J, Dilts DB. NLP II: The Next Generation. California (US): Meta Publications; 2010. p. 432. ISBN 10: 0916990497

[27] Dilts RB, Gilligan S. Generative Coaching Vol. 1: The Journey of Creative and Sustainable Change. Santa Cruz, CA: International Association for Generative Change; 2021. p. 236. ISBN 10: 0578896966

[28] Schumpeter JA. The Theory of Economic Development: An Inquiry into Profits, Capital, Credit, Interest, and the Business Cycle. London (UK): Harvard Economic Studies; 1934. p. 255. ISBN: 9780674879904

[29] Christensen CM. The innovator's Dilemma: When New Technologies Cause Great Firms to Fail. London (UK): Harvard Business Review Press; 2016. p. 288. ISBN: 978-1633691780

[30] Hicks J. Value and Capital: An Inquiry into some Fundamental Principles of Economic Theory. 2nd ed. Oxford (UK): Clarendon Press; 1946. p. 340. ISBN: 9780198282693

[31] Shah KJ, Pan S-Y, Lee I, Kim H, You Z, Zheng J-M, et al. Green transportation for sustainability: Review

of current barriers, strategies, and innovative technologies. Journal of Cleaner Production. 2021;**326**:129392. DOI: 10.1016/j.jclepro.2021.129392

[32] Zhuravleva NA, Panychev AY. Problems of economic speed assessment in transport and logistics systems in the new technological order. Transport Systems and Technologies. 2017;**3**(4): 150-178. DOI: 10.17816/transsyst 201734150-178

[33] Christensen CM, Overdorf M. Meeting the challenge of disruptive change. Harvard Business Review. [Internet]. March-April 2000. Available from: https://hbr.org/2000/03/meeting-the-challenge-of-disruptive-change [Accessed: 2021-12-02]

[34] Christensen CM, Anthony SD, Roth EA. Seeing what's Next: Using the Theories of Innovation to Predict Industry Change. 1st ed. Boston, Massachusetts: Harvard business school press; 2004. p. 352. ISBN 10: 1591391857

[35] Feldman F. Daniel Kahneman, Ed Diener, and Norbert Schwarz (eds.), well-being: The foundations of hedonic psychology. New York: The Russell Sage Foundation; 1999, pp. xii 593. Utilitas. 2006;**18**(2):192-196. DOI: 10.1017/ S0953820806231972

[36] Kahneman D. Thinking, Fast and Slow. 1st ed. New York (US): Farrar, Straus and Giroux; 2013. p. 499. ISBN: 978-0374533557

[37] Investment in Infrastructure. Ecology. 2020. InfraOne Research. [Analytical review]

[38] Analytical Center for the Government of the Russian Federation data. [Internet]. Available from: https:// ac.gov.ru/en [Accessed: 2021-12-02]

[39] United Nations. Resolution adopted by the general assembly on 6 July 2017. In: Work of the Statistical Commission Pertaining to the 2030 Agenda for Sustainable Development (a/RES/71/313). 2017

[40] On Approval of the Comprehensive Plan for the Modernisation and Expansion of Trunk Infrastructure for the Period up to 2024: Russian Government Decree No. 2101-p of 20.09.2018. [Internet]. Available from: http://staticgovernment.ru/media/files/ MUNhgWFddP3UfF9RJASDW9VxP8z wcB4Y.pdf [Accessed: 2021-12-02]

[41] About the National Development Goals of the Russian Federation for the period until 2030: Presidential Decree of 21.07.2020. [Internet]. Available from: http://kremlin.ru/events/ president/news/63728 [Accessed: 2021-12-02]

[42] Federal'nyi budget do 2022 goda. [Internet]. Available from: https:// minfin.gov.ru/ru/perfomance/budget/ federal_budget/budgeti/2022/ [Accessed: 2021-12-02]

[43] On approval of the State Programme of the Russian Federation "Environmental Protection". Decree of the Government of the Russian Federation of 15 April 2014 No. 326

[44] A comprehensive plan for the modernisation and expansion of backbone infrastructure for the period up to 2024. Approved by Russian Government Decree No. 2101-p of 30.09.2018

[45] The Russian national project "Safe High Quality Roads" [Internet]. Available from: https://bkdrf.ru/ [Accessed: 2021-12-02]

[46] National programme "Digital Economy of the Russian Federation" approved by the minutes of the meeting of the Presidium of the Presidential Council for Strategic Development and National Projects No. 7 of 04.06.2019

[47] Global Infrastructure Hub. 2020. [Internet]. https://www.gihub.org/

[48] Green Bond Database Methodology. 2020. [Internet]. Available from: https://www.climatebonds.net/certification/certified-bonds [Accessed: 2021-12-02]

[49] Bass B, Avolio B. Multifactor Leadership Questionnaire Manual. Third ed. Menlo Park, CA: Mind Garden, Inc; 2004

[50] Multifactor Leadership Questionnaire Product Specs. 22.11.2017 [Internet]. Available from: www.mindgarden.com. [Accessed: 2021-12-02]

[51] Singh SK, Del Giudice M, Chierici R, Graziano D. Green innovation and environmental performance: The role of green transformational leadership and green human resource management. Technological Forecasting and Social Change. 2020;**150**:119762. DOI: 10.1016/j.techfore.2019.119762

[52] Russian Railways' Environmental Strategy to 2020 and Beyond 2030 (21.05.2014, as edited by 22.06.2016). [Internet]. Available from: https://company.rzd.ru/ru/9353/page/105104?id=958. [Accessed: 2021-12-02]

[53] A systematic format for international business events in the 1520 area (22-23 октября 2020). PRO//Motion. [Internet]. Available from: https://railwayforum.ru/ [Accessed: 2021-12-02]

[54] Flammer C. Corporate green bonds. Journal of Financial Economics. 2021;**142**(2):499-516. DOI: 10.1016/j.jfineco.2021.01.010

[55] Stroebel J, Wurgler J. What do you think about climate finance? Journal of Financial Economics. 2021;**142**(2): 487-498

[56] Climate Change and Green Finance. Discussion paper. The UK's Financial Conduct Authority (FCA). 2018